OPERATIONS OF EIGHTH CORPS

NORMANDY TO THE RIVER RHINE

IN THIS ROOM
THE VIIIth CORPS
COMPOSED OF
THE GUARDS ARMOURED
DIVISION
THE XIth ARMOURED
DIVISION
AND
THE XV SCOTTISH DIVISION
PLANNED THEIR PART
IN THE
INVASION OF EUROPE
ON JUNE 6th 1944
UNDER
LIEUTENANT-GENERAL
SIR RICHARD O'CONNOR
K.C.B. D.S.O. M.C.

Non nobis Domine
sed Nomini Tuo da Gloriam

OPERATIONS OF EIGHTH CORPS

Account of Operations from Normandy to the River Rhine

BY

LIEUTENANT-COLONEL G. S. JACKSON

The Naval & Military Press Ltd

Published by

The Naval & Military Press Ltd
Unit 5 Riverside, Brambleside
Bellbrook Industrial Estate
Uckfield, East Sussex
TN22 1QQ England

Tel: +44 (0)1825 749494

www.naval-military-press.com
www.nmarchive.com

In reprinting in facsimile from the original, any imperfections are inevitably reproduced and the quality may fall short of modern type and cartographic standards.

ACKNOWLEDGMENTS

The extracts from "Normandy to the Baltic" were taken with the authorisation of Field Marshal Viscount Montgomery, K.G., G.C.B., D.S.O. and Messrs. Hutchinson & Co., Ltd. The quotations on pages 24 and 52 come from the book "Defeat in the West" by Mr. Milton Shulman and are reproduced by permission of Messrs. Secker & Warburg, Ltd. The broadcast on pages 92 and 93 from "War Report" is printed by permission of the B.B.C.

In addition, I would like to express my gratitude to Mr. Chester Wilmot for placing at my disposal the result of his detailed investigation into Operation "Goodwood" and also to many others who have helped with this account, notably Lt.-Col. A. F. Warhurst and Mr. C. V. Owens of the Cabinet Records Office, through whose kindness much valuable time was saved in research work, and Lt.-Col. J. G. Hooper who solved all the problems of printing and production.

Finally, the work of Sjt. R. W. Neale, Pte. Sheila Smith and Pte. C. G. Rossiter who typed this account, and of Sgmn. W. Webster and Mr. E. J. Peace who were responsible for the diagrams, was always greatly appreciated.

G. S. J.

FOREWORD

BY
GENERAL SIR MILES C. DEMPSEY,
K.C.B., D.S.O., M.C.

It is now nearly four years since the invasion of Normandy set on foot the fighting in N.W. Europe, which was to end with the total defeat of the German armed forces in May 1945.

8 Corps played a great part—in Second Army from start to finish—and this History will show what they did.

My thoughts go back to the intense armoured fighting around Caen; to the dramatic break-out at Caumont; to the winter fighting on the Meuse, and to the final glorious advance from the Rhine to the Baltic.

In all these great actions I seem to see "The White Knight" in the forefront, and I am glad indeed to pay my tribute once again to a great Corps.

General.

April 1948.

CONTENTS

PAGE

FRONTISPIECE
    COMMEMORATION PLAQUE ERECTED AT WORTH PRIORY.
    THIS WAS THE HEADQUARTERS OF EIGHTH CORPS
    IMMEDIATELY PRIOR TO THE INVASION   FACING PAGE iii

FOREWORD   v

CHAPTER 1   *"Early Days"*   1

CHAPTER 2   *Normandy and Operation "Epsom"*   18

CHAPTER 3   *"Goodwood"*   68

CHAPTER 4   *"Bluecoat"*   115

CHAPTER 5   *Normandy to the River Maas*   145

APPENDICES
    STAFF LIST, EIGHTH CORPS TROOPS AND ORDER OF BATTLE   166
    FORMATIONS UNDER COMMAND OF EIGHTH CORPS   172

DIAGRAMMATIC MAPS
    MAP I   19
    MAP II   69
    MAP III   71
    MAP IV   117
    MAP V   147

SURVEY MAPS
    CONTAINED IN THE POCKET AT THE BACK OF THE BOOK

CHAPTER 1

" Early Days "

IN 1942, although the threat of invasion from the Continent was no longer immediate, there was still in Great Britain a garrison of considerable size controlled from G.H.Q. Home Forces in London, via the Home Commands, through a series of corps headquarters. Most of these had been formed in the crisis year of 1940, to take charge of field formations on an area basis, but latterly, with the despatch of many divisions overseas to active theatres, some corps were beginning to possess only a very miscellaneous assortment of troops to command, ranging from training divisions to Young Soldiers battalions and the Home Guard. A number of these headquarters were thus becoming redundant and available for duties elsewhere. One of them was that of the Eighth Corps stationed at Taunton in Somerset, and responsible for the defence of the three south-western counties of England—Somerset, Devon and Cornwall.

Headquarters 8 Corps was originally formed in the early summer of 1940 at Aldershot by General Sir Harold Franklyn, and in August of that year had moved to the south-western defence area, where it had remained ever since, playing a useful if unobtrusive part in the military defence of Great Britain. The even tenor of this existence, however, was interrupted in November, 1942, when a letter was received from the then Commander-in-Chief, Home Forces, General Sir Bernard Paget, which announced:

" It is my intention to form an armoured corps in this country, and I have selected 8 Corps to be the Headquarters commanding it. 8 Corps will therefore be prepared to hand over its static commitments and move to a new location by the end of the year."

This news, as might be imagined, aroused much excitement and speculation as to the future. A sudden remarkable interest developed in the activities and training of the adjacent Guards Armoured Division, and many surreptitious trips were paid to it by those hoping to achieve the metamorphosis to armour. Few realised, though, at the time that these visits were the precursor of a long and happy association between the two formations, which formally beginning in the following spring when the division passed under command of 8 Corps, was strengthened by a year of mutual training and culminated in the heavy and victorious battles of Normandy.

By the end of 1942 the handover to the new South-Western District Headquarters was complete, and early in January, 1943, the main body of Corps Headquarters moved off to a new life, sped on its way by virtually the whole of Taunton lining the streets to say farewell. Until the day of embarkation for France in June, 1944, no better or more enthusiastic send-off was ever given to the Headquarters.

So passed Taunton.

The new sphere of activity was Yorkshire, and although the initial stay was short, to the Yorkshire Wolds the Corps was later to return for its major collective training, and its debt to this hospitable county is great. The actual location of the Headquarters was at a large modern hotel at Scotch Corner on the Great North Road and about six miles from the nearest town, Darlington. It was a bleak and isolated spot, but had housed a military Headquarters from the beginning of the war.

Life quickly began anew, running at a vastly increased tempo, for everything, of course, had to start again from scratch. Almost all the other rank personnel of low medical categories left and were replaced by younger men, whilst many new staff officers were posted and arrived.

Some of the old, too, who had survived the transition from Taunton began to drift away, notably Brigadier Jock Whitefoord, the B.G.S., who went to COSSAC (the forerunner of SHAEF), and Johnny Fass, his G.S.O.1 (Operations), who followed him there. On the "G" side, Lieutenant-Colonel Henry Carden became G.S.O.1 (Operations), with Nigel Birch, Ian Balmain, John Young and Douglas Paybody as the Operations and Staff Duties team, whilst in the Intelligence Branch, Graham Jackson was first joined by Michael Strachan, of the Inns of Court Regiment, whose ability was, unfortunately, far too soon appreciated elsewhere, for he was shortly afterwards whisked overseas to the planning staff of A.F.H.Q. in Algiers, being succeeded by Bryan Hunt from 42 Armoured Division. On the A/Q side, apart from Brigadier Geoffrey Lucas, the D.A. and Q.M.G., who was the first of the new senior officers to arrive at Scotch Corner, an old friend and former G.S.O.2 (Operations) of Taunton days, was welcomed back as A.Q.M.G. in the person of Lieutenant-Colonel Reggie Batt, whilst Michael Fitzalan-Howard became D.A.Q.M.G. and Ronnie Phillips D.A.A.G., with John Haslam as his very popular staff captain.

Among the supporting arms and Services, early arrivals included Brigadier L. C. Manners-Smith from Guards Armoured Division as C.C.R.A., Brigadier Cyril Knowles back from Italy as Chief Signal Officer, whilst Brigadier H. L. Glyn-Hughes, also from Guards Armoured Division, came as D.D.M.S., and Colonel Michael MacEvoy, from 11 Armoured Division, as D.D.M.E. Of these, Brigadier Manners-Smith was destined to stay at the Headquarters for a few months only, but the remainder served the Corps faithfully and well, and were a source of encouragement and help to all until the close of the campaign in Europe.

Brigadier Glyn-Hughes, in particular, became a famous character not only in 8 Corps but throughout Second Army, for his abilities were by no means confined to the practice of healing the sick and wounded. Most other aspects of army life attracted him also, for he was always ready to show interest in, or give advice (and extremely expert advice at that), upon matters not normally connected with the Medical Branch. At Corps Headquarters this almost became a joke, for if some difficult technical question arose, say an awkward bridging operation during an exercise, or the solution of a complicated tactical problem, the cry was always, "Send for the D.D.M.S.—he'll know the answer." And he normally did. Not only 8 Corps but the entire Second Army owes much to Brigadier "Glyn," for in the last days of the campaign it was he who took over, re-organised and cleared up the infamous concentration camp at Belsen, and thereby prevented a typhus epidemic in its midst.

No mention has yet been made of the Chief of Staff, or B.G.S., as he was then called, for though one was early nominated in the shape of a Brigadier Pyman, and a mass of teleprints announced his posting and imminent arrival, in point of fact he never came at all. The reason for this was that en route from Italy he had been selected to take charge of the Training Branch at G.H.Q. Home Forces, and General Paget, notwithstanding all appeals, was adamant in his refusal to release him. Despite the inconvenience this occasioned at the time, full compensation was later provided, for this act of chance was the direct cause of the arrival at Corps Headquarters as B.G.S. of Sir Henry Floyd. In the meantime Brigadier Manners-Smith combined the roles of C.C.R.A. and B.G.S.

The new Commander, Lieutenant-General Herbert Lumsden, arrived on the 20th January, and to attempt to describe the character and attributes of General Lumsden in a short paragraph is to do him less than justice. His reputation had, however, already preceded him, and his newly-constituted staff expected an awe-inspiring figure of great experience in armoured warfare of all kinds, particularly in the Western Desert, and now fresh from taking a major role as Commander of 10 Corps—the original armoured corps—in the battle of Alamein and the subsequent operations into Cyrenaica. What was discovered on his arrival, and during the months in which he commanded 8 Corps was, however, something far greater than this.

In appearance thin, wiry, of medium height, and with the most immaculate turnout, he possessed boundless energy and determination, and was quite relentless and ruthless in the attainment of any object he considered of importance to the Corps. He could never suffer fools gladly—nor for long— and extremely sudden outbursts would arise through the discovery of anything he considered slack or slovenly. He was, nevertheless, of a most kindly disposition, was always approachable, and would take great pains to help anyone in difficulty, particularly the more junior members of his staff. Of his charm of manner, his piercing look and quizzical smile, and the overall magnetic effect of his personality, only those privileged to have known General Herbert Lumsden can speak, but it can be truly said that he set a standard for 8 Corps surpassed by no other formation, and that those early months of training under his leadership enabled it to become a corps d'élite.

One anecdote concerning him will not be out of place, for it typifies his personality and outlook on life. Soon after his return to England from Africa, he lectured at the Staff College on the Battle of Alamein, and the pursuit into Cyrenaica. His final comment, and one which, incidentally, "brought the house down," was:

"Well, gentlemen, the race to Benghazi may not have been a 'classic,' nor was it run entirely as we had hoped, but at least it was a record for the course—by either side—either way."

By the accident of his tragic and untimely death on the bridge of an American battleship attacked by Japanese aircraft off the Philippines in 1944, Britain lost a soldier who could ill be spared.

With the arrival of the Corps Commander, the stage was now set for training, in order to begin the process of welding new and old into an efficient and unified body, fit to take the field and possessing the same confident outlook and enthusiasm as its commander.

One of the earliest steps General Lumsden took, in order to create this atmosphere, was to offer a prize for the best suggestion for a new Corps sign.

The choice of a good formation emblem is all-important, for it can do much to foster a feeling of pride and unity among those bearing it. One has only to think of the Crusaders's shield of the Eighth Army or the "Pegasus" badge of airborne units, to realise what an immense contribution they made to the esprit-de-corps of those privileged to wear them. So too, it was with 8 Corps. A happy combination of several separate suggestions finally produced the "White Knight," best described (though in regrettably un-heraldic language) as a "knight in armour, galloping full tilt ahead, lance in hand."

This design was manufactured with commendable speed in white on a red background, the Corps colours, and before many months were past, the new sign was known to the world at large. Though one of the last great army emblems to be evolved during the war, it is outstandingly apt and graceful in appearance, and really typified 8 Corps.

The first major event due to affect the army at home as a whole in 1943, was the second (and last) G.H.Q. exercise-with-troops, called "Spartan." Conceived on an extremely large scale, this was planned to test the system of command and supply which the British Army had evolved through experience in active theatres, and to find out whether our forces would be able to maintain a high rate of advance after a fast withdrawing enemy, in a situation such as might be anticipated on the Continent once a break-through from an original bridgehead had been achieved. On one side the Canadian Army in Britain, commanded by Lieutenant-General A. G. L. McNaughton with two Canadian corps (1 and 2 Armoured Corps) and one British corps (12 Corps) constituted the invading British force taking on a German occupation army. This consisted of 11 Corps (infantry) with 8 Corps (armoured) and its task was to withdraw, after the initial contact, with all speed northwards, leaving the Canadians to pursue, developing their supply installations and lines of communication in so doing.

For "Spartan" 8 Corps assumed control of 9 and 42 Armoured Divisions commanded by Major-Generals d'Arcy and Aizlewood respectively. 9 Armoured Division, with its well-known Panda sign, had been formed in early 1941, though it was never fated to see action, as in 1944 it had to be broken up to provide reinforcements for divisions already in the field. There is no doubt, however, that had it been permitted to fight, it would have acquitted itself well, since it possessed a fine spirit and tremendous élan under the leadership of General d'Arcy. 42 Armoured Division, an old Territorial formation with a long history stretching back before the first World War, had seen active service in France in 1940, and after hard fighting had been reconstituted at home, and then transformed into an armoured division under Major-General Dempsey, who was later to lead the Second Army.

On the conclusion of "Spartan," 9 Armoured Division took over the bleak North Yorkshire home of 42 Armoured Division, which was happy to exchange it for sunnier days in Somerset, in the area vacated by Guards Armoured Division on the latter's move to Norfolk.

"Bumper," the first of these large-scale G.H.Q. exercises, in the autumn of 1941, had been an unqualified success, and many lessons had been learned. General Paget hoped, therefore, that "Spartan" would be a worthy follower, but it proved to be rather too ambitious an undertaking for many useful deductions to be made from its results.

Considering that as a headquarters, formed only six weeks beforehand, this was its first attempt at carrying out its allotted role, the performance of 8 Corps in this exercise was, however, most encouraging. It moved reasonably easily, the wireless links were good, information flowed in and out in the best text-book manner and the Services functioned smoothly. It is true that when General Paget ordered the "cease fire" on 12th March, the exhaustion shown by most members of the Staff proved that they had not yet learned the supreme arts of working moderately and living as comfortably as possible—both of which, needless to say, came later—but nevertheless everyone felt proud to belong to a formation with a clearly defined future.

To sum up, Exercise "Spartan" was, so far as 8 Corps was concerned, a very thorough test of its abilities and capabilities at the start of its active life, and, by and large, it was equal to the task. Much, of course, remained to be done before it could be termed properly trained and fit to take the field, but it certainly compared favourably with some older formations on this exercise. Most important of all, it already possessed a spirit and a conscious superiority (perhaps at times a trifle too openly displayed) seldom felt in a large formation.

As soon as the message "Spartan, cease fire Spartan," had been received, an advance party was sent to reconnoitre a new location for the Headquarters. This was to be Didlington Hall in Norfolk, a fine old house with a homely atmosphere, situated a few miles from Thetford, and in the centre of what was at that time the principal tank training area in England.

Once settled in, delightful spring weather, a large swimming pool in the grounds and last, but by no means least, the special train to London which the L.N.E.R. obligingly put on at week-ends, made the three months there seem, in retrospect, among the most enjoyable of any in England. The nearest neighbour of the Corps was the Guards Armoured Division, an opponent in "Spartan," but which at the conclusion of this exercise moved to the North Norfolk-King's Lynn area and established new headquarters at Cockley Cley, two or three miles to the north. A Canadian formation, the 5th Armoured Division, was the next nearest, though it moved to Aldershot and subsequently to Italy at the beginning of April, whilst further south, in the Newmarket-Cambridge area, was the mobilised and fully trained 11th Armoured Division. The sailing orders of this division, which had been warned for service with the First Army in North Africa, had recently been cancelled at the eleventh hour, and after embarkation of some of its units had already started, as the cry for reinforcements from Tunisia had changed to "more infantry" and "less armour." At the beginning of March, therefore, it was in the throes of undoing all its carefully completed preparations for moving overseas and resuming normal training, though, as might be expected, without any great enthusiasm.

Neither Guards nor 11 Armoured Divisions were destined to be left very long to their own devices, however, for on 17th March 8 Corps received orders to assume command over them. Thus began that partnership which, joined in June by 15 (Scottish) Division, was always the firm base on which 8 Corps rested, and which lasted without interruption for over eighteen months and until the end of the campaign in Normandy.

In March, also, two major additions were made to the Headquarters, and whose influence henceforward cannot be overestimated. Their arrival might almost be described as accidental, in that they succeeded to appointments which, though filled in theory, in practice had not been taken up. For this twist of fate, 8 Corps can never be sufficiently grateful, for Providence certainly "batted for" the Corps on these occasions. The first was the long-awaited appointment of the B.G.S. or Chief of Staff. After "Spartan" the Corps Commander finally gave up hope of persuading General Paget to release Brigadier Pyman, and decided to select his successor nearer home, so that he would be less likely to be "lost" en route. His choice fell upon a cavalryman, Sir Henry Floyd, who after distinguished service with his regiment, the 15/19th Hussars, in the 1940 French campaign, had been Commandant of the Senior Officers' School, and latterly G.S.O. 1 of 9 Armoured Division. During his long and happy tenure of office, Sir "Harry" endeared himself to all with whom he came into contact in the Corps, and his inspiring leadership, foresight and imperturbable nature won the devotion, respect and admiration of every man in the Headquarters.

The second arrival was the new C.C.R.A., Brigadier A. G. Matthew, the successor to Brigadier Manners-Smith. Here, again, the Corps was singularly fortunate, for Brigadier Matthew not only brought with him the accumulated experience of four years' unbroken campaigning in France and the Middle East, but was also the possessor of a dynamic energy and singleness of purpose which it would be hard to equal—those who saw them will never forget the faces of his staff when they were set an exercise on the very evening of his arrival. If he was exacting in his demands, however, on his own branch or the Headquarters staff, he also never spared himself, and was always ready and willing to help and encourage them in their work. The debt of 8 Corps to "Hammer" is very great.

Several signal exercises, notably "White Knight," "Charger" and "Sabre," which involved the two new divisions, were undertaken in magnificent weather during April and May, and these, though less imposing in design than "Spartan," nevertheless were probably of greater benefit to the Corps. The emphasis in training now, of course, being entirely offensive, each one of these exercises dealt with some particular aspect of its intended role and the "break-out" battle was explored from every angle. Thus in "Sabre" 8 Corps practised the command and control of a break through enemy defences by armour following an initial penetration by infantry—a task later to be given to the Corps in its first battle—whilst "Charger" produced the problems of the approach march and a change of plan. These were, however, signal exercises only, and though they provided valuable tests for formation staffs, no similar collective training with troops was being carried out. East Anglia, moreover, with its flat landscape and numerous waterways, was not really suitable for armoured movement on a large scale. The so-called "battle area" around Stanford could deal with little more than a regiment of tanks at a time. Even so, it was the best armoured training area available.

For some months past, negotiations had been carried on behind the scenes between various Ministries over a much larger and more controversial project, namely whether a sizeable slice of the Wolds country, north of Hull in Yorkshire, should be placed at the disposal of the military authorities for armoured training purposes. This extremely valuable agricultural land produces some of the finest crops in England. It is also, with its firm soil and undulating wooded countryside, almost ideal for tank training. The battle was long and reached Cabinet level, but finally approval was granted, and 8 Corps was selected to be the first tenant. This news was given to the Staff on 22 May, 1943, simultaneously with a warning order for the move northwards in the following month, and accordingly on 1 June, 1943, the Corps Headquarters was established at Sandhutton Hall, six miles north of York, on the Scarborough road. 11 Armoured Division and Guards Armoured Division also began to arrive during June, and by the middle of July the whole Corps was concentrated in the Yorkshire Wolds, and ready to carry out large-scale collective training.

Sandhutton Hall cannot truly be termed an attractive house, though the surroundings are pleasant; nor was it sufficiently large, as was Didlington, to accommodate the whole Staff. Recourse had to be made to putting up Nissen huts in the grounds, and also to the establishment of a rear headquarters. It was, however, the place where the Headquarters was longest in residence, where the Staff received its final shaping, where the vicissitudes of intensive training were endured, where the many changes of command were suffered (and there were six in as many months), where the major planning for participation in the invasion of France was carried out, and where many of the "great ones" of the land came to say farewell before the Corps moved overseas. To most of the Staff, it would probably conjure up, in addition, a picture of General Herbert and Sir Harry, sometimes accompanied by Brigadier "Hammer," taking their early morning rides, or of Staff Serjeant-Major Lamond the chief "G" clerk and a famous "character," laying down the law to some luckless staff officer, or making one of his numerous démarches to the B.G.S. Insofar as a corps headquarters can be said to have one, Sandhutton was the home of 8 Corps.

The first event on arrival in Yorkshire was an exercise for the A/Q services and Corps troops. Entitled "Caviare," this was a test of mobilisation procedure which lasted from 2nd-16th June, and was felt to be a pointer to ultimate employment in an active theatre of the Corps at no very distant future.

On the 20th June the formation of 8 Corps was completed when the 15 (Scottish) Division, then lying along the Tyne Valley, was placed under command. This fine division was at that time constituted as that curious hybrid formation, evolved from theories at home, but never, it is believed, used in practice in operations, known as a "mixed" division. Instead of three brigades of infantry it had two only, together with one tank brigade, a cumbersome arrangement with the combined evils of the infantry and armoured divisions, and none of their virtues or strength. Almost as soon as the Scots joined 8 Corps however, mixed divisions were abolished, and 6 Guards Tank Brigade therefore left 15 (Scottish) Division, being replaced during July by the normal third infantry brigade—in this case, 227 (Highland) Infantry Brigade from the Orkney-Shetland defence area. The long period of co-operation and mutual training, however, had established between 15 (Scottish) Division and 6 Guards Tank Brigade a trust and confidence seldom achieved by different arms of the Service, the extent of which was to be clearly demonstrated during the fighting in Normandy and, in particular, during the break-through operations by 8 Corps south of Caumont.

8 Corps had now assumed its final shape for active service—Guards and 11 Armoured Divisions, 15 (Scottish) Infantry Division, 6 Guards Tank Brigade, 8 A.G.R.A., and 2 Household Cavalry Regiment as the Corps armoured car regiment. In addition there was, of course, the usual allotment of Corps troops. On this basis, all future training was carried out, on this basis the Corps sailed to France, and on this basis it fought its heaviest and most successful engagements.

The next exercise, called "Hawk," took place from 21st-24th July and, as usual, dealt with an aspect of the future of 8 Corps, in this case the break-out of an armoured division from a bridgehead held by an infantry corps, followed by an advance to contact and engagement with an enemy armoured division. During it, 11 Armoured Division in particular and 8 Corps in general, made their first acquaintance with that peculiarly bleak locality and dominating feature of the Wolds, known as the Octon Cross-Roads. Wherever an exercise was set in the Wolds, whether it ran from north to south or east to west, or vice versa, somehow the culminating point always took place astride these cross roads. Thither too, the "great ones" who visited us, were conducted to "spectate." As Calais was said to be engraved on Queen Mary's heart, so must "Octon Cross-Roads" have been on that of any average member of 8 Corps during the summer and (especially) winter of 1943.

At the conclusion of "Hawk," the Corps Commander held the usual Directors' conference for all officers, down to company commanders, who had participated. This took place in a theatre at Bridlington, and at the end of his brilliant summing-up, he announced abruptly, "Gentlemen, this is my swan-song as Commander of 8 Corps." This was the first official intimation that the Corps had received of General Lumsden relinquishing his appointment and it was a tremendous and unhappy shock. It is difficult for the commander of a large formation to become personally known to many serving under him, particularly at unit level. In the brief six months, however, in which he had commanded, General Herbert Lumsden had succeeded in impressing his personality on 8 Corps to no small degree, and a genuine feeling of loss and disappointment was felt throughout at this news. The whole Corps was very sorry to see him go.

With his departure began a period of change and uncertainty for 8 Corps, which extended over the next six months, and in retrospect seems more serious than was realised at the time. It might well form a separate chapter with the title "Under six Commanders," for five permanent or acting successors held their brief sway, before the General arrived who finally led it into battle, General O'Connor. However, in July, 1943, he was still a prisoner-of-war in Italy, and in Yorkshire in any case there was no idea what was immediately in store for the Corps.

At the end of July, 1943, General Lumsden's successor, Lieutenant-General Sir Richard McCreery arrived. It was known that he had served with great distinction in the Middle East, latterly as Chief of Staff to the Commander-in-Chief, General Alexander, during his successful campaign to drive Axis forces out of Africa. Like his predecessor he was a cavalry officer, shared his love of horses, and by a coincidence belonged to the same regiment, 12 Lancers. Quiet and unassuming in manner, the major impression which he gave to the Corps staff assembled in a Nissen hut in the grounds of Sandhutton Hall to hear his inaugural address, was of his idealism and sincerity.

General McCreery soon settled in, and his first engagement was to attend, accompanied by the B.G.S., D.A. and Q.M.G. and C.C.R.A., a study week held by the newly-constituted Second Army at its Headquarters at Oxford. This study week which was really in the nature of a pre-planning exercise, was the first of many outward signs that the design for the assault on "Fortress Europe" had passed from the theoretical to the practical stage, and that detailed planning had now been begun by one of the two assault corps (the other was not yet back from Italy), though 8 Corps, as an officially designated "follow-up formation," was not yet involved. In this study week, blank maps of the actual area chosen were used, but those attending had obviously made some shrewd guesses as to its location, for on their return to Sandhutton their lips were very tightly sealed.

Towards the end of the month, took place Exercise "Grouse," a companion exercise to "Hawk," but this time set for Guards Armoured Division. This was successfully held between 28th and 30th July, being attended by General Paget, the Commander-in-Chief, 21 Army Group (as G.H.Q. Home Forces was now called), and also by the newly appointed Second Army Commander, Lieutenant-General Anderson, just home from Tunisia.

In the middle of August, however, General Alexander asked urgently for General McCreery to be flown out to Italy to take over 10 Corps in the Salerno landings and on 20th August, 8 Corps once again found itself without a head.

Though now lost to 21 Army Group, General McCreery was subsequently to have a brilliant career leading the Eighth Army in the concluding phase of the campaign in Italy, and to become the first British High Commissioner and Commander-in-Chief in Occupied Austria.

Into the breach to act temporarily as Corps Commander, however, stepped the senior divisional general, Major-General M. Brocas Burrows of 11 Armoured Division.

EARLY DAYS

During the early part of September, 15 (Scottish) Division moved down from Tyneside to a somewhat miserable stretch of the West Riding, bordering Ilkley Moor. The division was, however, now better positioned for collective training with the remainder of the Corps, and the first combined effort took place at the end of the month in a very large scale exercise named "Blackcock" in which 15 (Scottish) Division and Guards Armoured Division, in the usual break-out situation, took on 11 Armoured Division representing the enemy. This began on 23rd September and lasted until 2nd October, and for it Lieutenant-General "Monty" Stopford, the commander of 12 Corps then situated in south eastern England, was brought up to take charge of the Corps. This exercise, the most realistic and the largest in scope since "Spartan," was designed expressly, as its preamble stated, "to exercise 8 Corps for an extended period at the fullest possible scale." Re-reading the general narrative, one cannot help being struck by the startling similarity of the situation envisaged in "Blackcock" with what actually was the case in France ten months later. Here is what the narrative said:—

"The north-east of England represents occupied France.

The Allied offensive in the West was launched on 7th September, 1943, by an assault on the north coast of France. The operation was entrusted to 30 Army Group consisting of British Fourth and Fifth Armies. The British Fourth Army comprising 17 Corps, 8 Corps and 19 Corps, assisted by 4 Airborne Division and Commandos carried out the initial assault.

Another large scale landing was made simultaneously by the American Army 60 miles to the west (i.e., Northumberland) with the result that only a portion of the enemy reserves could "build-up" opposite the British Army.

17 Corps composed of 20, 21 and 22 Divisions acted in the role of an "assault" corps, each division having under command one army tank assault brigade. The assault operation by 17 Corps assisted by 4 Airborne Division was successful and by the evening of 7th September, the covering position was firmly in the hands of the assault divisions.

8 Corps acting in the role of "follow-up" corps, successfully landed over the beaches, in rear of 17 Corps followed by 19 Corps acting in the role of a "build-up" corps. By 11th September the bridgehead position had been dominated and a main port captured. The whole of the British Fourth Army was landed by 17 September, 1943.

The R.A.F. provided complete air cover for the landing operations. Both before and since the assault on France the principal effort of Bomber Command has been directed on communications in central France to delay the arrival of enemy reinforcements in the battle area.

In the action to secure the bridgehead, 9 Panzer Division previously located in the York area launched an attack against our positions on the high ground north of Great Driffield. The attack was a failure and the enemy withdrew after being badly mauled.

The bridgehead position is held with two corps up—17 Corps right, 19 Corps left with 8 Corps in army reserve. It was decided that the break-out of the bridgehead should commence on 28 September, 1943."

Except for the numbering of the various formations, the fact that the actual assault was carried out by two corps, though the same number of divisions was employed as in the narrative, that the British Second Army was not landed quite so speedily as the exercise Fourth Army, and if "Mulberry Harbour" be substituted for "main port," a very fair summary of the early part of the Normandy campaign results. In one respect, however, 8 Corps did better than this prophetic forecast. The exercise denotes 7th

September as invasion day, and 28th September as the day on which 8 Corps is landed, which is twenty-one days later. Its actual operations began on 26 June, 1944, twenty days after "D" Day.

When this exercise was written the final shape of the invasion was by no means certain. If ever proof were needed, however, that the British High Command had the measure of their opponents, that their training methods were correct, and that they were methodically preparing their forces to fight the enemy on the best possible terms, this is certainly supplied by this exercise narrative. "Waterloo was won on the playing fields of Eton" is an old familiar saying. Equally true is its modern equivalent that "Normandy was won in the training areas of Britain."

At the end of "Blackcock" General Anderson delivered a favourable summing up of the exercise and 8 Corps returned in a satisfied frame of mind to billets for the winter.

During the summer and autumn, the Corps had trained energetically, had studied its future role from every angle, and had already provided solutions for many of the problems arising from it. By October, it felt ready to fight and confident of its ability to do so, and that was apparently the general opinion for henceforth there was only one more corps exercise with troops on so gigantic a scale—"Exercise Eagle" in the following February. The Wolds, however, were by no means idle, for there was still much to be done. The "Sherman" which had replaced the "Crusader," hitherto the principal tank in British armoured divisions, during the course of the summer, had to be thoroughly mastered, as henceforth it was to be the main equipment in British as well as American armoured divisions. Though heavier than the Crusader, it was being produced in vast quantities and this solved the ever-present difficulties of British tank production. Several other American equipments also arrived such as the "M 10 Tank Destroyer"—a 75 mm. gun on a Sherman chassis—and the "Weasel," an ingenious small armoured vehicle used in effecting safe passage through boggy or swampy ground. All of these required considerable "getting to know" involving much experiment. The Corps as a whole made the acquaintance, too, about this time, of two activities peculiar to the status of a "follow-up" formation in the invasion of France. For the readers' benefit, let it be explained that a "follow-up" formation was one which, while not actually making the assault on the French coast, followed the assaulting troops ashore as soon as possible, achieving its landing therefore, in the absence of a port, across the open beaches. The indispensable preliminary to this was, of course, to ensure that tanks and vehicles did not get "drowned" in so doing. The many necessary precautions for this purpose were therefore worked out in Yorkshire during the remainder of 1943, and involved "waterproofing" vehicles, by coating their vulnerable parts with a sticky substance and then conducting extensive wading trials with them in the adjacent pond or river. Though this procedure caused much exasperation among all ranks at the time, it later proved its value, for during the invasion few vehicles were "drowned" in landing over the open beaches. Many combined practice camps for the armour, infantry and artillery to perfect co-operation among the various arms were also held during these winter months.

During the summer there had been some changes in the Corps staff. Brigadier Geoffrey Lucas, the D.A. and Q.M.G., had departed to Italy, where, too, one other senior officer, Brigadier R. R. Keane, the Chief Engineer, later joined him. They were replaced by two very experienced officers in the shape of Brigadier E. P. Sewell and Brigadier H. H. C. Sugden, who were destined to stay with 8 Corps right throughout the campaign.

One other addition to the Headquarters must be mentioned, though it was provisional only, and not destined to last very long. In order to foster closer relations with the R.A.F., at every corps headquarters the post of "Air Adviser" was created, and it was the intention that he, in conjunction with the G.S.O.2 (Air), already a member of the General Staff, should advise on the employment of the R.A.F. in conjunction with operations by the ground forces. 8 Corps was very fortunate in having Group Captain Viscount Acheson as its first, and unfortunately last "Air Adviser," for the appointment was abolished shortly before "D" day, when John Acheson, to the great regret of all, left the Headquarters. His association with 8 Corps was by no means wasted however, for through his assiduous training of the worthy G.S.O.2 (Air) and the many courses which they attended together in all parts of the country, it is safe to say that Fred Beer had a knowledge of R.A.F. procedure and temperament unrivalled among his colleagues in other corps, which was a great help when the time came to make use of it.

On Armistice Day, 11 November, 1943, news of the appointment of a new commander was received, and a few days later, Lieutenant-General A. F. Harding arrived. He had had a distinguished career in North Africa and would undoubtedly have been most popular in 8 Corps, but Fate, in the shape of far-away General Alexander, again willed otherwise, for General Harding was very shortly afterwards summoned to be his Chief of Staff at 15 Army Group Headquarters, and left on the following Christmas Day. Major-General MacMillan, commanding 15 (Scottish) Division, took over temporary command, but once again it was an unsettling experience for the Corps. Christmas festivities were however, held as usual, and if a slight digression in a lighter vein be permitted, perhaps the outstanding memory of that last Christmas at home, is of the scene towards the end of the evening at the combined mess party in which the portly but dignified Education Officer, Major R. H. Tibbits, urged on by a circle of clapping and cheering officers led by Sir Harry, performed a small solo song and dance to the strains of "Why do I love you?" rendered equally uncertainly by the band. This "act" by "Tibby" became quite famous, and on appropriate occasions thereafter, he was always encouraged to perform it, which he usually did.

In January, participation by 8 Corps in the planning for "Overlord," as the invasion operations were now called, began in earnest. On 1st January the change to overseas documentation was ordered, and from the end of that month onwards, an officer of the Corps armoured car regiment, 2 Household Cavalry, travelled, suitably guarded, every day between Second Army Headquarters at Victoria in London, and Sandhutton, bringing instructions and orders in profusion, dealing with every aspect of the invasion. G (Operations) and (Staff Duties) Branches were soon heavily involved with the A/Q side on loading tables, movement to the concentration areas, and maintenance in the bridgehead. On the Intelligence side, security instructions of all types from censorship regulations to instructions on the "Bigot" procedure of dealing with "top-secret" documents, flowed into the Headquarters, and out to subordinate formations. Elaborate precautions were taken to preserve secrecy, a guarded planning flat was set up, and as officers were initiated, so they were given a pass admitting them to it. Everything "top-secret" had to kept in this flat, though one senior officer developed a penchant for studying the "Overlord" plan in his own room, to the consternation of the responsible custodian, when one day, at the usual evening check-up he was unable to account for it, until he bethought himself of looking under the blotting pad of the aforesaid senior officer, where sure enough, it was lying. The planning flat too was quickly overgrown with vast piles of maps, for in order to conceal the identity of the invasion area, when maps concerning it were forwarded, they were packed in bundles which included those of other parts of France, and even of Holland and Belgium.

In the midst of these excitements, on 21st January, Lieutenant-General Sir Richard N. O'Connor arrived, the commander destined to take the Corps overseas and who was to guide it during the most vital phase of its career, and through its hardest fighting. General Dick O'Connor was well known throughout the Army at home, for his brilliant defeat of the Italians under Marshal Graziani in Egypt and Cyrenaica, in the winter campaign of 1940 —the first British victory after the sombre days of Dunkirk. Through the mischance of a wrongly chosen route in the succeeding April, 1941, he, together with Lieutenant-General Neame, was made a prisoner-of-war and taken to Italy. There, after several efforts to escape, he had finally reached British hands in December, 1943, and thence returned to England on the following Christmas Day. Despite the handicap of his two and a half years in captivity, his immediate appointment to 8 Corps speaks volumes for the esteem in which he was held. Though slight of build and shy by nature, he combined a most kindly disposition with an inflexible determination, and commanded from the first the greatest respect from everyone in his Headquarters and throughout the Corps. Under him 8 Corps prospered and was happy.

As soon as General O'Connor had toured the divisions, met their commanders and become familiar with the Corps layout, the next item on the programme was a visit from the new Commander-in-Chief of 21 Army Group, General Sir Bernard L. Montgomery, who had been selected to take overall charge of the Allied land forces in "Overlord." In accordance with his policy of inspecting all troops in his new command, while at the same time showing himself to them and instilling confidence by means of a short address, in the early months of 1944 he made a tour of England and Scotland in which every man, British, Canadian and American, destined to take part in the invasion, had the opportunity of seeing and hearing his Commander-in-Chief.

These parades were simple in character, but nevertheless were laid on with the utmost precision. Most detailed instructions came direct to Corps Headquarters from General Montgomery's personal staff, specifying how the parade was to be drawn up, the dress to be worn, and the equipment to be provided. In view, however, of the importance the Commander-in-Chief attached to these visits, it is obvious that he could afford to take no chances with them. One for Corps Headquarters and Corps troops was held at Sandhutton in a large meadow adjacent to the house. The bulk of the audience came from 6 Guards Tank Brigade and the whole was drawn up along three sides of a hollow square in two ranks facing inwards, through which the Commander-in-Chief walked alone, pausing occasionally to talk to a soldier. He then moved to the centre of the square and mounted the bonnet of a jeep equipped with a microphone, at the same time motioning the troops to break ranks and gather round him, which they always did in a tremendous rush. Then followed a short and very simple address brimming over with confidence, an enthusiastic "three cheers" and finally the cavalcade moved away, headed by a Rolls Royce flying an outsize Union Jack. It was all very impressive.

A long and final exercise with troops called "Eagle," followed towards the end of February, which certainly proved a test of endurance and of fitness for battle. Starting off with dispositions as in a bridgehead, 8 Corps was launched in the usual break-out role in the most severe weather. Several of the opposing troops dug-in and awaiting the attack, are said to have died from exposure in the Arctic conditions prevailing. Every arm and service was employed in as realistic a representation of winter campaigning as the most enthusiastic writer of military exercises could desire, and 8 Corps came through with flying colours. One story which should be told is of the occasion during "Eagle" in which the G.S.O.2 (Intelligence), giving the Commander his appreciation of a certain phase of it, calmly and naïvely informed him that he, veteran of many successful battles, had "lost the initiative." The shocked surprise of Brigadier Hammer and the amused grin of Sir Harry, spectators of the scene, alone showed to him the enormity of his offence, for the Commander betrayed no emotion at the time.

The life of the Corps at Sandhutton was now drawing to its close, and two final events gave proof that its time for active service was very near—the visits on 23rd March, 1944, of their Majesties the King and Queen, accompanied by H.R.H. Princess Elizabeth, and one week later of the Prime Minister, Mr. Winston Churchill. The Corps Headquarters was set up as in the field, and the King, escorted by the Commander, and the Queen by the B.G.S., showed particular interest in the Command Post, though this was but a small version of what it later became. Of G (Operations) the King enquired whether they worked hard, of G (Intelligence) he asked whether they always "guessed right." History, unfortunately, does not record the answer to either question.

At the beginning of April, General O'Connor and the B.G.S. left Sandhutton to attend the well-named "Thunderclap," the Commander-in-Chief's presentation of his plan for "Overlord," held at St. Paul's School, London and at which almost everyone prominent in British and Allied circles at that time, was present. One week later, on 14th April, 8 Corps as a whole began to move to its concentration areas in Sussex and Surrey. The Headquarters was established in a very fine house, formerly the property of Lord Cowdray, but latterly a Roman Catholic school, called Worth Priory, about two miles outside Crawley in Sussex, and midway between London and the coast. Guards Armoured Division chose the Eastbourne area, whilst 15 (Scottish) Division was disposed round Worthing and Brighton. 11 Armoured Division probably had the worst of the deal, and was quartered rather closely and uncomfortably in the Aldershot area. A planning flat was once again established, at Worth Priory, but this time on a larger scale as now the divisions were brought into the planning and more space was required. The Corps also became increasingly security-minded and barbed wire was liberally used to safeguard this part of the house—even being strung round the first floor windows. It was rumoured, though doubtless the story is apocryphal, that the C.C.R.A. retired to a hill opposite the house and surveyed this flat through a telescope, to see what information could be obtained from the many maps on the walls. At all events, true or not, he recommended that the windows be whitewashed, which was duly carried out and was, after all, an elementary security precaution.

At Sandhutton, too, the Commander had ordered the making of a sand model of the future area of operations, which was beautifully carried out, to scale, just before the Corps moved, by Peter Low, the topography Intelligence Officer, and Theo Peters. Of course, at Worth Priory, to Peter's fury and dismay, this model had to be re-created. It was, however, constantly used by General O'Connor both for contemplation and reflection on the probable course of events, and also for some necessary but abortive planning with General Urquhart of 1 Airborne Division and his staff. Although the overall strategy for the Normandy fighting had long since been decided by General Montgomery, planning for certain eventualities had to be undertaken. One of these was a possible airborne landing by 1 Airborne Division astride the main Caen-Falaise road roughly in the wooded area of Bretteville-sur-

Laize, to coincide with an armoured break-out by 8 Corps south west of Caen. A plan was fully prepared and wireless exercises were held, practising the establishment of communications between 8 Corps and the airborne troops. However, the enemy situation in the bridgehead later precluded the use of airborne troops in this way, and the scheme was never put into operation.

One's attention when regarding this model of the Normandy countryside, always tended to be drawn to the dominating feature, a rocky massif stretching from south west of Caumont by the Foret de L'Eveque to the south east, in which the high points, two formidable hills called Pt. 309 and "Mont Pincon" stood out. Although at that time there was little thought of 8 Corps operating in this area, the Commander was fascinated by these hills, appreciating, very accurately as it turned out, that they would be the pivot of the enemy's final positions in Normandy. There was no idea, however, that in this area was to take place a great victory, one which would turn the German line, assisting the Americans to break out to the south and bring about their swing to the Seine.

By the middle of May, all marshalling and embarkation instructions had been issued, the Commander had addressed all three divisions and Corps troops in person, and there was nothing left to be done except to await the signal. London, being conveniently close, became a favourite Mecca for an evening's entertainment (approximately two million other British and Allied soldiers came to the same conclusion every day) though Brighton and the south coast were equally favoured and a notable "Highland Games" day was held there by 15 (Scottish) Division, which showed clearly how fit were the troops of this magnificent formation.

Many distinguished but last-minute visitors called, including General Crerar, the Canadian Army Commander, and General Eisenhower, who addressed a representative parade of the Corps. He gave the impression of an attractive personality and his tale of the private who refused to envy his commanding general on the grounds that the latter had no prospects of promotion, drew a laugh from the troops. General Montgomery, at the end of May, gave two addresses to all officers of 8 Corps down to battalion commanders—part of a series he made to the whole of 21 Army Group—in which he revealed not only his plan, but his faith that the actual invasion, despite Field-Marshal Rommel's latterly increased anti-invasion precautions (including under-water obstacles, which were causing a certain amount of alarm) would not only be successful, but as he put it, "easy, quite easy, not difficult at all." And in this he was, as always, accurate.

At the beginning of June it was decided to burn the many surplus or redundant papers concerning "Overlord," which had by now been accumulated, and this occasions a story against the Chief Engineer's branch, which though rigorously suppressed at the time is too good to withhold any longer. The Sappers claimed to have a speedy, effective and foolproof method of destroying papers by using explosives, which they had developed for the benefit of headquarters, which in battle might get overrun. Speed and efficiency in this matter were therefore essential to prevent secret documents falling into enemy hands. In short the Sappers made an offer to G (Operations) and G (Intelligence), both to deal with their secret waste, and to try out this scheme at the same time. Somewhat reluctantly, they agreed, and the resulting bundle of papers interlaced with slabs of gun cotton was stacked some three hundred yards behind the house in a convenient dell and (fortunately) out of sight of the occupants. Those present then retired to a safe distance and the charge was ignited. Their hopes received a rude shock for the air was immediately filled with snow flakes. Large scraps were lodged in the trees, and the ground round about for about 100 yards was littered with unburned remnants. The G.S.O.2 (Intelligence) and the S.O.R.E. were appalled, for every piece of paper seemed to have on it some such name as Caen, Bayeux or Falaise. Visions of trial by court-martial and subsequent shooting, appeared individually and simultaneously to all witnesses of this distressing spectacle. The whole area was immediately cordoned off, the two Corps field security sections, by the mercy of Providence, billeted nearby, were summoned, and after three hours of hard work including much climbing of trees to shake down refractory scraps, every shred of paper was collected and burned. To add to the troubles, a light wind sprang up in the middle of all this, complicating the task, and the C.C.R.A. also came out to enquire what the explosion was. Both were successfully dealt with. There were some guilty looks in the mess that night however, and the Sappers' method of destroying waste paper was never heard of again.

By the end of May, every final preparation was complete throughout the Corps. The weather was delightful and as the assaulting formations were now all in their marshalling areas, it was obvious that operations could not long be delayed. On Sunday, 4th June, a church parade was held at Worth Priory, after which the Corps Commander gave an address. In this he spoke of the coming hardships and difficulties of battle and stressed that a headquarters exists only as the servant of the fighting troops. During the afternoon, Corps Headquarters sports and a fête were held in the grounds and were much enjoyed, many wives and friends being present.

On the following day, as if drawn by a magnet, most of the Staff motored down to the coast to see the state of the Channel. Weather conditions had considerably worsened, for though it was bright and warm, a fresh breeze had sprung up on 4th June and persisted, making the sea very choppy indeed, not to say rough. The B.G.S. on seeing it, remarked, as did everyone else, that it looked as though the invasion was not destined to take place on the morrow. However, shortly after his return to Worth Priory, a message came in from Second Army, with the appointed code name and " D " Day was fixed for all taking part, and for history too, as 6th June. Sir Harry's only comment on being shown the telegram was " Well, I couldn't be more surprised."

It was, of course, intended that the Headquarters should be in close touch by wireless with those of the assaulting corps and also Second Army, which had been established in one of Palmerston's forts overlooking Portsmouth—the relics of an earlier invasion scare, now at long last having a period of usefulness. The whole of " D " Day was spent in listening to wireless bulletins of one sort or another, and in discussing with some degree of excitement, how well the operations appeared to be going, but finally in the afternoon, orders were issued for the move of the advance party to Horndean and thence to its marshalling area.

The move overseas of the Corps Headquarters, a body of some considerable size, owning several hundred vehicles, was in itself quite complicated. The move had been worked out on the basis of a number of parties, the first of which, in this case, was called " Tac Headquarters," though it bore no relation to that later used in the field. It consisted of the Commander, B.G.S., D.A. and Q.M.G., C.C.R.A., C.E., C.S.O., G.S.O.2 (Operations), G.S.O.2 (Intelligence), G.S.O.2 (Liaison), S.O.2 (Signals), G.S.O.3 (Operations), and the O.C. Headquarters Squadron. It was, in effect, the Command Group of the Headquarters, and its task was twofold—first, to reconnoitre a suitable area for the full Corps Headquarters on arrival in Normandy, and generally to act as an advance party, and secondly to liaise with the formations in situ in France, learning the day to day situation so that when the time came for participation in operations, the principal staff officers would be, to use a popular military phrase, "in the picture."

On the morning of 7th June, a slow cavalcade (since the roads were crowded with military traffic) moved off from Worth Priory to an intermediate stop at a house in a small village called Horndean, near Chichester, where two days were spent, and, at length, on the afternoon of 10th June, it reached the marshalling area at Gosport, near Portsmouth. No embarkation was possible that night and the vehicles remained, therefore, aligned along the streets of a rather humble dockside quarter of the town. It thus appeared as though the first of probably many uncomfortable nights in store for the Headquarters had arrived. This reckoned, however, without the local population, who had obviously been immensely cheered and relieved by the successful beginning to "Overlord." No one in any of the cars or trucks was permitted to stay in them for long. Every house was opened, food, drink and refreshments of all kinds were constantly brought out, and a most happy time was spent by all. Several impromptu concerts started up, there was dancing in the streets to wireless and gramophone, as well as to home-made music from an astonishing collection of musical instruments carried by the troops, and it is doubtful if any member of "Tac Headquarters" had much sleep that night.

The following morning, 11th June, the party was re-assembled, and made its way to the dockside, and some two hours later, towards midday, it embarked in an L.C.T. of American construction, manned by the Royal Navy. Personal kit had been cut to a minimum, as had also the number of vehicles, and one could not help a slight feeling of chagrin therefore, that when completely loaded—there was also on board a troop of Light A.A. guns as protection against air attack during the crossing—the hold was only two-thirds full and could easily have accommodated another twenty vehicles. However, it was too late for any changes. In the middle of the afternoon, the L.C.T. made its way out into the Solent, and took up its allotted position in the immense convoy stretching in every direction as far as the eye could see.

In retrospect, that short voyage seems as fantastic now, as then, for it had nothing so much about it as the air of a holiday cruise. The weather was sunny and calm, jazz music was played on the ship's loudspeakers all day long, the troops were not unduly crowded and there was no enemy air activity. Some were indeed lucky enough to occupy cabins, of which there were a fair number on that hospitable craft. For the next three months, living in a narrow bridgehead on hard rations and with only an occasional visit to a mobile bath unit, two memories predominated of that astonishing trip—the ship's shower baths and the American food. The latter really brought home for the first time, how stereotyped and unappetising Britain's war-time diet had become. Hard rations on the other side, however, soon cured one of any hankering after American food, for the eternal "biscuit and bully" made the memory of even English food seem veritable ambrosia, and it is beyond the power of any pen to depict the relief generally felt at the introduction of white bread in the place of biscuits, some six weeks after the start of the invasion.

The voyage was completely without incident, though an American Liberty ship is said to have all but rammed the L.C.T. in the middle of the night, the main witness being the C.C.R.A. Towards midday on the following day, 12th June, the French coast with its beached landing craft, its wrecked houses and bombarded defences came into view and the L.C.T. anchored about a mile off shore. There seemed no activity apart from unloading, although this was the extreme east end of the invasion area. An occasional circle of white foam five or six hundred yards away showed, however, that the enemy coastal battery on the far side of the River Orne, at Merville, was endeavouring, without success, to reach the L.C.T. This enemy battery was later destined to become a thorn in the side of the local Beach Group, and eventually this particular beach was given up, since to use it, proved too costly in lives and equipment. Overshadowing everything, especially to those in operations for the first time, was the rumble of guns along the whole front.

CHAPTER 2

Normandy and Operation "Epsom"

TOWARDS evening, the L.C.T. was beached near the mouth of the River Orne, at a small seaside resort called Rivabella, and the Headquarters landed dryshod, being welcomed on arrival by the G.S.O.2 (Liaison), who, with the Commander and the B.G.S., had made the crossing earlier in the day in H.M.S. Glasgow, in the convoy of destroyers escorting Mr. Churchill, Sir Alan Brooke and General Smuts on their visit to the Commander-in-Chief at his Tactical Headquarters in Normandy.

The first essential was to remove the various waterproofing impedimenta to vehicle movement, and this was easy, for the work of weeks was undone in as many minutes. Then, having been given a map reference of the proposed location for the night, the party moved off along the road bordering the Caen Canal. Missing the very narrow turning for Douvres in the one-way circuit, possibly owing to attention being riveted on the many gliders, wrecked and otherwise, which littered the area as evidence of the previous week's airborne landings, the convoy approached Benouville Bridge (or Pegasus Bridge as it is now called) at the time apparently undergoing one of its periodic enemy counter attacks. The arrival of the party seemed as unpopular with the troops of 6 Airborne Division holding it, as with the enemy, and somewhat hastily the vehicles were turned about and made their way, more correctly, westwards, first of all to a kind of staging area for parties arriving, and finally after a night in the open, early on the morning of 13th June, to what was intended should be the first location for the whole Headquarters—the chateau of Lantheuil, six miles north-west of Caen and three miles north of the main lateral road from Caen to Bayeux. This fine 17th century French house had been the pre-invasion headquarters of the German 716 Coastal Division, in whose sector the first landings had taken place. It was, however, owned by a French count, who with his mother, was still in residence, and whose reception of the Headquarters in the early stages was distinctly cool. He had been a naval officer under the Vichy régime, and present at both Oran in 1940, when the Royal Navy sank part of the French fleet, and Toulon in 1942, when the remainder of it had been scuttled. His sour outlook was therefore understandable. It was, moreover, the general attitude of the Normandy population, who were afraid of reprisals, if the Germans succeeded, as they had boasted, in driving the Allies out again. The manner of the French changed once operations became mobile, and they were certain of the outcome of the struggle, but not until then. For the moment the Allies were " capturing " places and not " liberating " them.

It was not the intention of the Commander, however, that his Staff should occupy the house, though this was occasionally to be used for conferences. The woods surrounding it were to be its home, and well-spaced (though inconveniently), the various caravans and L.C.V.s were dotted about the grounds, for there was as yet no thought of a central Command Post, which evolved somewhat later. On the following day, 14th June, the second

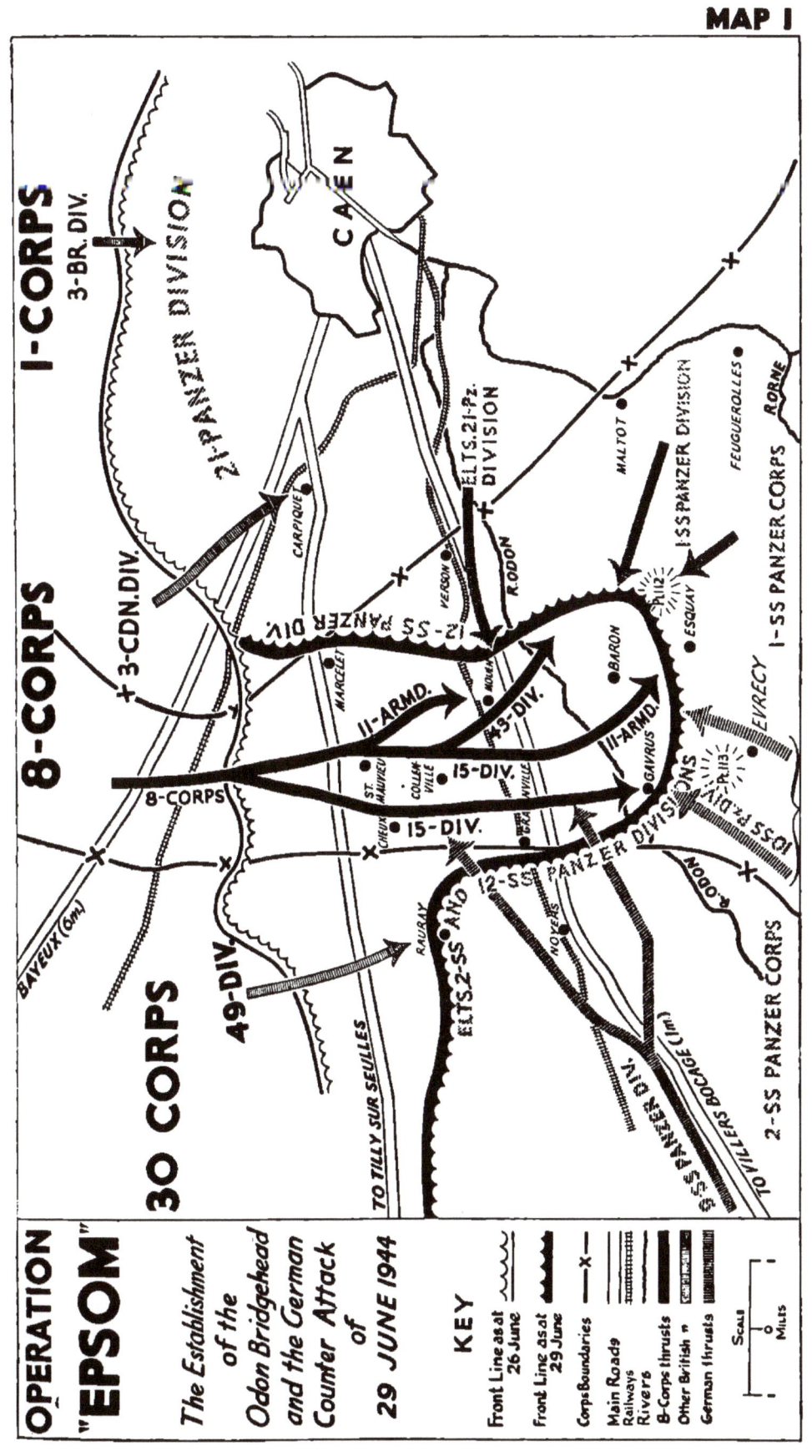

party of Corps Headquarters arrived, and thereafter for the next ten days, detachments trickled in, and were absorbed.

The territory held by Second Army was still extremely narrow—it was only just about to link up with that of the Americans on the right flank, who up to now had undergone a severe struggle to maintain their own bridgehead, and the whole area was rapidly becoming very congested. Indeed, by the end of June, when over a million Allied soldiers had been landed, as well as hundreds of thousands of tons of stores and equipment, there was not one single unused piece of ground to be seen anywhere.

At Lantheuil, Corps Headquarters was centrally placed for liaison with Second Army Headquarters, as well as those of 11 Armoured Division, now set up in the adjacent village of Cully, and 15 (Scottish) Division at St. Gabriel. A glance at the map, however, shows that Lantheuil woods are the most prominent ones for some distance round about, which in itself should have aroused the suspicion of the enemy. Moreover, a brief reconnaissance of the area soon after arrival, revealed the Headquarters to be nicely positioned between a landing ground under construction by the R.A.F. on one side, and a deception unit of several scores of dummy tanks, made of rubber and inflated, and representing the Guards Armoured Division (at that time still in England) on the other. Why the Corps was never shelled or mortared, for Lantheuil was well within enemy range for either, will always be a major mystery. Possibly the enemy artillery was already too heavily committed to attempt harassing tasks of this nature. At all events, save for one bombing attempt which achieved nothing more lethal than breaking the windows of the B.G.S.' caravan, in this location 8 Corps was never molested.

The countryside looked peaceful and relatively undamaged, and except for the nightly air raids and the sound of the "flak" by which Lantheuil was surrounded, the casual observer might have considered the general effect to be that of one of the more pleasant exercises at home. It was, however, a period of great strain and tension for the Corps Commander and B.G.S., for 1 and 30 Corps, having carried out the invasion, were now withstanding considerable enemy pressure and urgently required help for their tired divisions. This 8 Corps was unable to give until its own formations had completed their arrival, and in this matter Fate was unkind, for the great storm which raged from 19th to 22nd June greatly delayed the landing of units, notably those of 15 (Scottish) Division.

It was, of course, no part of the Commander-in-Chief's plan that 8 Corps should remain inactive for long. From 15th June onwards some brief attention was paid to planning an operation entitled "Dreadnought," which involved a breakout east of the River Orne, by 15 (Scottish) Division and 11 Armoured Division, through the sector held by 51 (Highland) Division. In view of the confined area of the Orne bridgehead, it was at length decided that this manœuvre was not a feasible proposition, and finally the idea was abandoned on 18th June. One day later, on 19th June, a conference was held at the Mairie in Creully, presided over by General Dempsey, at which the main intentions of Second Army were revealed for the new phase of operations about to begin. The Allied foothold on the soil of France was now firm enough to withstand any attack the enemy might choose to launch against it. Moreover, so swift and devastating had been the early blows struck at the German framework of defence, that from the moment of landing, the initiative had rested with the British and American forces, and the enemy had never even momentarily regained it. By now, however, the German High Command had had ample opportunity to size up the full nature of the threat to "Fortress Europe," and it was reasonable to suppose that their hasty "roping-off" policy of dealing with the invasion would give way to a more co-ordinated effort, in which a series of deliberate counter-attacks would attempt a systematic reduction of the Allied bridgehead. Let us examine the overall situation, from the enemy point of view, in the middle of June.

Thus far, of the sixty or so German divisions of all types in the West, about a dozen had been drawn into the Normandy fighting. The remainder, of which the bulk were in the Fifteenth German Army, garrisoning the Pas de Calais area (where the greatest threat was felt), were still scattered around the coast of France. All available local divisions had thus been used to contain the Allies, and this had entailed the committal in an infantry role, of first class Panzer divisions, such as 12 SS Panzer Division and 21 Panzer Division, a course which must have been anathema to von Rundstedt and Rommel. Prudence and the principles of war alike demanded, therefore, that fresh infantry divisions be brought in to relieve these panzer formations as soon as possible, so that the Germans could reform their armoured reserve as the indispensable preliminary to a counter offensive.

From the Allied standpoint, this was exactly what General Montgomery was determined to prevent, for the launching of any counter offensive would regain the initiative for the enemy and thus upset the general lines of the strategy he had already worked out, and announced, for the battle of Normandy.

Hitherto, so far as Second Army was concerned, the fighting, which as more troops were brought in by the enemy was steadily becoming fiercer, had been borne by formations which had carried out the original assault on "D" Day. It was understandable that these were by now somewhat tired, and that their casualties were already appreciable. It was therefore a matter of some urgency both to expand the bridgehead and at the same time to relax the pressure on 1 and 30 Corps. At this juncture too, reports began to circulate of the return to France of 2 SS Panzer Corps, fresh from a brief but successful visit to the Eastern Front where, as the spearhead of a surprise counter attack, it had brought the Russian advance on Poland to a halt and relieved the threat to the important industrial area of Lvov. The Germans thus had in the two tried and proven divisions of this corps—9 SS (Hohenstaufen) and 10 SS (Frundsberg)—a formidable nucleus towards their greatly desired strategic reserve.

Some quick stroke, therefore, was necessary if the Allies were to retain freedom of action. Factors of geography and strategy, as well as the shape of the bridgehead, which was deepest in the British sector on the right flank, dictated that the major effort should be directed against the Caen area, the possession which was vital to the development of any future threat to the Seine basin, and to the east generally. The Seine basin was, of course, of supreme importance to the enemy for a variety of reasons, the chief of which he considered to be the following:—

      (a) It was the last major barrier protecting the V.1 and V.2 sites.
      (b) At the mouth of the river was Le Havre, his chief naval base in the Channel.
      (c) If the British succeeded in reaching Paris, then his forces in Normandy would be cut off.

Finally, Allied deception plans had been sufficiently good to make the German High Command believe that a further assault in the Pas de Calais was to be expected, and that any link up between the two forces landing must be prevented at all costs. This flank was, therefore, the very lynch pin of the whole enemy position in Normandy. Once it had gone, there was nothing to prevent his entire forces west of the Seine from being trapped.

The declared Allied strategy was, however, to attract as much German strength as possible, particularly in armour, to the British sector, so that the break through and subsequent sweep round to the Seine and Paris, might be more easily accomplished by the Americans. Not, of course, knowing this, but fitting the Allied operations into his pre-conceived notions of our aims, the enemy played exactly into the hands of General Montgomery. As the SHAEF report on the campaign in North-West Europe later stated:—

> "The resultant struggle around Caen, which seemed to cost so much in blood, for such small territorial gains, was thus an essential factor in ensuring our ultimate success. The very tenacity of the defence was sufficient proof of this. Every foot of ground the enemy lost at Caen, was like losing ten miles anywhere else."

At the Creully meeting, General Dempsey, on instructions from the Commander-in-Chief announced that he proposed as soon as possible, to initiate a three corps attack (though not as a co-ordinated army operation), in which 1 and 30 Corps would conduct subsidiary operations, designed both to help the main effort, and to divert the enemy's attention from it, whilst the major attack was to be carried out by 8 Corps with its fresh, if untried, troops. This would be known as Operation "Epsom," and was to take place as soon as possible, being provisionally fixed for 23rd June. Every assistance would be given to 8 Corps, including maximum support from both the R.A.F. and the Royal Navy. A series of staff conferences were then held with Second Army and subordinate formations, and at 1500 hours on 23rd June, the Corps Commander explained the general situation and his plan to all officers in the Corps of the rank of lieutenant-colonel and above, at Corps Headquarters at Lantheuil.

The weather, which in general had been changeable since "D" Day, had greatly hampered the unloading of stores and the disembarkation of troops. The result was, therefore, that some of 8 Corps' subordinate formations, notably 15 (Scottish) Division were not as yet at their full strength, whilst there had also been a temporary ammunition shortage. Many of the Staff will remember the C.C.R.A. predicting this latter eventuality, before the Headquarters left Worth Priory and urging that every vacant space in vehicles and L.C.T.s be utilised to take across shells of all types, over and above the normal "Q" supply arrangements. Though this was not accepted at the time, there must have been many regrets over that decision at this juncture. "Epsom" was therefore postponed, first, for twenty-four hours, and then tentatively to 26th June, so that the deficiencies in manpower and material could be made good. Formations moved forward to their assembly areas and forming-up points, however, on 24th and 25th June, and at 2205 hours on 25th June, confirmation was received from Second Army Headquarters that the operation would take place at 0730 hours on the following morning, 26th June. A telephone call a short while afterwards depressed everyone somewhat with the information that in view of the steady deterioration in the weather in England, the full programme of air support, arranged between the R.A.F. and the Corps Headquarters, could not be carried out. This was a considerable disappointment, but it made no difference to the decision to launch 8 Corps into its first battle on the next day.

So far as the subsidiary operations to "Epsom" were concerned, these were three in number, and were planned as follows:—

(a) 30 Corps.

30 Corps was instructed to capture Rauray, a village on a spur overlooking Cheux, one of the first objectives of 8 Corps, by midnight on 25th June, and on the following day to continue the advance southwards with the object of taking and clearing Noyers by the evening. Thereafter its axis of advance was directed on Aunay-sur-Odon, touch being kept with 8 Corps by frequent patrols up to the inter-corps boundary. In view of its dominating position vis-a-vis Cheux, the capture of Rauray was felt by General O'Connor to be absolutely necessary, and in the event of 30 Corps failing to reach and take it, then this task would undoubtedly fall to 15 (Scottish) Division in addition.

(b) 1 Corps.

The operations by 1 Corps, unlike those of 30 Corps, were not due to begin until two days after 8 Corps had started, and may be summed up by saying that it was the intention first, as a diversion to the attack by 8 Corps, to take a series of small but strongly-held villages, forming part of the outer perimeter defences of Caen, as a useful preliminary also to an ultimate assault on the city itself. With these villages in British hands, the task of capturing the formidably defended airfield at Carpiquet would be facilitated, and once this was achieved, the British left flank was secured from counter attack by enemy armour known to be in this area. 3 Canadian Division, therefore, had been ordered to carry out this undertaking at the same time as the other operations by 1 Corps.

The Enemy Situation on the "Epsom" Front

From 3 Canadian Division, one of the original assault divisions, which had been in the line from "D" Day onwards, a clear picture was obtained of the enemy facing 8 Corps in the area chosen for its first attack. It appeared that a sector extending from roughly Bronay to St. Contest was held by an SS formation, 12 SS Panzer Division (Hitler Jugend), its boundaries roughly coinciding with those of the Canadians. This SS division belonged to the crack 1 SS Panzer Corps, commanded by that colourful figure, old party member and former butcher, Sepp Dietrich, a personal friend of the Fuehrer, and who, despite his humble origin and lack of education, military or otherwise, had nevertheless had an interesting and successful army career. From the early days when he had been engaged by Hitler to keep order at his meetings, Sepp Dietrich had prospered with the rise of the Nazi Party, and after being successively the creator and peacetime commander of Hitler's bodyguard regiment, the "Leibstandarte Adolf Hitler," had also continued as the wartime commander of these troops on their expansion to divisional size as 1 SS Panzer Division (Adolf Hitler). In this position he had been conspicuously successful, and under him the division had fought brilliantly, usually in a spearhead role, as befits élite troops. Moreover, despite their heavy casualties, Sepp Dietrich was much liked by his men, to whom his toughness and rough humour appealed, and he remained the most popular Waffen SS commander until the end of the war. At the end of 1943, when 1 SS Panzer Corps had been created, comprising 1 SS Panzer Division and 12 SS Panzer Division, Dietrich had received command of it and, at the same time, promotion to the rank of Oberstgruppenfuehrer, or Colonel-General in the Waffen SS.

It is interesting to note at this juncture the rise to predominance on the German side in Normandy, of field commanders belonging to the Waffen SS, and not to the German Army proper, for the two bodies were quite separate and little love was lost between them. In view of the increasing disasters the Wehrmacht was everywhere suffering, it was only natural that Hitler should come to rely more and more on his own Praetorian Guard and on commanders whose dependance on him and the régime made their loyalty beyond question. This inclination received a great stimulus after the bomb plot of 20th July, in which so many of the German General Staff were implicated. Henceforth the Fuehrer's whole trust reposed in his Waffen SS, for we find men like Dietrich and Hausser becoming army commanders; Himmler, Commander-in-Chief of the Home Army, and later in charge of army groups in the more threatened sectors, whilst the Waffen SS received absolute priority in replacements of men and material. They, moreover, led such limited counter offensives and forlorn hopes as the Ardennes and Hungarian operations, which the Germans were able to organise. A remark by Hitler to the luckless General von Choltitz when despatching him in early August to take over command of the Paris area, then already virtually invested by the Allies, is most revealing. The Fuehrer's rage at the events of 20th July was apparently extreme, for von Choltitz relates:

"When the Fuehrer told me how he hates Generals, a sadistic hatred which I can never forget, was in his eyes."

In Hitler's defence it must be admitted that the Waffen SS were by far the best German troops, and fought always with the intensity of fanatics.

These were the type of troops therefore that 8 Corps was destined to meet in its first engagement, for though composed largely of soldiers 17-19 years of age, 12 SS Panzer Division, with its youthful commander of 33, Brigadefuehrer Meyer, and leavening of experienced, battle-trained officers and N.C.O.s from its parent formation, 1 SS Panzer Division, fought with a tenacity and a ferocity seldom equalled and never excelled during the whole of the campaign in the West.

It was estimated that although this division had been in action since 7th June it had not suffered unduly heavy casualties, as, apart from one abortive attempt at a counter-attack and some fairly severe engagements with 2 Canadian Armoured Brigade in the early days, it had latterly been on the defensive. Indeed, it was firmly dug in by now, and there had been many reports of mines and wiring, and also of occasional booby-traps. So far, therefore, as its infantry personnel were concerned, it was probably at 75% strength. As regards armour, the same was also true, for while 3 Canadian Division claimed 83 tanks knocked out up to 20th June, not all these necessarily belonged to 12 SS Panzer Division. In any case, as the enemy had retained possession of the ground over which the engagements were fought, his excellent maintenance organisation would have restored many of these to the condition of "runners." The strength in armour of 12 SS Panzer Division was, as a result, somewhat difficult to assess, but at the time was put at between 140-160 tanks, mainly "Panthers," but with possibly a battalion of "Tigers" in addition. This estimate in retrospect seems a trifle high, but at all events this division must have had over 100 tanks, and the emphasis was therefore in the right direction to bring home to the troops the formidable nature of their first opponent.

In passing, it may be mentioned that just prior to "D" Day, General O'Connor had been much exercised by the many reports of last minute intensification of anti-invasion preparations, and in particular by the increase in the German tank build-up opposite the British landing area, which, moreover, already expected to receive the lion's share of enemy armoured counter-attack. It was also considered that the German field army in the West, by the late spring of 1944, would be equipped largely with two types of tanks only—" Panthers " and " Tigers "—both of which were superior in armament and armoured protection to any on the Allied side. He had therefore caused to be prepared a comparative table of German and British tank build-up, which was somewhat disquieting, as the following figures show:—

FRONT HELD BY SECOND ARMY AND INCLUDING 5 U.S. CORPS SECTOR.

GERMAN AND BRITISH TANK BUILD-UP.

Available	Enemy					Own Troops		
	Formation	Tanks		Running Total		Formation	Tanks Fire-flies	Running Total
		Panthers	Tigers	Panthers	Tigers			
D Day	21 Pz Div	93	50	—	—	1 Corps and 30 Corps	93	—
	12 SS Pz Div	80	—	173	50			
D+1	116 Pz Div	80	—	253	50			
D+2-3	No change	—	—	—	—			
D+4	2 Pz Div	80	—	333	50		94	187
D+5	No change	—	—	—	—			
D+6	2 SS Pz Div	80	20	413	70			
D+7 to D+14	—	—	Nil	—	—	8 Corps 11 Armd Div Gds Armd Div	36 36	— 259
D+15 onwards	—	—	?	—	—	12 Corps	Nil	259
		TOTAL ...	413	70		—	—	259

Additional armoured formations likely to be employed against U.S. forces in the Cotentin Peninsula:—

Panthers

Pz Lehr Division 80

17 SS Panzer
Grenadier Division } .... nil (Mark IV's only)

Balance of German armour in the West after D+6 (excluding Mark IV's):

Panzer divisions and separate formations, including training establishments:—

    Tigers   *Panthers*
    140   480

Grand Totals:

German Tanks—Panthers...... 973   British Tanks—Fireflies...... 259
                 Tigers......... 210

In point of fact, so far as the Germans were concerned, these figures were not an over-statement, for they did not take into account the return to France of 2 SS Panzer Corps with its corps tank regiment and two first class divisions, which at the time was in progress, though unknown to the Allies. On paper, the contrast was therefore a marked one, for the only answer in tanks which they had to the "Panther" and the "Tiger," was the "Firefly."

The "Firefly" was a Sherman tank, equipped with a 17-pr. gun, and was a recent innovation available, so far, only in comparatively small numbers on the basis of one per troop of tanks, or 36 in all to each armoured division. The majority of these had naturally fallen to the assaulting corps, but 8 Corps had 72 and the total for Second Army was 259. This figure, however, did not seem sufficient to General O'Connor, who expressed his anxiety to the Army Commander.

There was a second answer to these formidable German A.F.Vs. in the shape of ordinary 17-pr. guns, either tractor drawn, or self-propelled, providing they were equipped with a special type of ammunition, known as "Sabot." This was ammunition with a tremendous "boost" to the normal charge and thus a far greater penetrative effect, but it was hardly reckoned to be so effective an answer, as the guns were not so mobile, nor the crews so well protected, as in the "Firefly." Moreover, "Sabot" shells were in extremely short supply, and none had so far been allotted to 8 Corps. The reply from General Dempsey showed, nevertheless, that whilst every effort was being made by the War Office to remedy this state of affairs, Second Army was compelled to reckon in every 17-pr. to redress the balance. Thus he stated:—

> "17-prs. in all forms and 'Sabot' ammunition are absolutely first in our priority for equipment. The Q.M.G. and all those concerned are quite clear about this. I attach a note showing the total number of 17-prs. which we will land by day."

This note gave the build-up of these guns from 167 landing on "D" Day and rising by an average of 40 per day to 711 on D+17, when all would have been brought on shore. Before going into its first action, however, 8 Corps received on 23rd June, 240 rounds of Sabot, which was allotted to 31 Tank Brigade for its 42 x 6-pr. Churchills, as well as a further allocation of 300 rounds on the following day. Though the enemy in the early stages was never able to attempt a co-ordinated attack with anything like the amount of armour at his disposal, the result of "Overlord" might have been very different, had he been in a position to do so.

Composition of 8 Corps for Operation "Epsom"

For Operation "Epsom" 8 Corps was not to be constituted exactly according to the normal set-up, as the second of its armoured divisions, Guards Armoured Division, was still far from complete, the majority of its tanks having yet to arrive in France. Its place was taken by 43 (Wessex) Division, commanded by Major-General G. I. Thomas, an infantry formation which had hitherto trained with, and formed part of, 12 Corps, of which it was the first troops to arrive in Normandy. The resultant loss of armour was, however, more than made up, when 4 Armoured Brigade, a formation with a very fine battle record in Africa, and 31 Tank Brigade, which had hitherto not been out of England, were placed under command. The Corps was also allotted two squadrons of "flail" tanks for use in clearing a passage through enemy minefields, from the Westminster Dragoons and 22 Dragoons respectively, as well as a large assortment of heterogeneous R.E. units for dealing with the various engineer problems anticipated.

The composition and strength of 8 Corps therefore at 0600 hours on its first day of battle, 26 June, 1944, was as follows:—

Formation	Strength	
	Officers	Other Ranks
Headquarters 8 Corps and Corps troops	338	4,821
11 Armoured Division	665	12,050
15 (Scottish) Infantry Division	790	15,001
43 (Wessex) Infantry Division	798	14,821
4 Armoured Brigade	243	4,300
31 Tank Brigade	179	2,986
8 A.G.R.A.	151	3,101
TOTAL:	3,164	57,080

It will be noted that whilst it numbered upwards of 60,000 strong, and therefore may be reckoned as a strong corps, some of the subordinate formations were as yet not fully up to strength, notably 43 Division, where the unhappy accident of a floating mine sinking the L.C.T. conveying the reconnaissance regiment of the division, had occasioned great loss of life to this unit, forcing it to be re-formed in England. This was by far the worst disaster among the relatively few which, thanks to the Royal Navy, took place in ferrying the armies over from England to France, but it left 43 Division somewhat weakened at the start of its career in the field.

The General Situation in the " Overlord " Area and Outline Plan for " Epsom "

Despite the slowdown of operations occasioned by the great storm of 19th June, and the precarious supply position it created for a few days, by the time "Epsom" was being organised, the overall situation for the Allies in Normandy was good. Events were working out as anticipated in the Overlord plan. The lodgement area was now securely established, and the British sector, against which the weight of German pressure had, as foreseen and indeed desired, been brought, had held firm in the face of attack by four panzer divisions. U.S. forces, after a shaky start on "Omaha" beach, had recovered their balance, linked up with the British Second Army and were now over-running the weakly defended Cotentin Peninsula. The German Supreme Command did not like the shape of affairs at all, and on 17th June, Hitler, belatedly realising that far from being a side-show, the campaign in Normandy was to be decisive for the outcome of the war, tore himself away from his pre-occupation with the Eastern Front at his headquarters at Rastenberg in East Prussia, and journeyed to France to see Field Marshal von Rundstedt. At the headquarters of the Supreme Command West at Soissons, he held a conference with both von Rundstedt and Rommel, in which running true to form in rejecting their advice to withdraw his armies behind the River Seine, he ordered that Normandy be held at all costs, and that in order to regain the initiative, von Rundstedt's alternative plan of a massed armoured counterattack by all available panzer divisions, with the object of driving a wedge between the British and American armies, be put into effect as soon as possible.

This was exactly, however, what General Montgomery foresaw and was determined to prevent. Every effort was made, therefore, to launch "Epsom" as soon as the supply build-up was assured.

The attack by 8 Corps was to take place across the front held by 3 Canadian Division, running through Le Mesnil Patry-Norrey en Bessin-La Villeneuve, on the left of which the line turned north-eastwards to Rosel, and thence went approximately eastwards as far as the Caen Canal. On the right, 30 Corps had for some days been conducting operations in a southerly direction and by a series of small jabs, had succeeded in advancing its line to roughly Point 102, south of Cristot by 24th June.

The British positions in Normandy were therefore deepest on the right, and shallowest in the Caen sector, but Caen being the nodal point and lynch pin of the German defence system in Normandy, this was not surprising. It was the area in which the hardest fighting had up till now taken place, for here the enemy had so far deployed his major strength. This, too, had been the only sector in which the enemy, by sustained pressure, had improved his position since "D" Day, though this had involved using two panzer divisions (21 Panzer and 12 SS) in an infantry role, making it a costly undertaking. Nevertheless, in the three weeks that had gone by since "D" Day, the Germans had temporarily succeeded in stabilising the front or, as they preferred to say, "they had sealed off the invasion area preparatory to the decisive counter-attack which would annihilate the Allied bridgehead." The German troops, now well dug in and protected by numerous minefields, were thus a tough proposition, the formidable nature of which was not underrated by the British High Command.

The break-out operations planned for 26th June provide a remarkable illustration, therefore, both of the determination of the Commander-in-Chief to retain the initiative and his confidence in 8 Corps in planning "Epsom" on so ambitious a scale. Here is the Corps intention for its first battle, as laid down in the first Corps operation instruction to be issued in Normandy, on 23rd June, 1944.

> "On 'D' Day (26th June) 8 Corps will break out of the existing bridgehead on the front of 3 Canadian Division with a view to the Corps forcing crossings over
>
> (a) The River Odon,
>
> (b) The River Orne,
>
> so that at a subsequent date the Corps can be positioned on the high ground north-east of Bretteville-sur-Laize, thereby dominating the exits from Caen to the south."

It was necessary, of course, that these operations should take place in successive phases, which were planned as follows:—

(a) *Phase I.*

The capture of the area Evrecy-Esquay and the seizure or construction of crossings over the River Orne.

(b) *Phase II.*

Positioning 8 Corps on the high ground north-east of Bretteville-sur-Laize, from which area it was in a position to exploit towards Falaise if called upon to do so.

At this point it will be useful to reflect upon the nature of the country over which the fighting was to take place. Any participant in planning "Overlord," and certainly those who later fought in Normandy, will be familiar with the word "bocage." This French word, present in many of the place names of this part of France, notably "Villers Bocage" and "Le Beny Bocage," denotes country divided up into small hedge or tree-lined pasture fields, which provide obstacles hindering cross-country movement. These hedges are usually several feet high, dense and either ditched on both sides or growing on a thick earth bank. Many small copses flourish, as well as the apple orchards for which Normandy is famous. This type of country extends from roughly the valley of the River Orne to the west, and is seen in full flower to the south and south-west of Caumont and Villers Bocage respectively. East of the River Orne it is not found at all. In the "Epsom" area, therefore, the "bocage" was just beginning, but despite this, the country is definitely enclosed with limited vision and comparatively short fields of fire. Hedges and copses abound to the south, as far as the first major obstacle, the River Odon, which is a sluggish stream averaging twenty feet in width, with flat shallow banks, and lined for most of its course with trees and small thick woods, the clearance of which was to prove a troublesome matter. South of the River Odon, and as far as the next water obstacle, the River Orne, the ground becomes more open and undulating, the highest point being a comparatively slight knoll called Hill 112. This, however, is sufficiently high to dominate its surroundings, and a bitter struggle later took place for the possession of it.

From this, it can be seen at once that this type of country is ideal for the defender, for if well dug in, resolute and battle experienced, he has a tremendous advantage over troops, however well-trained and enthusiastic, who are attacking for the first time in their lives.

8 Corps Plan for Phase 1

The Corps plan was a flexible one, for it was so framed that, in the event of comparatively light opposition in the early stages, the armour could be unleashed quickly to take advantage of the fact. If, on the other hand, stubborn resistance were encountered, then the infantry would be readily at hand to fight forward as far as the first river, and secure crossings over which the armour could later pass.

1. Divisional Tasks

(a) 15 (Scottish) Infantry Division.

The first part of Phase I of "Epsom" was allotted to 15 (Scottish) Division, and the task was to attack at 0730 hours on 26th June to secure crossings over the River Odon between Gavrus and Verson. This operation was to be carried out in two parts:

(i) *First objective*—the villages of St. Mauvieu and Cheux.

(ii) *Second objective*—the crossings over the River Odon.

This second objective for the Scots was contingent on the armour not succeeding in rushing the crossings, though, if this were accomplished, 15 (Scottish) Division would in any case take over responsibility for the protection of the bridges over them as soon as possible. Should the crossings not be intact, through the bridges being destroyed or for some other reason, then it became likewise its responsibility to construct four Class 40 crossings, and one Class 9 bridge for the passage of the armour.

For all these tasks the following additional troops were placed under command of 15 (Scottish) Division:—

31 Tank Brigade (Churchills) less one regiment.

B Squadron, 22 Dragoons.

C Squadron, Westminster Dragoons.

81 Squadron Armoured R.E.

25 Field Regiment R.A.

One self-propelled battery 91 Anti-Tank Regiment R.A.

(b) 11 *Armoured Division.*

11 Armoured Division was given the armoured role, and was ordered to be so positioned that it was able to exploit the success won by 15 (Scottish)

Division, and ready to pass through bridgeheads gained over the River Odon at the earliest possible moment.

As soon as conditions permitted after the capture of Cheux and the high ground to the south of this village, and, it was hoped, while the enemy was still disorganised, 11 Armoured Division was to attempt to rush the crossings over the River Odon and establish itself east of the river. In the event of this failing, then the armour would cross as soon as possible after the Scottish attack, being prepared first to dominate the area Evrecy-Esquay and subsequently to undertake Phase II of the whole operation, namely, forcing a passage over the River Orne.

The additional troops placed under 11 Armoured Division for both these phases were: —

>4 Armoured Brigade Group.
>One self-propelled battery 91 Anti-Tank Regiment R.A.
>One survey troop 10 Survey Regiment R.A.

There was a restriction on the use of 4 Armoured Brigade, however, since the eastern flank, always open and menaced from Caen, had to be strong. This formation was therefore to remain in the area between the two rivers as flank protection, but able either to act offensively in the direction of Caen, or to the west if favourable circumstances arose.

The divisional axis of advance was: —

>Cheux-Mondrainville-Esquay-Feuguerolles-sur-Orne.

(c) 43 (Wessex) Infantry Division.

43 (Wessex) Division provided the firm base for the Corps, so necessary in an operation of this nature, and was later to relieve 15 (Scottish) Division in the area of Cheux and St. Mauvieu.

So much, therefore, for the individual tasks of subordinate formations. Now let us turn to a brief examination of the fire support in all the forms in which it was available to 8 Corps for this operation.

2. Fire Support

(a) Artillery

This was organised by the C.C.R.A. on an impressive scale and involved use of the largest concentration of guns so far employed on the whole Allied front. As a start, the artillery under command of the Corps was: —

11 Armoured Division ...	... Two field regiments totalling 48 guns.
15 (Scottish) Division ...	... Four field regiments totalling 96 guns.
43 (Wessex) Division ...	... Three field regiments totalling 72 guns.
4 Armoured Brigade Group ...	One field regiment totalling 24 guns.
8 A.G.R.A.	... One heavy regiment totalling 16 guns.
	One medium regiment totalling 16 guns.
	One heavy A.A. regiment totalling 24 guns.

A total of 240 field guns, 16 medium guns, 16 heavy guns and 24 heavy A.A. guns.

In addition to the guns of 8 Corps, others in support of "Epsom" were: —

From 1 Corps.
>Nine field regiments totalling 216 guns.
>Two medium regiments totalling 32 guns.
>One heavy regiment totalling 16 guns.

From 30 Corps.
>Four field regiments totalling 96 guns.
>Four medium regiments totalling 64 guns.
>One heavy regiment totalling 16 guns.

In all, therefore, a grand total of 552 field, 112 medium, 48 heavy and 24 heavy A.A. guns were employed in the "Epsom" area. The artillery plan consisted briefly of a heavy creeping barrage to cover the initial advance of the Scottish troops on St. Mauvieu and Cheux, and thereafter concentrations and counter- battery fire in the area generally, including the flanks.

Over and above this very extensive programme, the Royal Navy was also lending a helping hand, for the bridgehead was still sufficiently shallow at this point to permit its co-operation with the land forces. Working under the supervision of 1 Corps, three cruisers and the monitor "H.M.S. Roberts" which had taken part in the "D" Day bombardment of the coast, were available to add the weight of their guns in support of the advance.

(b) *Royal Air Force.*

A detailed programme of bombing was arranged by Second Army, with the R.A.F. in accordance with requests put forward by General O'Connor, the principal features of which were:—

>(a) An attack by heavy bombers on Verson at 0200 hours 26th June.

>(b) An attack by a strong force of medium bombers on the area of Carpiquet at 0730 hours to safeguard the left flank at the moment when the Scottish troops were beginning to move forward behind the barrage.

>(c) A second attack by mediums between 1730 and 1930 hours against the area of Bretteville-sur-Odon, it being hoped that the Corps would, by that time, be within striking distance of the river line.

As well as the above effort, fifteen squadrons of fighter bombers, some based in England, and the remainder belonging to 83 Group R.A.F. (the tactical air force operating with Second Army from landing strips in the bridgehead), were initially to maintain strong fighter cover over the Corps forming-up areas and subsequently were to be directed against enemy headquarters and hostile batteries. By the evening of 25th June, however, the weather had deteriorated to such an extent that at 2300 hours intimation was received from G (Air) Branch at Second Army Headquarters that the full programme of air support could not be carried out, as the heavy bombers were unable to take off from their airfields in England. The medium bombers might fly later and if visibility allowed, would attack their allotted targets, failing which they would return home with their bomb loads. Fighter bombers would also operate if humanly possible.

During the night, conditions worsened and at 0645 hours on 26th June, Second Army Headquarters telephoned to say that the mediums and also any fighter bombing effort from England had been cancelled. 83 Group R.A.F., however, were able to produce twelve Spitfire and three Mustang squadrons, and these would give strong fighter cover over the forming-up areas, and fighter-bomber support until the weather broke.

There was thus a big curtailment of support from this direction and it was an object lesson in not placing too great a reliance in land operations upon automatic co-operation with an air force. Man may have conquered the air, but he certainly has not conquered the weather, and it is astonishing how quite minor vagaries of climate can cause considerable dislocation to the performance of aeroplanes. If bomber support is considered vital to any operation, then those directing must be prepared for postponements until the necessary climatic conditions are available. Otherwise it must be reckoned during the planning stage, as a useful adjunct but not an indispensible necessity. There were to be many instances of this nature throughout the campaign.

A further disappointment was in store for 8 Corps also, for during the night of 25th June, 30 Corps failed to take the Rauray spur overlooking Cheux, and thus the right flank, as well as the left, was exposed during the earliest stages of the attack. Rauray in point of fact was to prove a very tough proposition indeed and possession of it was bitterly contested by both sides. It was not until 28th June that 30 Corps was able to state that Rauray was finally cleared of enemy and firmly in its hands.

Summing up therefore on the design for Operation "Epsom" there are certain salient features which should be borne in mind:—

1. It was the first operation undertaken by troops of 8 Corps, and for the vast majority of them their first actual battle experience.
2. The plan was an ambitious one, involving an attack by an infantry division through which an armoured division was later to pass, against a resolute enemy in strongly prepared positions.
3. The objectives, several miles deep in enemy territory, were such that, if gained, the Corps would be in a very pronounced salient. Remembering the Commander-in-Chief's policy of endeavouring to attract as much enemy armour to this flank as possible and away from the Americans, the reaction of the enemy could be expected to be violent, and it was obvious that heavy fighting would ensue.
4. Deterioration in the weather limited the powerful air support which otherwise would have been at the disposal of 8 Corps.

Let us now pass on to a study of what actually happened.

26th June

The morning dawned dull and hazy and despite the curtailment of the air support, 15 (Scottish) Division, preceded by an intense barrage, attacked at 0730 hours with two brigades forward, right 46 (Highland) Infantry Brigade supported by 7 Royal Tank Regiment, directed on the village of Cheux and the adjacent spur, Le Haut du Bosq, and left, 44 (Lowland) Infantry Brigade directed on St. Mauvieu and La Gaule, also with a unit of 31 Tank Brigade, 9 Royal Tank Regiment, in support.

Right Brigade Attack

46 (Highland) Brigade moved off with 9 Cameronians on the right and 2 Glasgow Highlanders left, and it had been intended that the two squadrons of tanks with these battalions should lead the attack. To avoid being held up in passing through Le Mesnil Patry, evacuated by the enemy a couple of days previously and where mines and booby traps had been discovered, the tanks were ordered to by-pass this village on both sides. Unfortunately in so doing, each squadron encountered mines on its south-west and south-east flanks and was delayed until the limits of the minefields were discovered and a way round worked out. Thus the Scottish infantry advanced from their start line at zero hour without the armour, which was unable to get ahead of them until the main Caen-Fontenay le Pesnil road was reached.

Meanwhile, opposition had been encountered from enemy infantry dug in and concealed with great ingenuity, so that locating them was extremely difficult. In the early stages of the advance, however, the Germans were thin on the ground and the artillery effectively neutralised it, for as one of them remarked on being taken prisoner, "We were caught in the fury of the barrage, had gone to ground and emerged only to find ourselves surrounded by tanks or furious Scotsmen throwing grenades." The opposition at this point was fiercest from the right flank and clear of the barrage, but steady progress was made and by 1000 hours the Glasgow Highlanders had reached the northern outskirts of Cheux where, assisted by their tank squadron, they were endeavouring to gain a foothold in the village.

Their neighbours, 9 Cameronians, were on approximately the same alignment except to the extreme right, where the advance was slower, owing to heavier opposition from that direction from well-hidden parties of tanks and anti-tank guns.

By 1230 hours, 2 Glasgow Highlanders had penetrated Cheux and was clearing houses and orchards in this long straggling village, whilst the Cameronians were similarly engaged in dislodging Germans from buildings and enclosures on the northern tip of Le Haut du Bosq.

Left Brigade Attack

44 (Lowland) Infantry Brigade likewise had two battalions up, 8 Royal Scots right and 6 Royal Scots Fusiliers left, plus tank support, and their advance was steady, and without the initial difficulties of 46 (Highland) Brigade or any active interference from the enemy, until a streamlet called the Muc was reached. Here some machine gun fire was encountered and a slight check imposed, but despite the fact that the opposition from now onwards became stiffer, by 0835 hours 6 Royal Scots Fusiliers reached the fringes of St. Mauvieu, which proved to be heavily defended. Here bitter hand-to-hand fighting took place all the morning, but the enemy was gradually eliminated, house by house, along the line of advance, often with the help of the flame-throwing tanks known as "Crocodiles." 8 Royal Scots reached La Gaule at about 0930 hours, but here again hard fighting was necessary to penetrate the village.

By shortly after noon therefore, both battalions had reached the southern edges of their respective villages, and it appeared that their objectives were firmly in their hands, but it subsequently turned out that only buildings and ground actually covered, had been cleared of enemy, so that a number of pockets of resistance, all stubbornly defended, had later to be mopped up.

Situation at Mid-day 26th June

So far, everything had gone according to plan. The attack by 15 (Scottish) Division had taken its objectives, initially against light opposition, but once the built up area had been reached, to the accompaniment of heavy house to house fighting, and at the cost of considerable casualties.

Enemy positions forward of the confines of the four villages had, in point of fact, been manned as outposts only, the main strength of the unit defending this sector being located among the ruins of the houses themselves. This unit proved to be 12 SS Engineer Battalion which, having lost its bridging equipment in an R.A.F. bombing raid some days previously, had been put into the line to act as infantry, pending relief of 12 SS Panzer Division, which all prisoners stated had been promised in the near future. In German military circles, engineers have always been looked upon as élite troops, and to find these specialists in an infantry rôle showed that the resources in Normandy of the enemy were already strained. At all events, these SS sappers certainly lived up to this reputation, for whilst most of those taken prisoner were under twenty, they fought desperately to avoid capture, having been warned, they said, that the British always shot their prisoners. Even their wounded were suspicious of attention from our medical personnel, for just as an injured wild beast when first shut up, backs to the limits of its cage and snarls at all comers, so the reaction of these youths was a similar mixture of fear, hatred and defiance.

About this time, too, a "werfer" brigade which, from captured documents was known to be under command of 1 SS Panzer Corps, realised that the area of Cheux and St. Mauvieu had fallen and began mortaring it heavily. The German Army did not develop its artillery arm to anything like the extent that we achieved during the war, the result being that ours was overwhelmingly superior. The Germans did, however, do something to redress the balance by the employment of a multi-barrelled mortar which, organised in brigades, was very accurate up to a range of about 6,000 yards and a most effective anti-personnel weapon. It is probably true to say that more casualties were caused to the Allies through mortaring than from any other cause in the western campaign. Moreover its simplicity of construction (whereby mass production was possible), mobility, ease of supply and moral effect, made the "nebelwerfer" one of the best weapons at the disposal of the enemy.

It now began to take a heavy toll of 8 Corps.

Unleashing the Armour

By 1230 hours 29 Armoured Brigade of 11 Armoured Division, which had followed up the Scottish advance, had positioned its tanks, ready for the dash to the River Odon, in the area south of Norrey-en-Bessin. 2 Northamptonshire Yeomanry, the divisional reconnaissance regiment, which was to spearhead this move, was deployed due north of Cheux and at 1250 hours one squadron was ordered to reconnoitre toward the river astride the Corps axis of advance. 29 Armoured Brigade then began to move down to Cheux preparatory to advancing.

Owing to debris, the result of shelling, all thoroughfares through Cheux were seriously obstructed, and this caused much traffic congestion. The situation was further complicated by the discovery of a minefield covering the northern approaches, which delayed the passage of the Northamptonshire Yeomanry so that it was almost 1400 hours before it began to shake itself clear of the village. Before this was completed, however, it became involved in a general mêlée, being attacked at short range by grenades, sticky bombs and anti-tank weapons. Nevertheless, at the cost of some casualties, by 1430 hours the squadron was on the ridge a short distance to the south of Cheux when enemy tanks made their appearance from the south-east and south-west. Though its centre troop was knocked out, the remaining two held their positions, whilst in the meantime, the fourth troop, which had made a wider detour of Cheux, managed to slip through to the outskirts of Grainville by 1600 hours, though it withdrew with the rest of the squadron about an hour later.

At 1400 hours 29 Armoured Brigade was ordered to advance, being directed on Gavrus and Tourmauville. 2 Fife and Forfar Yeomanry moving west of Cheux soon became engaged in the confused fighting there, which resulted from the many pockets of enemy not as yet mopped up. 23 Hussars, moving through the centre of Cheux, with one squadron by-passing it to the east, made better progress, though rubble in the village itself and cratering on the outskirts both caused difficulty. As with the Northamptonshire Yeomanry, however, any attempts to deploy south of Cheux met with determined opposition, and by the end of the afternoon it was apparent that, in view of the strength of the enemy position here, the situation was not favourable for continuing the advance by 29 Armoured Brigade. The Odon crossings could not thus be rushed by the tanks.

Moreover, whilst St. Mauvieu and Cheux were firmly in the hands of the Scottish infantry, the limit of their advance to the south was only three or four hundred yards clear of these villages, and the leading battalion, 7 Seaforth Highlanders, was having a very unhappy time in its small salient. The wooded areas from the southern slopes of Le Haut du Bosq to the west and south-west were also unsubdued and filled with small parties of infantry, supported by tanks, often dug in, and anti-tank guns which, through their effective concealment and rapid change of position, gave much trouble.

At 1800 hours, therefore, orders were given to 15 (Scottish) Division to continue the advance and commit its reserve brigade, 227 (Highland) Infantry Brigade, with 10 Highland Light Infantry making for Grainville-sur-Odon and 1 Gordon Highlanders for Colleville, an appreciable bound forward, considering battle conditions. Once these villages were secured, 2 Argyll and Sutherland Highlanders was to pass through 10 Highland Light Infantry and take Le Valtru, and in the whole action 227 Brigade was to be supported by the leading regiments of 29 Armoured Brigade, 2 Fife and Forfar Yeomanry on the right and 23 Hussars on the left.

The situation around Le Haut du Bosq remained as sticky as ever unfortunately, and as both the Highland Light Infantry and the Fife and Forfar Yeomanry became involved in the desultory fighting in this area, they were unable to get their attack going in the direction of Grainville. By this time it was getting dark and rain, which had been threatening all day, began to fall heavily, adding greatly to the discomfort of the troops. It was, therefore, decided that the operation should be postponed until the following morning.

On the left, the two leading companies of the Gordons had made good progress and were on the northern outskirts of Colleville at 2100 hours, but this provoked a series of spirited counter attacks from the east, which cut them off from the main body, now held up along a stream called the Salbey. After heavy and confused fighting one of these companies managed to extricate itself and rejoined the battalion, which then consolidated for the night.

At last light the situation was:—

15 (Scottish) Division

    44 (Lowland) Brigade.

Firmly holding the area of St. Mauvieu-La Gaule, having eliminated most of the enemy in the vicinity and beaten off several small but spirited counter-attacks with tanks from the direction of the enemy strongpoint of Marcelet. It was now expecting to be relieved by 129 Infantry Brigade of 43 (Wessex) Division during the night.

    46 (Highland) Brigade.

In Cheux, having mopped up the main part of the village during the afternoon, and awaiting relief by 214 Infantry Brigade of 43 (Wessex) Division.

227 (Highland) Brigade

The two forward battalions, 10 Highland Light Infantry and 2 Gordon Highlanders, south-east of Cheux and in contact with the enemy.

31 Tank Brigade

7 Royal Tank Regiment and 9 Royal Tank Regiment had rallied in the rear of 46 and 44 Brigades respectively.

11 Armoured Division

29 Armoured Brigade and 2 Northamptonshire Yeomanry—north of Cheux.

4 Armoured Brigade—area Le Mesnil Patry—Norrey-en-Bessin.

159 Infantry Brigade—still in the concentration area of Secqueville.

43 (Wessex) Division

Two brigades were moving up to relieve 15 (Scottish) Division and the third, 130 Infantry Brigade, to take over the position of 8 Canadian Infantry Brigade in Bretteville.

As darkness came, so fighting died down throughout the battle area, and except for occasional mortaring and shelling no further incidents took place.

Summary 26th June

Thus ended the first day's operations by 8 Corps. As a baptism of fire it had been a gruelling experience for 15 (Scottish) Division, who had borne the lion's share of the fighting, and the casualties sustained by this magnificent division were the highest it was ever called upon to suffer in one day throughout the campaign. No pen can, however, adequately describe the gusto and dash with which the Scots went into their first attack, and though all evidence goes to show that formations and units were tactically well handled, the natural eagerness and high spirits of the troops must have caused some losses. All the more so, too, as the enemy fought with fanatical tenacity in country which he knew well and had had time to prepare, and which, moreover, was ideally suited to defence. Most of the fighting took place at close range, the enemy sitting tight in thick cover until he had every hope of a " kill " with the first round or burst of small arms fire, whereafter he was quick to change over and come rapidly into action again from an alternative position.

There were many examples in the day's fighting and subsequently, of the use by the German of what might be termed tactics of " inverted infiltration," i.e., unless actually attacked, knocked out or over-run, he stayed put in his slit trench and allowed the advance to flow past him, coming to life only when worth-while targets offered themselves or when he was located. This alone speaks much for the morale of 12 SS Panzer Division, and indeed some isolated SS posts were still being discovered two or three days later, when the tide of battle had surged on several miles to the south, though hunger and exposure gradually reduced their will to resist.

Long after objectives may have been taken, therefore, the intervening area over-run had to be methodically " beaten," the close country making this process a long and difficult matter.

As the operation was in the nature of a break-through on a narrow front, both flanks of the advance were exposed, and here again the close country helped the defenders, for no opportunity of harassing was neglected, whilst every effort was made to infiltrate between tanks and infantry and between forward troops and those following up.

To sum up, therefore, 8 Corps during 26th June had broken into but not through the main positions of 12 SS Panzer Division, both infantry regiments of which had been identified; it had not been possible to rush the Odon crossings in view of the strength of the resistance, but by last light it was well positioned to continue the advance on the following morning. Moreover, the gains achieved so far were firmly held, despite the salient they created and there was no question of any counter attack catching it off balance. Morale and spirits remained high. As far as prisoners were concerned, two officers and one hundred and sixteen other ranks had passed through the Corps cage by last light, of whom the greater part belonged to 12 SS Engineer Battalion, though three had strayed over from the formation adjoining 12 SS Panzer Division, 130 Panzer Lehr Division.

Casualties suffered by 8 Corps were:—

	Killed	Wounded	Missing
11 Armoured Division	3	4	4
15 (Scottish) Division	86	470	19
43 (Wessex) Division	6	1	—
31 Tank Brigade	5	33	—
4 Armoured Brigade	2	6	—
8 A.G.R.A.	2	3	—
8 Corps Troops	—	1	—

The most serious loss was the commander of 4 Armoured Brigade, Brigadier John Currie, D.S.O., M.C., who after a long and distinguished career with this brigade in Africa, had the ill luck to be killed by a shell while on reconnaissance on its first day of action in North West Europe.

27th June

The Corps intention for 27th June remained the development of the original plan. At first light 15 (Scottish) Division supported by 29 Armoured Brigade and two battalions of 31 Tank Brigade was to resume the advance and establish a bridgehead over the River Odon. As soon as crossings had been secured, 11 Armoured Division would pass through the Scots and, as planned, first dominate the general area of Evrecy and Esquay and subsequently force a passage over the River Orne four miles to the south. Providing the weather improved, general support to these operations would be given by the R.A.F. and, in particular, medium bombers would attack Carpiquet airfield not later than 1100 hours. Night brought no change however, in the dismal weather, and at 0355 hours Second Army intimated that the projected air plan with the mediums could not be carried out. Arrangements were therefore made for additional artillery support from 3 Canadian Division, which provided another four field regiments to compensate for this disappointment.

On the right flank of the Corps, Rauray was to be subjected to another assault at 0630 hours and 30 Corps anticipated being able to clear this village by 1000 hours. This would be a big help for the exposed right flank, which had been the cause of much delay on the previous day, and remained a source of weakness, the farther south the Corps advanced. Rauray and Le Haut du Bosq were, however, complementary spurs, the importance of which the Germans, with their customary tactical ability, had not been slow to realise, and to which they were determined to cling as long as possible.

The morning dawned dull and cloudy, with intermittent rain, and 15 (Scottish) Division did not get off to quite so early a start as had been expected. However, on the right of 227 (Highland) Brigade, 10 Highland Light Infantry with a squadron of Churchill tanks under command, resumed the offensive at 0645 hours with the object of crossing the Odon north of Gavrus, whilst on the left, 2 Argyll and Sutherland Highlanders moved off at 0730 hours to cross near Tourville. 2 Gordon Highlanders after the heavy fighting of the previous evening, remained in situ as a reserve.

It was obvious that the Highland Light Infantry had a difficult task ahead, for quite apart from the question of enemy opposition, their objective was no less than four thousand yards distant and the difficulties of maintaining control of the battalion as well as communication with the tanks would be exceedingly awkward in view of the heavily wooded country through which they were to pass.

To get clear of their start line immediately south of Cheux, however, proved to be the most awkward task of all, for in attempting to move off they at once came under heavy fire from the area of Le Haut du Bosq. Indeed, throughout the day the Highland Light Infantry were engaged in fierce fighting in the built-up area and the close country due west and south of Cheux, and made little progress from their original start line.

2 Fife and Forfar Yeomanry, which was also supporting this attack, endeavoured to outflank the enemy pinning down 10 Highland Light Infantry, but was likewise held up, and eventually towards midday was ordered to position a squadron on the northern tip of Le Haut du Bosq to protect the rear of the hard-pressed Highlanders. While carrying out this role, it drove back a number of small tank attacks, which from identifications and prisoners' statements made it clear that 12 SS Panzer Division had obtained reinforcements in the shape of a battalion of "Panthers" from 2 Panzer Division. Fortunately as yet no strong armoured counter attack had been delivered, though the enemy had lost a number of tanks on the previous day. These, however, had been used defensively in the majority of cases, and had been dealt with effectively by the Scottish infantry. During the morning a number of reports had come in of "Tiger" tanks operating on various parts of the front, and as these tanks were always organised in corps tank battalions it was clear that the enemy was concerned to do everything possible to halt the advance. With 12 SS Panzer Regiment down to some 60 or 70 runners, the battalion from 2 Panzer Division estimated at 40-50 "Panthers" and with the probable addition of the "Tiger" tank battalion some 36 strong, of 1 SS Panzer Corps, the armour available for employment against the enlarging salient achieved by 8 Corps had risen to between 130 and 160 tanks, and these began to be used in a more enterprising, though as yet unco-ordinated manner.

Despite this increase in enemy tank strength, one squadron from 2 Fife and Forfar Yeomanry managed to nose its way against fairly stiff opposition into Grainville-sur-Odon, nearly a mile to the south of the infantry, by midday and gallantly hung on there for several hours.

Meanwhile on the left things were going better, for 2 Argyll and Sutherland Highlanders met less resistance, and by 0930 hours approximately had passed through Colleville and reached the outskirts of Tourville, crossing in so doing the main lateral road from Caen to Villers Bocage. This, astonishingly enough (something which illustrates how little the German High Command intended to give ground on this front), was still being used by enemy transport between the two cities, and this now received a rude shock at the hands of the Scots. Pushing on from there, the Argylls pressed their advance as far as Mondrainville, where at 1220 hours a pause was made for reorganisation, for the battalion had become somewhat scattered in fighting through this very enclosed country. As the river was within reasonable striking distance, however, this prudent course was entirely justified if this very fine penetration was to be maintained. Moreover, 23 Hussars of 29 Armoured Brigade, following them up, had fought numerous small "tank v. tank" encounters, especially to the left of the advance, and as a result had no very clear picture of the infantry situation, being virtually out of touch with the Scots.

Let us now glance at what was happening in the rear, around Cheux and St. Mauvieu. Here 44 (Lowland) and 46 (Highland) Brigades were being relieved by 43 (Wessex) Division, and against one of its battalions, 5 Duke of Cornwall's Light Infantry, came at 0930 hours the sharpest and heaviest armoured counter attack yet experienced, delivered by a full company of the 2 Panzer Division "Panthers." Striking from the west, this attack penetrated Cheux itself, knocking out several 6 and 17-pr anti-tank guns and inflicting some personnel casualties, including unfortunately the commanding officer of the D.C.L.I., before it was beaten off with the loss of three tanks to the Germans. Smaller enemy thrusts were also repulsed from the east.

However the base of the salient was everywhere secure and at 1015 hours orders were given to 159 Infantry Brigade of 11 Armoured Division to be prepared to move, embussed, to the River Odon.

By the end of the morning therefore, despite increasing enemy resistance and bolder attempts at counter attack, marked progress had been made on the Corps left flank, whilst though the state of affairs on the right was far from satisfactory, at least the position was organised and firm. Moreover, fresh troops had replaced the Scots and the dangers of the tank run leading in from the south-west were by now fully appreciated.

The whole front had been, and indeed, remained, a mass of small engagements and disconnected fighting on both sides, whereby the operations of one part of the force had little or no effect on the local situation of the other. This, of course, was only possible through the close nature of the country but even the ripening corn was sufficiently high to restrict mobility. Everything favoured the defence, for progress was greatly delayed by the advancing troops being forced to fight these countless small eliminating actions, even in rearward areas.

At 1330 hours, the Argylls, then on the point of resuming their southernly advance, were counter-attacked, but this proved to be a local affair of no great strength and was soon repulsed, permitting them to begin their move forward. By 1700 hours leading troops of the battalion reached the river banks and by great good luck discovered intact the bridge north-west of Baron. Covered by the tanks of 23 Hussars, which had now joined up with them, a small bridgehead was quickly seized and by 1900 hours securely established.

In the meantime the remainder of 29 Armoured Brigade was tapping out to the east in an endeavour to widen the area of advance. On the outskirts of Mouen, about half a mile east of Colleville, they were finally held, but remained in observation of this flank whilst over on the other side the regiments of 4 Armoured Brigade, 44 Royal Tank Regiment and the Scots Greys, were deployed south-west of Cheux in a similar protective role, as it was felt that a major threat still emanated from the west. With the sides of the salient thus protected, 46 (Highland) Brigade moved forward to thicken up the Grainville-Colleville area with 9 Royal Tank Regiment in support, as a backing to 227 (Highland) Brigade, now somewhat scattered, with 2 Argyll and Sutherland Highlanders on the Odon, 2 Gordon Highlanders in Mondrainville and Tourville, and the third battalion, 10 Highland Light Infantry, still held up far to the north-west, around Le Haut du Bosq.

Further back 43 (Wessex) Division had spent the day organising a strong position in the triangle St. Mauvieu-Cheux-Le Haut du Bosq, using two of its brigades for the purpose, the third, 130 Infantry Brigade completing the relief of 8 Canadian Infantry Brigade in Bretteville and Norrey-en-Bessin.

32 Guards Brigade, the first formation of Guards Armoured Division to arrive in the theatre, was also promised to 43 (Wessex) Division for the following day, and the newly won area thus began to fill up with infantry, in conformity with the Commander-in-Chief's policy of maintaining a firm base. Never allowing oneself to be caught off balance is a very wise doctrine, as events were to demonstrate.

During the late evening 159 Infantry Brigade was brought down in lorries from behind Cheux as far as Tourville where the troops debussed and made their way down the narrow track leading to the newly-won bridgehead. It is always desirable when a unit goes into battle for the first time for it to be introduced in such a way that the resultant shock is minimised as far as possible and there is time for a reasonably gradual adjustment to war conditions. Thus in the attack it is preferable to have seasoned troops in the leading role, whilst in defensive fighting, the gradual "feeding in" of fresh troops to quieter sectors is the best policy.

159 Infantry Brigade was, however, not so lucky in its battle inoculation, for with darkness falling it had the unenviable task of enlarging the hard-won bridgehead during the night, under constant harassing fire from enemy artillery and mortars, and conscious that by daybreak the position must be consolidated against attack so that the armour would have a firm base from which to operate on the morrow. That this was successfully accomplished was a fine achievement for troops in action for the first time.

The increasingly spirited German counter attacks, the continued presence of the enemy in various bitterly defended localities west of the river, the fact that no bridges had been destroyed and, most significant of all, the stream of enemy traffic towards the Odon battlefield, revealed by last light Tac R, showed clearly that the enemy proposed to make a still bigger effort to halt 8 Corps.

So far as the overall strength of the Corps and casualties during 27th June are concerned, the addition of part of 32 Guards Brigade and the arrival of some delayed echelons of the three divisions and Corps troops, had increased its numbers to some 66,000 all ranks, whilst casualties, though still heavy for 15 (Scottish) Division, were somewhat less than the previous day, being as follows:—

	Strength		Killed	Wounded	Missing
	Officers	O.R.s			
11 Armoured Division ...	689	12,608	19	58	5
15 (Scottish) Division ...	753	14,169	23	180	290
43 (Wessex) Division	813 ...	15,197	13	34	2
31 Tank Brigade	163	2,885	5	19	1
4 Armoured Brigade	244	4,373	2	6	—
32 Guards Brigade	132	2,806	—	... —	—
8 A.G.R.A.	170	3,182	2 ...	3	—
8 Corps Troops	435 ...	7,042 ...	1 ...	3 ...	—
	3,399 ...	62,262 ...	65 ...	303 ...	298

28th June

During the night and early hours of the morning, steady progress had been made with the passage of 11 Armoured Division across the River Odon. By 0500 hours 1 Herefordshire Regiment and 4 King's Shropshire Light Infantry were over and organising a wider bridgehead, thereby helping to relieve some of the pressure on the first occupants, 2 Argyll and Sutherland Highlanders. A considerable amount of sniping and mortaring took place during these operations but, in general by day-break, the position was organised with 3 Monmouthshire Regiment protecting the north bank of the river.

The Corps intention for the day was still to carry on with the offensive, completing Phase 1 of " Epsom " and starting Phase 2, the establishment of forces astride enemy communications south-east of Caen, so that this city could be speedily reduced, and thereby the hinge of the German positions in the west destroyed. This involved an advance from the Odon to the Orne of some 3-4 miles across, for a change, open country in the form of an undulating plain. From the confines of the first river line, however, the ground rises quite steeply for a thousand yards, before starting to level off, and results due east of the bridgehead in a flat topped summit known for ever to Second Army as Hill 112, which despite its seeming insignificance, in reality dominates both the Odon valley and the country to the north. Two miles to the south-west and just north of the small town of Evrecy, a similar knoll called Hill 113, likewise commands the approaches from north and north-east, and from the defence angle forms an effective complement to Hill 112.

Early on the previous evening two squadrons of 23 Hussars had crossed the river and, as soon as it was possible to see on the morning of 28th June, one was ordered to advance and establish itself on Hill 112. Skirting the ruins of the village of Baron, and covered by the remaining squadron, these tanks, accompanied by a company of infantry from 8 Rifle Brigade, approached the hill from the north, since the bulk of opposition came from its southern slopes. For some time going was good and reminiscent of the Yorkshire Wolds and, eventually, though not without casualties, the northern slopes were over-run and 23 Hussars established on them, the Germans on the crest being dislodged in the process. No one ventured to take their place, for it was now quite untenable and so they remained in possession of the southern half of Hill 112. Here, positioned in a small wood and with " Tiger " tanks dug-in and able to move into alternative positions under cover, they proved impossible to move, though everything from self-propelled guns to medium artillery and rocket-firing Typhoons was tried without effect. Later in the morning the remainder of 23 Hussars arrived but were still unable to get forward. The enemy, by being in possession of Esquay, was able to deny the southern slopes of Hill 112 to 29 Armoured Brigade in conjunction with the comparatively few troops and tanks which he had on the hill himself. The Germans seemed everywhere, for armour-piercing shot and H.E. were coming from all directions, including the woods to the rear ; nor were the British tanks hesitant to reply, and thus in the afternoon, 23 Hussars began to run short of ammunition. There being no question of bringing forward lorries to replenish their stocks, it was decided to relieve them by 3 Royal Tank Regiment. This relief took place about 1500 hours and 23 Hussars was pulled back to the vicinity of Tourmauville, on the other side of the Odon, for a well earned rest.

Whilst this bitter and abortive contest for Hill 112 was in progress, General O'Connor held a conference at Headquarters 15 (Scottish) Division in Putot-en-Bessin, at noon, since from reports during the early hours of the day from various formations of the Corps, it was clear that enemy pressure was increasing on both flanks and particularly on the right between Cheux and the Odon. It was known that 30 Corps eventually, after fierce fighting, late on the previous afternoon had succeeded in taking Rauray, but much mopping up remained to be done, and it was unlikely that further advances would be easy in this sector in view of the strong enemy resistance on the Haut du Bosq position. The capture of Rauray therefore, did not now bring the same relief to the right flank as it would have done if this operation had been achieved on time, in view of the subsequent enemy build up.

On the other hand the eastern flank was somewhat easier, for patrols had found the northern half of Marcelet empty during the night, the enemy having pulled back to a general line running from Carpiquet airfield to the River Odon.

The morning, however, brought a number of additional signs of a new formation moving in from the south-west against the right of the Corps. An increase in "flak" in the vicinity of Villers Bocage, a major traffic bottleneck for the Germans, was noticed. Then, very significantly, the hard-pressed Luftwaffe provided some fighter cover over the same sector. The Corps Commander, therefore, warned of the probability of this new arrival, decided that if 11 Armoured Division continued its advance to the River Orne, before the enemy still north of the Odon had been eliminated, its maintenance might become a serious problem. 11 Armoured Division was therefore ordered to maintain and improve its bridgehead over the Odon and to position 29 Armoured Brigade ready to advance to the Orne but not to move until the Corps Commander ordered it. In the meantime 15 (Scottish) Division and 43 (Wessex) Division were to concentrate on wiping out enemy posts north of the Odon, back into which there had been some infiltration by 12 SS Panzer Division.

159 Infantry Brigade in its bridgehead, now rather over 1,000 yards in length, was providing firm backing for the armour ahead, but it was considered that an attempt should be made to widen the area of penetration, by striking down the right bank of the Odon in the direction of the village of Gavrus, some half mile to the south, and above which there were two further undestroyed bridges. Once these were taken, the object was to wheel north and join up with 46 (Highland) Brigade, at the same time catching the enemy fighting it in the rear, and thus materially assisting in clearing Le Valtru and Grainville. The battalion chosen to carry out this ambitious little scheme with its text book pincer movement was 2 Argyll and Sutherland Highlanders, now rested after its praiseworthy performance of the previous day. Starting at 0900 hours, the Argylls moved astride the Le Vilains-Gavrus road and after much heavy and confused fighting took the village and one bridge to the north, but this effort was exhausting, and nothing further could be done that afternoon to join up with its neighbours to the north. As will be seen, this left the battalion in an extremely exposed position, which the enemy was not long in realising. However, Gavrus and the newly won bridge were organised for defence by last light and no further incidents took place during the night.

So far as 29 Armoured Brigade was concerned, its three armoured regiments were positioned by early afternoon ready to advance, with 3 Royal Tank Regiment and 2 Fife and Forfar Yeomanry on the northern slopes of Hill 112, and 44 Royal Tank Regiment (from 4 Armoured Brigade and replacing 23 Hussars) on the high ground north of Evrecy. The enemy kept up throughout the afternoon a constant and murderous mortar and anti-tank fire, and at 2000 hours covered by what, in fact, amounted to a barrage of mortars, launched a counter attack, supported by tanks, of battalion strength. This was beaten back but provided a prisoner who, under interrogation later in the evening at the Corps cage, told an interesting story shedding considerable light on Rommel's reactions to 8 Corps' threatening advance. Complete possession of Hill 112 remained however a prize to which neither side could aspire.

Elsewhere in the Corps sector progress had also been made during the day, and enemy counter attacks beaten off, notably and principally from west of Le Haut du Bosq and Grainville. This flank remained, as always, the most uneasy part of the front, and 46 (Highland) Brigade had a heavy task all day long in clearing the many snipers' nests that still clung on obstinately in the quadrilateral formed by the four villages—Colleville, Grainville, Le Valtru and Mondrainville. In view of the likely enemy reinforcements from the Villers Bocage area, 2 Northamptonshire Yeomanry (the armoured reconnaissance regiment of 11 Armoured Division) was brought in here to thicken up the defence, whilst 44 (Lowland) Brigade organised a two battalion drive, with tank support, from west of Cheux to beat the area to the south as far as the railway leading from Caen to Aunay. Very heavy resistance to this drive was encountered about half a mile from the railway and some hand-to-hand fighting took place, so that at last light a halt was called and plans were made to continue the advance on the following morning.

The reason for the increased opposition here was not far to seek, for identifications of prisoners taken in this area showed that a new and very formidable opponent had joined in the fray in the shape of 2 SS Panzer Division (Das Reich). Both its infantry regiments were identified and men from them stated that the division had moved hotfoot from St. Lo in the American area during the previous night with the intention of assembling during 28th June and finally launching a co-ordinated counter attack at dawn on 29th June. In view of the precarious nature of the German positions however, units of 2 SS Panzer Division were flung in to plug the gaps immediately they arrived in the battle area, a clear illustration of how the Wehrmacht was being made to dance to the British tune.

The eastern flank was slightly quieter, though still potentially aggressive, for twice during the morning a concentration of tanks and vehicles in Verson was bombed by the R.A.F. on request. At 1600 hours an attempt by 10 Highland Light Infantry and 3 County of London Yeomanry to extend their operations to beyond Mouen, proved that reinforcements had been hurried to this side too, for a swift counter attack by a battle group of 21 Panzer Division with between 20-30 tanks put an end to any ambitions in this part of the world. This was beaten back, and these tanks again bombed in the Verson area, for good measure, towards dusk.

43 (Wessex) Division spent the day quietly, consolidating its positions around Cheux and St. Mauvieu. 32 Guards Brigade was placed under command and took over a sector alongside 129 Infantry Brigade. Reconnaissance having shown that Marcelet, a small village a mile to the east of St. Mauvieu, had been abandoned by the enemy, a mobile force of carriers and anti-tank guns moved into it as well as into the adjacent wood, where unfortunately it was continuously shelled and mortared.

Summing up the day's operations therefore, although there had been much confused fighting, with brigades and even battalions carrying on isolated actions in different areas, steady progress had been made towards achieving the Corps intention. The bridgehead over the River Odon had been widened and consolidated. The Cheux-St. Mauvieu-Haut du Bosq triangle was well on the way to being organised as a firm base. Many of the enemy pockets between this position and the bridgehead had been eliminated, and the flanks had been strengthened. Much remained however to be done, for the Germans remained as active and enterprising as ever, and 28th June provided unmistakable evidence that one of the most important objects of " Epsom " was being achieved—that of attracting enemy armoured strength to the British sector. Fresh formations identified against 8 Corps so far had included a tank battalion from 2 Panzer Division, the bulk of the infantry of 2 SS Panzer Division, and a battle group of 21 Panzer Division. Nor was this all, for late that night, the detailed interrogation of a prisoner revealed that at least one unit of still another panzer division, 1 SS Panzer Division (Adolf Hitler) had also been flung into the fighting south of the Odon. The story of the first prisoner from this renowned division was most revealing, for it showed that after a slow journey by rail and always at night, from Brussels via Compiègne and Paris—the Seine bridges north of the French capital having been destroyed by the R.A.F.—his unit had detrained at the nearest railhead—Conches, no less than sixty miles away in Eastern Normandy. Thence it travelled by lorry to the front where immediately on arrival and without any adequate briefing, a reconnaissance patrol including the prisoner, was sent to find out if any British were in Baron, which was conclusively proved to be the case. The picture emerged therefore of units of various enemy divisions being moved, in the greatest haste, to the Normandy front and flung in piecemeal and without preparation, in a desperate bid to halt 8 Corps' advance. The decisions of the Fuehrer's conference at Soissons now being implemented were already disrupted and foredoomed to failure.

Casualties during 28th June were lighter than on previous days, amounting to 61 killed, 228 wounded and 22 missing. The strength of the Corps rose by the addition of the remaining echelons of 32 Guards Brigade to 3,514 officers and 64,957 other ranks.

As far as the enemy was concerned 12 SS Panzer Division had suffered heavy losses in infantry and been forced to call in the aid of other formations, whilst it was estimated that at least sixty of its tanks had been knocked out by the end of the first three days' fighting.

29th June

The weather, which had improved considerably during the previous day, now favoured us, for the morning dawned bright and clear, and the R.A.F. was early abroad in the skies. The Corps intention remained unchanged, since the Corps Commander, convinced by the reinforcements reaching the enemy opposite, that something in the nature of a major counter attack was in the offing, was determined not to be caught off his balance. The pronounced salient in which 8 Corps still found itself, owing to the position of 30 Corps still held up to its right rear, made this possibility only too easy, in the event of any serious penetration of the flanks. The Canadian attack on Carpiquet airfield had for the moment been postponed whilst 30 Corps, though now firmly established in Rauray and Le Manoir, had not succeeded in gaining further ground southwards, despite heavy and fluctuating fighting. 8 Corps could not, therefore, expect any relief, and it became, as nearly always in its operations, a case of " Heaven helping those who help themselves." 8 Corps passed to the defensive and prepared for the storm to come. At 1000 hours General O'Connor held a conference at Headquarters 15 (Scottish) Division in which he announced that in view of the general situation any further advance to the River Orne would be temporarily stopped, and present positions maintained. A general consolidation would take place with particular stress on the co-ordination of anti-tank defence, and the positioning of the armoured brigades. Certain re-grouping too, on account of the nature of operations since " Epsom " had begun, was urgently necessary, for formations had become strung out with a certain amount of intermingling of units. Areas of responsibility were re-assigned and every effort was made to "tidy up" the sector in order to take the shock of what had every appearance of becoming the first major enemy offensive since the Allies had landed. Much had also to be done generally to improve communications in the area over-run so far and the Sappers had a heavy task in front of them in widening the narrow lanes, bulldozing rubble aside in the villages and locating and clearing enemy minefields. Last but not least, one necessary but unusual duty also fell on them—namely disposal of the hundreds of dead cattle littering the area, whose continued presence was certainly not beneficial to the health of the troops.

From dawn onwards, air reports had been flowing in showing large scale enemy movement northwards towards Second Army from Flers, Argentan and Vire. This could mean one thing only—the last reserve divisions of Army Group " B " at the disposal of Rommel were being flung into the breach. As German operational moves, on account of the overwhelming Allied superiority in the air, had since the beginning of the invasion, taken place only by night and on secondary roads, this daylight movement was in itself significant of the importance the German High Command attached to their quick arrival. The bulk of these formations of course had, by daylight, already reached their assembly areas in the triangle formed by Evrecy-Noyers-Villers Bocage, and this traffic largely represented their supply echelons. The occasion was nevertheless a field day for the R.A.F., for by early afternoon over two hundred enemy vehicles of all types had been shot up and destroyed on the roads, whilst concentrations of tanks and transport discovered on the outskirts of Villers Bocage had also been successfully dealt with—in common with the few Luftwaffe planes which attempted to intervene.

It is difficult for Allied soldiers to realise just what is meant by "mastery of the air," although during the subsequent advance into Belgium, the many hundreds of burnt out wrecks lining the roads bore mute witness to our air striking power. German troops however, in Normandy, could have given an accurate definition without calling on their imagination. Again and again in their letters home, references to the overwhelming strength of the R.A.F. and U.S.A.A.F. are encountered, whilst on the rare occasions when the Luftwaffe is induced to put in an appearance, the surprise and pleasure expressed is almost pathetic.

Thus a sergeant from 272 Infantry Division writes:—"The R.A.F. rules the skies. I have not yet seen a single plane with a swastika. Despite the material superiority of the enemy, we Germans hold firm and the front at Caen holds. Every soldier at the front is hoping for a miracle. . . ."

And a private from 331 Infantry Division:—"We saw several hundred burnt out trucks along the road. If 'Tommy' had not such a strong air force everything would be different. . . . We had only been marching for 500 metres before fighter bombers attacked us."

Whilst an SS corporal from 10 SS Panzer Division is more bitter, even surprisingly so, for morale in the Waffen SS was at all times higher than in the Wehrmacht. "We are now 30 kilometres behind the front after a nightmare journey across France which has taken a fortnight under the most frightening conditions on account of the enemy planes. For the last fortnight

I have hardly slept at all and have forgotten how many times the enemy has strafed us. We have suffered many casualties in men and vehicles, but our so-called Luftwaffe has not ventured to put in an appearance. There was nothing like this in Russia, and we are all wondering whether life at the front will be as bad."

On the other hand once the Luftwaffe did show up, a certain amount of enthusiasm is discernible as the following extract from the pen of an SS man of 12 SS Panzer Division illustrates:—"Last night the sky was covered with German aircraft of all types and they saturated 'Tommy's' positions with so many bombs that there was a red glow all around us. I have never before experienced such a nice firework display, and the enemy's anti-aircraft was firing from all his guns at the planes, which passed over us at a height of only 100-150 metres. We immediately sent up flares to warn them not to drop their loads on us. Let's hope they'll come every day, then we'll have some peace."

Perhaps the best summary of the air situation is contained in a report by the commander of 2 Panzer Division, Major-General Baron von Luttwitz, on the battle experiences of his division in Normandy during June. He writes:— "The enemy have complete mastery of the air. They bomb and strafe every movement, even single vehicles and individuals. They reconnoitre our area constantly and direct their artillery fire. During the month the *total* number of German aircraft over the divisional area was six!

"Our soldiers enter the battle in low spirits at the thought of the enemy's enormous material superiority. They are always asking 'where is the Luftwaffe?' The feeling of helplessness against enemy aircraft operating without any hindrance has a paralyzing effect, and during the bombing this effect on inexperienced troops is literally 'soul-shattering'—and it must be borne in mind that four-engined bombers have not yet taken part in attacking ground targets. It is therefore essential for troops to be lifted out of their state of distress the moment they begin to counter-attack. The best results have been obtained by the platoon and section commander leaping forward, uttering a good old-fashioned 'Hurrah,' which spurs on the inexperienced troops and carries them along. The revival of the practice of sounding a bugle call for the attack has been found to answer this purpose, and this has been made a divisional order. An attack launched in this manner is an experience which our troops will never forget, and stimulates them into action again."

Further comment on this praiseworthy but one-sided proposition is superfluous, but after the introduction of heavy bombing in direct support of 8 Corps in Operation "Goodwood" few German soldiers encountered were the type to shout "Hurrah!"

Before the start of "Overlord" there had been much talk of using air power to "isolate the battlefield." In so far as this is ever practicable, by 6 June, 1944, the Allies had achieved it in Normandy. Above Paris, all bridges over the River Seine had been destroyed and reinforcements from the north could only cross in small numbers at night by using improvised ferries. The unceasing bombing of railway junctions had virtually paralyzed the French railways, so that weeks were spent on journeys which in normal times took only hours. Thus 9 and 10 SS Panzer Divisions on their return to the West at the end of May had taken as long to cross to Normandy from the east of France as to reach the French border from Lvov on the outskirts of Russia. Once the Allied bombings had begun, the Germans had to bear an additional trial in the increased activity of the "Maquis" or French Resistance Movement. Before "D" Day this had largely consisted of isolated but fairly extensive sabotage. After 6th June the French became bolder and more useful to us, for they were able to harass enemy formations on a much larger scale, especially in the centre and south of France, where whole German divisions were forced to conduct punitive expeditions against them with indifferent success.

As the campaign progressed, so the paralysis affecting enemy communications and movement spread, and towards the end of it the most sure and safe method of moving enemy formations was by bicycle, a fact which aroused a certain amount of derision at the time, but which nevertheless did much to solve the reinforcement problem for the Wehrmacht.

To compare therefore this state of affairs with the peaceful condition of the restricted and grossly overcrowded Allied bridgehead, in which virtually any bomb dropped would have found a reasonable target, so close were units packed together, is to experience a feeling of profound thankfulness that the maxim of the Commander-in-Chief of "winning the air battle first" had been so thoroughly carried out.

Whilst the R.A.F. was attacking the enemy moving up from the south, the Corps artillery, fed with unusually plentiful information from its Air O.P. and counter-battery sources, fired heavy concentrations on likely enemy assembly areas and forming-up places, in addition to giving maximum aid to the forward troops in response to an increasingly large number of calls for direct support from them.

At this juncture (which is a very appropriate one since the events of 29th June so well illustrate the complete Allied superiority in these matters over the enemy), having discussed the air-striking power, let us pass to an examination of the complementary and no less effective weapon—artillery. If the R.A.F. was most feared for the destruction it spread outside the immediate battlefield area, the ordinary German soldier in his slit trench was terrorised by the British and U.S. artillery, whilst the amount of ammunition expended on even minor tasks dismayed and depressed his superiors.

Thus we find in that same despondent report by Baron von Luttwitz the following appreciation of the British artillery arm:—

"The incredibly heavy artillery and mortar fire of the enemy is something new both for the seasoned veterans of the Eastern Front and the new arrivals from reinforcement units. Whereas the veterans get used to it comparatively quickly, the inexperienced reinforcements require several days to do so, after which they become acclimatised. The average rate of fire in the divisional area is 4,000 artillery rounds and 5,000 mortar rounds. This is multiplied many times before an attack, however small. For example, when the British made an attack on a sector of only two companies, they expended 3,500 rounds in two hours. The Allies are waging war regardless of expense. Our own artillery can only fire one-tenth of the amount fired by the enemy."

Nor was the German writing home in any doubt about the inferiority of his army in that respect. Listen to an SS Corporal from 1 SS Panzer Division:—". . . Things here are fair. If it were not for the continued artillery fire one might call it peaceful. Yes, their artillery is a subject on its own. If it had not been for their artillery, we should have taught the 'Tommies' how to swim."

Whilst the last entry—from which the obvious conclusion can be drawn— in the diary of a member of 363 Infantry Division recorded this:—"The enemy artillery is terrific. I can count sixty impacts in a minute. This is the worst night I have ever lived through. But it will come worse—of that I am sure."

After this discussion of the effect on the enemy of the twin Allied weapons of air and artillery, let us return to events within the Corps sector. Here, in contrast to what was happening outside its borders, comparative quiet at first reigned. On the eastern flank, 43 (Wessex) Division, having been partially relieved during the afternoon of 28th June in the St. Mauvieu area, was able to move 129 Infantry Brigade south with the object of stabilising the position in Mouen and the surrounding woods. It was hoped that the battle group of SS Panzer Grenadiers from 12 SS Panzer Division operating here, having received a bloody nose on the previous day from the Scots, would not put up so spirited a resistance, and the more so as its tank component from 21 Panzer Division had twice been subjected to R.A.F. bombardment. Accordingly a battalion attack by 1 Worcestershire Regiment was put in against Mouen at 0830 hours, and this deduction proved to be correct, for within an hour this village and its eastern hamlet Bas de Mouen, was in its hands. Subsequently, on a brigade basis, a large scale clearance operation was conducted southwards, first to uproot the remaining enemy in the intervening woods and then to consolidate on the general line of the road Baron-Gournay as further backing for the armour forward of the River Odon.

The German High Command was itself not clear, as statements from prisoners revealed, as to whether or not British troops were in occupation of the Baron area, and presumably communications with its troops in situ there had broken down. At all events, this large and very difficult wooded area was not reinforced at all, and by 1830 hours had been cleared of its sniper contingent with 43 (Wessex) Division firmly on its objective.

To the west, similar beating and mopping up operations were intended, for it was far more necessary to stabilise the situation on this flank in time to meet any attack by fresh enemy troops brought up for the purpose. This was not to be so easy in view of the development by mid-morning of considerable German pressure from the south-west. However, at first light 44 (Lowland) Brigade resumed its advance of the previous night with 8 Royal Scots leading, and by 1040 hours the Caen-Villers Bocage railway line due west of Grainville-sur-Odon had been reached without violent opposition. Here this battalion was ordered to halt and organise a defensive position, whilst 6 Royal Scots Fusiliers passed through to continue the advance as far as the main Caen-Noyers road. Before this manœuvre had been carried out, however, an infiltration on the right combined with some heavy mortaring forced 8 Royal Scots to pull back its two leading companies from the neighbourhood of a farm called Les Nouillons. In order to ease this pressure the attack by 6 Royal Scots Fusiliers was diverted to this flank and the situation restored.

In the meantime reports from the neighbouring 46 (Highland) Brigade were far from satisfactory, and showed that the enemy north of the River Odon was by no means subdued. In fact there had undoubtedly been some strengthening of this sector, for identifications were made of the second brigade of 1 SS Panzer Division, and it was apparent that there was now a formidable force between the southern tip of Le Valtru and the river west of Gavrus bridge, to which 2 Argyll and Sutherland Highlanders still clung, though Gavrus itself was no longer held. The Argylls were by now tired, having spent the last twenty-four hours isolated and virtually cut off, under continual and increasingly heavy mortar and artillery fire, in addition to frustrating repeated attempts at infiltration by enemy infantry. It was a matter of some urgency, therefore, to join up with this battalion from the north, and this remained the main intention for 46 (Highland) Brigade.

Unfortunately, a sharp counter attack against the Le Valtru position, about 1630 hours, put back any thought of this for the day, for after heavy fighting to oust enemy panzer grenadiers, who succeeded in penerating between 9 Cameronians and 7 Seaforth Highlanders, the position here was not restored until the early evening. 2 Argyll and Sutherland Highlanders, therefore, remained for the moment " in the blue," but the remainder of 227 (Highland) Brigade was now concentrated south of Mondrainville, preparatory to moving at first light to reinforce the Gavrus sector.

Forward of the river, 29 Armoured Brigade spent an exhausting day in constant engagements against enemy tanks—both mobile and dug-in—and anti-tank guns. By careful fighting and some clever manœuvring a certain degree of progress was made, particularly during the afternoon, when 8 Rifle Brigade, supported by 3 Royal Tank Regiment, succeeded in taking the obnoxious wood on the southern slopes of Hill 112, which thus for the first time, was firmly in British hands. 2 Fife and Forfar Yeomanry operating on the right, extended its area of penetration and, in conjunction with 44 Royal Tank Regiment, reached the Esquay-Evrecy road and even threatened these twin enemy bastions. However, this provoked a rather sharper counter attack than hitherto from the woods south-west of Bougy and after quickly losing six tanks, 44 Royal Tank Regiment was forced to withdraw to their original positions.

In view of the enemy build up, the weight of which was now beginning to be felt by 29 Armoured Brigade, the retention of only one armoured brigade across the River Odon was proving both expensive and dangerous. The original plan had, of course, provided for two, for 4 Armoured Brigade was to have been brought forward to protect the right flank of 8 Corps in the area between the Rivers Odon and Orne, but owing to the developing threat from the south-west towards the main position north of the Odon, events had forced the retention of this armoured brigade in support of the Scottish infantry there. In the early afternoon 4 Armoured Brigade, less 44 Royal Tank Regiment (still under command of 29 Armoured Brigade), was positioned in the west of the Corps sector in direct support of 44 (Lowland) Brigade, in order to defeat any enemy armoured threat in that area.

The day had been remarkable for the increase in shelling on both sides. The enemy artillery had obviously been greatly stepped up and, coupled with the augmented and very accurate mortar fire, had caused considerable casualties and no small discomfort. Nevertheless, whatever the troops of 8 Corps experienced in this direction, must have been slight compared with the treatment meted out to the Germans. Repeated calls for DF support were made on the Corps artillery, which responded magnificently. Time and again, enemy parties forming up to attack had a " stonk " brought down on them, which effectively put paid to any activity of that nature. Yet it was not until long afterwards, when the opposing Corps Commander was interrogated as a prisoner of war, that the real truth of the success won by the Gunners was revealed, for it is to them that the main honours of the day must go in frustrating the enemy's efforts. Nor must the neighbouring Canadian artillery and the distant aid from the Royal Navy be overlooked, for all combined together to take a terrible toll of German lives and equipment.

The main enemy assault broke at 1800 hours, against the sector held by 44 (Lowland) Brigade, and at a moment when the relief of one of the battalions was in progress. In the late morning, because of the great increase in strength of the opposing enemy, it had been decided not to proceed further with the southwards drive once matters along the railway west of

Grainville-sur-Odon had been stabilised, since 8 Royal Scots had sustained appreciable losses in the day's fighting. Orders were accordingly given for the position to be taken over and consolidated by the relatively fresh 6 Royal Scots Fusiliers. The situation did not, however, permit of this relief taking place for some time and, in fact, it did not actually begin until 1700 hours. Whilst it was in progress and shortly before 1800 hours, the expected enemy counter attack came in.

An SS officer captured on a reconnaissance mission on the Haut du Bosq feature just prior to this, at 1600 hours, very imprudently carried the plan of his own brigade with him, and this foreshadowed an attack by all three battalions along the axis Feuguerolles-Brettevillette from a start line Vendes-Le Valtru and with its objective Cheux, which it was intended should be captured and held. This, however, was only one part of an offensive planned on much more ambitious lines. It was, in fact, nothing less than the attempted fulfilment of Hitler's demand to von Rundstedt at the Soissons conference for an all-out effort against the Allies. From subsequent examination of the various inter-related engagements the grand design was revealed as follows:—

A feint attack against the Odon bridgehead from the south, a subsidiary effort against the eastern flank from the Carpiquet-Verson area, whilst the main blow was to be delivered from the south-west along the natural tank runs provided by the two axes Villers Bocage-Caen and Noyers-Cheux. All these moves were to be co-ordinated and simultaneous, and the overall object was to reach the Caen-Bayeux road. The German High Command had intended to use Sepp Dietrich's 1 SS Panzer Corps of three or four panzer divisions to carry out this undertaking, in conjunction with the newly arrived 2 SS Panzer Corps, in the hope that the combined weight of some five hundred tanks in a massed blow would regain the initiative for the Germans. The original plan had been to launch this mass of armour against the junction between the British and American forces in order first to split and then to defeat them in detail. "Operation Epsom," however, had not only forced the abandonment of this idea but, like a magnet, had attracted in piecemeal, and thus whittled down, good panzer divisions such as 12 SS, 1 SS and 2 SS which, now the time had come for a major effort, were not in a fit condition to respond. Nevertheless it was decided to make the attempt, relying chiefly on the new arrivals, but with Dietrich's troops participating in a subsidiary role.

2 SS Panzer Corps, consisting of 9 SS Panzer Division (Hohenstaufen) and 10 SS Panzer Division (Frundsberg), was commanded by Colonel-General of the Waffen SS Paul Hausser, a former Wehrmacht officer who was reputed to have the best tactical brain among the senior SS commanders. The latest exploit of this redoubtable corps had been to inflict a heavy defeat on the Russians in front of Lvov in Eastern Poland during April, after which it had returned fresh and at full strength to Normandy. Its favourite and much practised accomplishment—as at Lvov—had been to attack the enemy suddenly through the sector of a corps already in action, and this manœuvre was attempted in this case, for from the south-west the main attack developed through the lines of Panzer Lehr, 2 SS and 12 SS Panzer Division.

North of the River Odon, 9 SS Panzer Division made the best progress, for two companies of 8 Royal Scots were quickly over-run (though many of the troops collected together and rejoined their battalion during the night) and heavy fighting ensued, which involved, in addition to 44 (Lowland) Brigade, 31 Tank Brigade and 4 Armoured Brigade. The complementary attack south of the river by 10 SS Panzer Division was so disrupted by shelling that it never got going at all, though a number of small tank and infantry sorties were launched against 29 Armoured Brigade from the Esquay area, and there was some localised but heavy fighting there. However, the main attack was held, and by last light the enemy had been driven back and the situation restored. Some Panther tanks did nevertheless get through as far as Cheux where they were destroyed. A threat to the eastern flank failed to materialise at the same time, since a concentration of approximately forty tanks which had moved from the outskirts of Caen to Carpiquet was shot up by R.A.F. Typhoons and did not venture to make any further movement.

As soon as the enemy had broken off and disengaged, 2 Northamptonshire Yeomanry was ordered to sweep south-west from Cheux to the railway west of Grainville during the night, in order to keep contact with the Scots and prevent any surprises from this quarter whilst 29 Armoured Brigade was moving back to concentrate round Norrey-en-Bessin. Unfortunately in carrying out these orders enemy tanks and anti-tank guns were encountered, and much shelling and mortaring sustained, resulting in a number of tanks being knocked out.

During the course of this action, General Dempsey, believing these attacks to be rehearsals for a more co-ordinated effort on the following day, confirmed the Corps Commander's appreciation of the general situation and ordered 8 Corps to consolidate in its present area. In addition, in view of the exposed position of 29 Armoured Brigade, he instructed that it was to be withdrawn north of the River Odon. The bridgehead was not, however, to be given up but indeed maintained at all costs by the infantry holding it, 159 and 129 Infantry Brigades. Hill 112 was thus once again to become a "no mans land." This move of the armour was carried out between 2300 hours and 0400 hours without attracting the attention of the enemy and was a masterpiece of good staff work and unit march discipline. The operation of withdrawing four armoured regimental groups as well as brigade headquarters back over the river, across only one bridge with steep narrow approaches, and on sudden orders received as daylight was failing, would have been commendable in any circumstances, but was particularly so in view of the torrential rain which fell throughout the night.

There is no doubt that to 11 Armoured Division, the decision to withdraw 29 Armoured Brigade—a formation undefeated and which had now very much the measure of its opponents—came both as a surprise and a blow, for it appeared as though the hard fighting of the first four days had proved abortive. It must be remembered however that in units, it is (fortunately) rarely possible to know the overall picture or the concealed aims of the High Command. In this case the two principal objects of the operation far outweighing any other factors were (1) to retain the initiative, and (2) to attract enemy armour on to the front of Second Army and these had been overwhelmingly achieved.

Had General O'Connor allowed 8 Corps to be caught off balance by the events of the day, the result might have been very different, for there is no doubt that 29th June was "D" Day for the enemy—we have it on the authority of the enemy Corps Commander himself, for here is what General Hausser said of this attack under interrogation later in England:—

"It was scheduled to begin at seven o'clock in the morning, but hardly had the tanks assembled when they were attacked by fighter bombers. This disrupted the troops so much that the attack did not start again till two-thirty in the afternoon. But even then it could not get going. The murderous fire from naval guns in the Channel and the terrible British artillery destroyed the bulk of our attacking force in its assembly area. The few tanks that did manage to go forward, were easily stopped by the British anti-tank guns. In my opinion the attack was prepared too quickly. I wanted to wait another two days but Hitler insisted that it be launched on 29th June."

Such was the story of the second and more ambitious of the only two enemy attempts at armoured counter offensive along the entire Normandy front during June. Both, as the Allied strategists desired, had been directed against the British sector of the line and both had been thoroughly beaten there. The failure of the second was as proportionately more serious for the German High Command as it was larger in scope, for henceforth scant success was ever achieved in again building up a mobile reserve. Eight out of the nine panzer divisions in France had been hurled against the British Second Army and of these, elements of no less than seven had been identified on the 8 Corps front during 26th-29th June. Of the estimated 350 tanks that the enemy had lost during June, well over 100 must have been knocked out as the result of ground or air operations during "Epsom." Personnel losses were even higher in proportion, for already documents were being captured showing that company strengths of one-third or one-quarter were becoming normal. Yet the morale of the SS troops, particularly in 9 and 10 SS Panzer Divisions, was extraordinarily high, for prisoners stated that they had all received a "pep" talk before going into action in which they were assured that a victorious end to the war was near as their V.1 bombs had destroyed London and killed twelve million people in England!

However, the hopes of the field soldiers no longer extended to the Staff, for one last anecdote afterwards recounted by General Blumentritt, at that time Chief of Staff to Field-Marshal von Rundstedt, gives some idea of the despair occasioned in the German High Command by the failure of the attacks, and as soon as it was realised that henceforth the precious panzer divisions were doomed to a costly battle of attrition.

Keitel, chief of Hitler's Combined Staff, on 1st July telephoned von Rundstedt, and discussing the situation in desperate tones asked: "What shall we do? What shall we do?" Von Rundstedt replied in his cool impassive voice "What shall you do? Make peace, you idiots, what else can you do?", and calmly hung up the receiver. Twenty-four hours later an order arrived from Berlin relieving von Rundstedt of his command, and replacing him as Supreme Commander in the West by the unfortunate Field-Marshal von Kluge, hitherto known as the "apostle of victorious defence," though not after the battle of Normandy.

At the same time that he ordered the withdrawal of 29 Armoured Brigade, General Dempsey also acceded to the request of the Corps Commander for additional infantry to be placed under his command. At 2200 hours Major-General R. K. Ross, commanding 53 (Welsh) Division reported at Corps Headquarters and during the night the first Welsh brigade arrived and was concentrated around Putot-en-Bessin and Le Mesnil Patry. The Army Commander meanwhile, as always, cautious, instructed 1 Corps to strengthen the junction between its right flank and the left rear of 8 Corps, so that in the event of an increased threat from the direction of Caen, the front was properly integrated and able to bear the shock. Some additional anti-tank artillery was also placed under command so that at the end of the day the strength of 8 Corps rose to 4,247 officers and 78,732 other ranks. Casualties had however increased considerably in wounded and missing, though fortunately not in killed. The figures were:—

	Killed	Wounded	Missing
11 Armoured Division	5	33	—
15 (Scottish) Division	37	219	87
43 (Wessex) Division	25	108	13
32 Guards Brigade	10	32	—
4 Armoured Brigade	10	35	21
31 Tank Brigade	1	5	—
8 A.G.R.A.	—	2	—
8 Corps Troops	—	2	—
	88	436	121

No estimate can be given of the losses sustained by the assaulting enemy, but in view of the complete repulse of all his attacks, coupled with the statements afterwards made by German commanders, of the slaughter caused by the Corps artillery in their assembly areas, there is no doubt that they were infinitely higher than those suffered by 8 Corps.

30th June

If the previous day had marked the official end of the plan to exploit forward and force the crossing of the Orne, the Corps intention for 30th June and subsequently, showed clearly that, in the opinion of the Commander-in-Chief, "Epsom" had now achieved its maximum offensive usefulness, and henceforward, by and large, activity on this part of the front would be allowed to die down for the moment, in conformity with his strategy of alternate hammer blows in different sectors. The immediate aim became, of course, to free the armour from its present task for precisely the same reasons as von Rundstedt and Rommel had in endeavouring to extract their panzer divisions from an infantry role—to reform a mobile force with which to strike elsewhere. Fortunately for the Allies, possessing the initiative and working to a definite plan, this was not difficult.

So far as armoured divisions were concerned, at this time Second Army had in the theatre 7, 11 and Guards Armoured Divisions complete (though in the case of the two latter their infantry components were detached and holding part of the front of 8 Corps) whilst 4 Canadian Armoured Division was in process of landing and 1 Polish Armoured Division was expected by the middle of July. Several independent armoured and tank brigades (notably 4, 8, 31, 33 and 1 and 8 Canadian) were also fighting in France as well as that astonishing creation of General Hobart—79 Armoured Division. The authorised war establishment of a British armoured division was considerably higher than that of its German equivalent, but in any case the actual British numerical superiority was far greater, for in most cases the panzer divisions, entering the campaign below strength, had also been unable to make good their losses. By the end of June it is reasonable to say that the British armoured division was numerically at least twice as strong as its average opponent and that the total British tank strength in Normandy at that time approximated to the total German tank strength in the West. This does not take into account the armoured divisions at that time operating with First U.S. Army, nor those building-up with Third U.S. Army and destined to become operational a month later.

The Commander-in-Chief had at his disposal, therefore, a comfortable superiority in armour already by the end of June, and was considerably aided thereby in following the strategy he had laid down. It is true that the enemy was able to redress the balance to a certain degree by employing two tanks which were appreciably better than anything the Allies possessed—namely the "Tiger" and the "Panther." Providentially, however, German industry, despite the miracles it was achieving under the guidance of Albert Speer, in the face of continual bombardment from the air had been unable completely to equip every panzer division with them.

Henceforward the remaining operations conducted by 8 Corps west of Caen were to be infantry battles only, 'holding' for the moment, though with limited objectives later, and every effort was now made to perfect its defensive preparations before the expected German attack materialised, so as to ensure that the position would withstand any shock which the enemy was capable of administering. The general plan for consolidation ordered by General O'Connor at his morning conference hinged on the tightest co-ordination of anti-tank defence together with the correct siting of the armoured brigades in relation to it, and was as follows:—

1. *Armour.*

(a) 4 Armoured Brigade would remain north-west of the Cheux position, prepared to engage any enemy tank attack which developed from the south-east or south-west.

(b) 29 Armoured Brigade was to move and position itself north-east of the Cheux position, ready to deal with any tank attack from the east.

(c) Either of these armoured brigades must be able to support the other.

2. *Artillery.*

(a) Field, medium and heavy guns were already well sited for the defensive battle and would not need to be moved.

(b) Anti-tank defence throughout the Corps area was to be co-ordinated under the supervision of Lieutenant-Colonel Cockburn, commanding 91 Anti-Tank Regiment.

(c) One additional anti-tank regiment from 12 Corps was placed under command of 53 (Welsh) division.

3. *Infantry.*

(a) 53 (Welsh) Division on arrival in the Corps sector would relieve 15 (Scottish) Division, during the nights 30th June, 1st July and 2nd July.

(b) 15 (Scottish) Division, which had assumed command over 159 Infantry Brigade at 0300 hours, was ordered to extend the Odon bridgehead, using 227 (Highland) Brigade (though this plan was subsequently not carried out).

(c) Elsewhere 43 (Wessex) Division and 32 Guards Brigade were adjusting and improving their sectors, notably that of 129 Infantry Brigade which as neighbour to 159 Infantry Brigade, now held a firm bridgehead from Baron to Gournay and thence back to the river.

The whole of the area for which 8 Corps was responsible now literally bristled with troops, tanks and guns echeloned in depth, for while the armour in the main was kept concentrated, small detachments under command of the infantry brigades were scattered throughout the area, since their presence not only gave additional confidence to the infantry, but confused the enemy as to the dispositions of the main bodies.

The textbook idea of a position strongly held in depth could not have been better illustrated. From the Odon as far back as the main Caen—Bayeux road, interspersed with the infantry in their slit trenches, every few yards one saw either a tank carefully sited hull-down, a dug-in anti-tank gun or a battery of field guns camouflaged but firing repeatedly, and the sharp crack of these coupled with the deeper bark of the mediums and heavies, the whine of the German mortars and the occasional bursts of machine-gun fire, combined to form an unforgettable memory for those who witnessed the scene. Everyone was braced for the expected blow, but in strength it never came. The enemy was doubtless licking his wounds, and regrouping his units after the terrible losses of the previous day. At all events no major effort was developed against 8 Corps during the whole of 30th June, though its opponents remained active and launched several probing attacks on a small scale. Thus at 1150 hours 159 Infantry Brigade repulsed two companies of panzer grenadiers, supported by a squadron of tanks coming from the direction of Esquay, whilst towards the middle of the afternoon the enemy tried again in a different sector—that held by 46 (Highland) Brigade, and for a short while succeeded in penetrating its southern-most positions. Within the hour, however, 7 Seaforth Highlanders had effectively dealt with this attempt.

The Germans then turned their attention once again to the bridgehead, emboldened perhaps by the absence of 29 Armoured Brigade, and sent, shortly before 1900 hours, what in fact amounted to a strong reconnaissance patrol against 5 Wiltshire Regiment in the vicinity of Gournay, but this was nevertheless soon driven out. A more serious effort was delivered at the same time against the unfortunate 2 Argyll and Sutherland Highlanders still around Gavrus bridge, which succeeded in infiltrating between the companies and battalion headquarters, resulting in a very confused situation and alarmist reports that the unit had been over-run and the commanding officer killed. Happily these were later proved false, but the Argylls had an unpleasant time, in common indeed with the whole of the forward areas of the Corps that day, for mortaring and shelling was constant, and perhaps heavier than hitherto.

So far as casualties were concerned, 30th June as a result was more expensive than any of the previous four days, for losses totalled over one thousand of all types, made up as follows:—

	Killed	*Wounded*	*Missing*
11 Armoured Division	27	160	130
15 (Scottish) Division	52	299	102
43 (Wessex) Division	55	192	8
53 (Welsh) Division	1	2	—
32 Guards Brigade	2	12	—
4 Armoured Brigade	11	24	1
31 Tank Brigade	1	10	—
8 A.G.R.A.	2	1	—
8 Corps Troops	1	2	1
	152	702	242

Patrols and air observation reports showed that there was still much enemy movement close to the battlefield, whilst Tac R reported that strong concentrations remained further to the south and south-west. Such movement and concentrations were, of course, effectively shelled by the Corps artillery, and thereby a number of impending attacks undoubtedly disrupted and broken up before they could get going. H.M.S. Rodney helped in this good work by bombarding three villages suspected of containing enemy headquarters, and during the afternoon fired fifty 16-inch shells into Feuguerolles, St. Andre-sur-Orne and Fontenay-le-Marmion. The first-named was later confirmed as the headquarters of 1 SS Panzer Corps.

The Commander-in-Chief too at this juncture, considering Villers Bocage to be the vital traffic centre through which all German moves to this part of the front had to pass, decided to have it thoroughly bombed, and asked R.A.F. Bomber Command to perform this service. Air Chief Marshal Harris concurred, for this was a target after his own heart, and at 2030 hours 250 heavy bombers from England removed this little town, in all but name, from the map. It had been hoped that considerable bodies of enemy troops would be caught in this bombardment in the act of moving up to the line, but whether this was achieved is doubtful, for prisoners later declared that only French civilians were in the town at the time of the raid. Nevertheless, considerable inconvenience to enemy supply arrangements must have resulted from the dislocation to their traffic, however temporary this may have been, and it was the high spot for the Allies on the last day of the fateful month of June.

Summary of Operations during June

For the Allies, general progress to date had proved most satisfactory. A firm lodgement area had been seized on the European mainland and developed according to plan. The enemy, despite elaborate precautions, had been unable to prevent this, and in fact within three weeks of the start of the fighting had committed almost the whole of his mobile reserves in attempting to "rope off" the British and U.S. Armies. Allied casualties, contrary to all expectation had been light, whilst German losses, on the other hand, were heavy, and already amounted to 62,000 all ranks in killed, wounded and captured. Finally, the Allies were working to a definite strategic plan, whilst the Germans were not only unable to do this, but in their day to day reactions to events constantly misappreciated Allied aims. Thus Rommel's Chief-of-Staff, Lieutenant-General Speidel, in his report to Hitler for the week ending 1st July, showed clearly that what the German High Command in Normandy was thinking was almost exactly one hundred per cent. wrong. Here are his comments on "Epsom" and the situation around Caen:—

"The most significant event of the week was the enemy's large-scale attack to obtain possession of the Caen area in order to acquire *a base for future operations in the* direction of Paris.

"The enemy employed 5 Infantry Division, 1 Armoured Division and 3 Armoured Brigade (sic—identifications were evidently not his strong point). A resumption of the enemy attack may be reckoned with in the break-through area, and various signs seem to indicate that the area east of the Orne will also be involved. The enemy's main objective is still the concentrated thrust at Caen.

"The enemy's plan after taking possession of the area surrounding Caen, possibly by encircling it from both sides, and after closing up again, will be to advance on Paris. At the same time he will attempt a concentrated attack on the St. Lo-Coutances area *for the consolidation of the land base.*

"There is no fresh evidence concerning the objective set for First American Army Group in Great Britain, but from the point of view of strategic co-operation with the 'Montgomery' Army Group for the thrust on Paris and the elimination of the long-range weapon, *a descent on both sides of the Somme up to the Seine* will have to be reckoned with."

The real Allied aims and intentions were, of course, the very contrary of the portions in italics.

From the point of view of 8 Corps, if its contribution then did not seem unduly spectacular, certainly the evidence concerning it which has since come to light, together with the more detached consideration which only the passage of time can ensure, compel the re-valuation of its achievements. To have broken through a strongly entrenched enemy, carried out a fighting advance of upwards of six miles against ever increasing opposition through the most difficult country, and finally over a considerable water obstacle, and all this with open flanks, would at any time be regarded as creditable for seasoned troops. However, for soldiers in battle for the first time in their lives, it was a very fine performance indeed, and reflected both the high state of training and the confident feeling running through the Corps. The passage through 15 (Scottish) Division of 11 Armoured Division showed that the attention paid to this particular operation in England had been well worth while, for it is doubtful whether in the face of such strong opposition it could have been successfully carried out by two divisions which had not accustomed themselves to working together over a period of many months. From the defensive aspect the Corps as a whole learned much in the course of heavy fighting, while the Scots in particular soon discovered the value of their PIAT guns, and that, if they stood their ground, even if enemy tanks were able to infiltrate temporarily, the latter were invariably knocked out. The next stage, the decisive repulse of all enemy attacks, including the attempted grand offensive on 30th June, was especially a tribute to the skill of the Corps artillery and to the accuracy and speed in which it answered calls for support from the infantry. Finally, despite the salient which 8 Corps was left holding, the enemy was never successful, even for a moment, in disturbing the overall balance of the Corps, despite employing all available armour to achieve this object.

July

The month of July opened inauspiciously, for the Corps intention of consolidating its gains and repulsing all enemy attacks was to be adhered to for several more days. No major moves were therefore to be expected in the near future. From the point of view of the enemy, however, the necessity for achieving some success was growing more desperate, for every day that passed found the Allies stronger and the Germans weaker. Accordingly, having had the whole of the preceding twenty-four hours to regroup and recover from their heavy defeat on 29th June, on 1st July the SS formations opposing 8 Corps tried again. This time they were luckier in the weather, for it had become dull and overcast, with a low cloud base, and air activity was, as a result, much hampered. In fact few fighters flew at all, and the enemy was enabled thereby to move with greater freedom in daylight than usual. In view of the rumoured but undelivered attack of 30th June, every precaution to strengthen the Corps front had been taken. In particular, the whole of the artillery of 43 and 53 Divisions as well as that of 8 A.G.R.A. had been placed in support of 15 (Scottish) Division, on whom the anticipated blow would undoubtedly fall. Arrangements for the co-ordination of direct support on the troublesome right flank were also tightened-up, for there had been an occasion during the recent fighting when fire had been brought down on British troops through difficulties of liaison.

During the night 30th June/1st July, reports were received from various parts of the forward areas, of increasing enemy activity, mainly around Esquay and to the south-west of Cheux and Grainville. Heavy mortaring was experienced in the bridgehead sector of 129 and 159 Infantry Brigades, and also in that of 227 (Highland) Brigade, and the Corps artillery was constantly kept busy on counter-mortar tasks. By 0330 hours enemy mortaring had reached a high pitch of intensity and covered by this, an attack was launched against the right of 159 Infantry Brigade. By 0400 hours it had spread also to its centre front, although not to that of the neighbouring 129 Infantry Brigade, which was, however, subjected to heavy shelling. This thrust was pressed hard, but in the face of overwhelming artillery fire could never get properly started, and at no time penetrated the forward positions to come to grips with the defenders. By 0500 hours this enemy effort had petered out and the sector became quiet once again. Ten field and two medium regiments, firing an average of 90 rounds per gun, had provided the fire power instrumental in breaking up this potentially formidable attack, which from identifications proved to have been delivered by infantry and tanks of 10 SS Panzer Division. Patrols later discovered on the northern slopes of Hill 112 between 300-400 German dead, as well as a number of knocked-out tanks, which gives some indication of the cost to the enemy of this abortive attempt.

While the enemy was being repulsed south of the River Odon, the first contingent of 53 (Welsh) Division to arrive in the forward areas, began to relieve the hard pressed Scots, and by 0550 hours 160 Infantry Brigade had taken over from 46 (Highland) Brigade—the brigade which had perhaps seen the heaviest fighting of any since the start of "Epsom." Soon after this, however, a further enemy attack astride the Corps boundary came against both 44 (Lowland) Brigade and the left formation of 30 Corps, 49 (West Riding) Infantry Division. Advancing up the convenient tank run from the south-west, the main blow was delivered against Rauray, but some penetration of the Scottish positions enabled both enemy tanks and infantry to get as far as the Haut du Bosq feature, where they were stopped by 4 Dorsetshire Regiment. The enemy remained in situ, however, and was only finally driven out in the early evening by 8 Royal Scots supported by a squadron of 7 Royal Tank Regiment and a troop of self-propelled guns. The fighting around Rauray was far more severe and occasioned severe losses in tanks to 9 SS Panzer Division, which jointly with infantry of 2 SS Panzer Division had undertaken this venture. By the end of the day over 30 German tanks had been destroyed, of which the bulk had fallen victim to 49 (West Riding) Division and 8 Armoured Brigade, and all positions remained intact. Prisoners complained of lack of artillery support due to shortage of ammunition, and this was probably the limiting factor in the remainder of the small offensive actions which the Germans endeavoured to carry out. Thus at 0800 hours 129 Infantry Brigade in the bridgehead repulsed a squadron of tanks and at the same time 1 Welsh Guards of 32 Guards Brigade beat off a slightly bigger effort by armour later identified as belonging to 12 SS Panzer Division.

At 1000 hours a further tank-cum-infantry attack developed against 44 (Lowland) Brigade from the south-west, which was continued about 1130 hours against the newly arrived 160 Infantry Brigade in the vicinity of Grainville, but by 1200 hours this too had been driven back with considerable losses, and the front quietened down somewhat.

The afternoon produced no changes or surprises, though elements of 1 SS Panzer Division made some sporadic and weaker efforts against the Odon bridgehead in the sector of 129 Infantry Brigade, and an enemy force forming up to the south of Hill 112 was dispersed by shell fire.

In his account of operations in the book, "Normandy to the Baltic," the Commander-in-Chief states that on 1st July the enemy made his "last and strongest attempt against the salient." It is true that at the time there was a very clear impression that a major effort had been made, for the Corps Intelligence Summary issued that same evening says: "The exact purpose of these attacks is not clear, though from prisoners' statements it would appear that they were intended to be on a much larger scale, but that concentration had been prevented by our bombing and artillery fire. As it was, the enemy achieved nothing and suffered heavy casualties both in men and tanks." Only later through identifications and captured strength returns was it made clear that all the SS formations—1, 2, 9, 10 and 12 SS Panzer Divisions had once more done their best to form up their panzer grenadiers and tanks, and launch simultaneous blows. Once again, as two days previously, the massed guns of the Corps, with devastating effect had engaged, delayed and dispersed these attacks, of which only one had been able to come to grips with the infantry. The Germans had certainly not recovered to the full the strength which they had been able to employ on 29th June, whilst the Corps artillery, reinforced and co-ordinated along the entire front had proved even more effective. The fanaticism of the SS was no match for the hurricane of shot and shell which poured down upon them and to which their only reply was personal courage and blind obedience to impossible orders.

The casualties of 8 Corps on 1st July, though still fairly heavy, were better than the previous day and amounted to 488 killed and wounded and 227 missing. The strength of the Corps had increased once again with the arrival of 53 (Welsh) Division and now totalled 4,401 officers and 82,414 other ranks. The number of enemy tanks which had been knocked out in the six days of fighting to midnight 1st July (excluding "possibles") had already risen to the respectable total of 126, of which 41 were "Panthers" and 25 "Tigers."

Operations 2nd July—9th July

The failure of the second German all-out attack, combined with the departure of Field Marshal von Rundstedt, which took place on the same day, marks the turning point in German policy in the conduct of the war in the West. The belated realisation that not only was the Allied lodgement area now proof against anything that the Wehrmacht could hurl against it, but that the daily increase in Allied strength might soon permit breakthrough operations, which in view of superior British and American mobility and overwhelming air power, would prove irresistible, had at last forced itself on Hitler and his Staff. The new Supreme Commander, Field Marshal von Kluge, who arrived on 2nd July, in contrast to his predecessor had largely made his reputation in defensive successes on the Eastern Front and his orders were to stand fast at all costs. Although the idea of a withdrawal to the River Seine was still vetoed by Hitler, the Germans now abandoned all offensive intentions and thought only in terms of containing the Allies and stopping any further advances. Unfortunately for them, this change of policy at once brought about the recrudescence of the old problem of freeing their armour and bringing in infantry divisions to hold the line in its place.

Early on 2nd July patrols from 15 (Scottish) Division produced the first evidence of this change of policy, for they reported that to the south of the Odon bridgehead generally, the enemy had begun to dig in. Air photographs, which the weather at length permitted to be taken two days later, confirmed this activity and showed large numbers of newly-dug weapon pits, which in each successive air coverage, gradually took shape as a line, and by 8th July extended along the entire Corps front. The enemy obviously regarded the 8 Corps salient as still the major outflanking threat to the defences of Caen, for similar defensive preparations had not yet appeared opposite other formations in Second Army.

On the British side although 8 Corps remained on the defensive, vigorous patrolling in the forward areas kept the enemy on the alert for any resumption of the advance. On 3rd July the Corps sector was extended when 158 Infantry Brigade of 53 (Welsh) Division took over the Rauray area from 49 (West Riding) Division, and this necessitated some slight re-grouping though no material changes were made. A few small local attacks were also attempted by the enemy but were broken up, as usual, by artillery fire.

Operation "Windsor," the project to take Carpiquet airfield originally planned for 27th or 28th June but postponed, was now revived as a preliminary to the capture of Caen itself. This was undertaken by 3 Canadian Division under 1 Corps on the left, but 8 Corps, in view of the fact that the salient it held, abutted on to the western side of the aerodrome, was instructed to provide a firm base for the Canadian attack. This task was allotted to 43 (Wessex) Division, which was ordered to occupy the small villages of Verson on the main Caen-Villers Bocage highway and Fontaine Etoupefour immediately to the south of it, in order to prevent enemy interference with the Canadian operation. Major-General Thomas, appreciating that no great strength would be necessary to achieve this small expansion, instructed 214 Infantry Brigade to carry it out by means of a night attack without previous artillery preparation. This was entirely successful and the seizure of these villages took place virtually unopposed. It was not so with the main Canadian attack, however, for Carpiquet airfield was found to be very strongly held, and with its long sweeping fields of fire, most difficult to take. The German air force too, put in some low level strafing attacks in one of its increasingly rare appearances, and in general the Canadians endured a most unpleasant experience, suffering very considerable casualties. Eventually the operation was temporarily abandoned and, in order to avoid leaving them in an awkward exposed position, the troops in Verson and Fontaine Etoupefour were withdrawn on the following day, 5th July.

After this there are no incidents of any importance to record for several days, except that advantage was taken of the lull in the fighting to effect the relief of 159 Infantry Brigade by 130 Infantry Brigade of 43 (Wessex) Division on 6th July. 159 Infantry Brigade had formed the original infantry bridgehead south of the River Odon and had held it since 28th June. During the whole of this time the enemy had subjected it to constant shelling, mortaring and sniping and to continuous attack varying from vicious probing of its defences to full scale tank and infantry assaults. Under its commander, Brigadier J. B. Churcher, 159 Infantry Brigade had stood firm and resolute under extremely trying and tiring conditions, and yet had rapidly established tactical dominance over the experienced SS formations facing it. It is true to say that there was a marked decrease in the Germans' efforts against this sector, each successive day that 159 Infantry Brigade held the Odon bridgehead.

Meanwhile the enemy was also profiting by the lull to strengthen his defences along the front and to bring up fresh infantry divisions to replace the prized panzer divisions in the line, and in this he was greatly aided by the wretched weather, which hampered air operations. The first of these formations, 16 G.A.F. Field Division, appeared as part of the garrison holding the Caen perimeter about this time, whilst almost simultaneously 30 Corps reported the arrival of 276 Infantry Division, which had moved up slowly by bicycle from Dax, in the Pyrenees region. It was to be expected that something of this nature would also take place on 8 Corps front as soon as the enemy considered it to be sufficiently quiet, and sure enough two deserters came over in the vicinity of Baron on 9th July, reporting that they belonged to 277 Infantry Division from the south of France, and now in process of relieving 9 SS Panzer Division.

Two days previously at dusk the Corps as a whole had a grandstand view of the first application in the campaign of heavy bombing in immediate support of a major land assault. The Commander-in-Chief had obtained the assistance of the R.A.F. Bomber Command in connection with the operations by 1 Corps against Caen, and between 2150 hours and 2230 hours on 7th July, two waves of heavy bombers, totalling altogether more than 450 aircraft, blasted the northern defences of the city, making a wonderful sight in the late sun of a perfect July evening. A general barrage, in which 8 Corps artillery also took part, then opened up, and at 0420 hours on 8th July, the main infantry assault began. By the morning of 9th July, Caen had been taken by 1 Corps, after bitter fighting, though much mopping up of isolated pockets of enemy remained to be done. The western thrust in this attack had been made by 3 Canadian Division simultaneously with a renewal of the attempt against Carpiquet, which this time was completely successful. As a result of this move, whereby its left flank was materially strengthened, 8 Corps was enabled to take the preliminary steps necessary to launching an operation christened "Jupiter," which had been planned contingent upon success by 1 Corps against Caen. Accordingly at 2300 hours on 8th July, when the result of the Caen battle was already beyond doubt, 214 Infantry Brigade moved back without unduly heavy opposition into the area Verson-Fontaine-Etoupefour-Gournay, which it was intended should be the start line for "Jupiter." By the evening of 9th July, the position had been consolidated and everything was ready for this latter operation to begin.

Operation "Jupiter" and the General Situation on 10th July

Second Army was still carrying out all its operations with the same primary object of drawing to itself and containing, the maximum number of enemy divisions, particularly the armoured variety.

From the enemy aspect, the overall situation was eminently satisfactory for the Allies but two recent developments were temporarily disquieting. The first was the arrival of new infantry divisions, which might enable the Germans to withdraw their panzer formations from the line and secondly, the identification of 2 SS Panzer Division in the American sector around St. Eny, showed the enemy's determination, despite Second Army's attempts to prevent it, to strengthen his resistance against U.S. forces in this area and consequently increase their difficulties when they attempted break-out operations later.

It was therefore necessary to maintain the impetus of the British effort at maximum pressure, and with the capture of Caen possibly allowing this to slacken somewhat, it was urgent quickly to strike elsewhere. In the period 10th-18th July, therefore, several operations, of which "Jupiter" was one, were undertaken to achieve this purpose and though limited in scope, they nevertheless also assisted materially in the favourable development of the campaign by increasing the space for manœuvre at Second Army's disposal.

For "Jupiter," the Corps intention was laid down as follows:—

> "At 0500 hours Monday, 10th July, 8 Corps will attack and seize the area Baron-Hill 112-junction with the River Orne (east of Maltot) with a view to a subsequent exploitation south-west of the high ground east of the River Ajon."

The main attacking role was this time given to 43 (Wessex) Division, though the remaining divisions in the Corps held watching briefs in case of major enemy reactions.

Task of 43 (Wessex) Division

43 Division with under command:—
- 4 Armoured Brigade
- 31 Tank Brigade (less one regiment)
- 46 (Highland) Infantry Brigade

was ordered to carry out this attack in four phases as follows.—

Phase 1. The capture of the area Fontaine-Etoupefour-Chateau de Fontaine-Hill 112-Baron.

Phase 2. The capture and clearing of Eterville.

Phase 3. The capture of the area Maltot to the River Orne.

Phase 4. On completion of Phase 3 an armoured regimental group from 4 Armoured Brigade was to pass to the south through the infantry and report the presence or otherwise of the enemy in the area of the half dozen or so villages to the west of the River Orne. Infantry was to follow up 4 Armoured Brigade quickly in order to consolidate the final line as soon as possible.

So far as timings were concerned, these were forecast as follows:—

- 0500 hours ... H (or Zero) hour.
- 0600 hours ... Completion of Phase 1.
- 0615 hours ... Commencement of Phase 2.
- 0715 hours ... Completion of Phase 2.
- 0800 hours ... Commencement of Phase 3.
- 0900 hours ... Completion of Phase 3.

4 Armoured Brigade was to be prepared to operate in Phase 4 from 0900 hours onwards.

Artillery and Air Support

In addition to 8 A.G.R.A., 3 A.G.R.A. was placed under command to support this attack, in which the artillery of all divisions in the Corps likewise participated.

The R.A.F. agreed to take part in the operation, being given the task of preventing enemy movement on roads leading to the area of operations whilst in addition fighter bombers were to attack continuously throughout the day selected targets such as Maltot, Evrecy, Esquay, Bully, etc.

Operations 10th July—11th July.

The attack began, as planned, at 0500 hours, and met with considerable initial success. The area to be captured, unfortunately, was most difficult, in that it was overlooked from east of the River Orne, whilst its principal feature, Hill 112, was also commanded to a great extent by the high ground north and south of Evrecy, which, had troops been available, should certainly have been attacked at the same time. 8 Corps was thus operating once again in a salient, and moreover one that was at all times under enemy observation. Nevertheless, by 0900 hours the first two phases, except for the seizure of Hill 112, were successfully completed against moderately stiff opposition from 22 SS Panzer Grenadier Regiment of 10 SS Panzer Division. Over 200 prisoners were rounded up in the early part of the morning, mainly from Eterville and the Chateau de Fontaine, which proved to be an enemy battalion headquarters.

Hill 112, however, was another story. A heavy battle for this elusive prize went on all day; but it was never possible to claim it as fallen, for any movement by the troops over the crest immediately brought down an inferno of mortar and artillery fire from Evrecy upon themselves, rendering any advance quite impossible.

5 Duke of Cornwall's Light Infantry fought extremely bravely and spiritedly, but circumstances were against these troops, and despite heavy casualties, in the late afternoon a reverse slope position had to be accepted. Thus they held the northern side of the hill, the enemy in dug-in tanks remained masters of the southern half, and in between, the crest was a most effective no-man's land. This state of affairs was by no means to the liking of the enemy, however, for several counter-attacks were launched, but were driven off, and the position firmly maintained.

Nor were the troops carrying out Phase 3 any happier, for 130 Infantry Brigade found Maltot untenable. 7 Hampshire Regiment, with a squadron from 9 Royal Tank Regiment, succeeded in entering the village, though at the cost of heavy tank casualties (9 Royal Tank Regiment losing 12 out of 14 tanks supporting the attack), but a quick counter-attack by "Tigers" from 2 SS Panzer Corps heavy tank battalion coupled with severe mortaring drove them out again. Although another battalion, 4 Dorsetshire Regiment, with a fresh squadron of tanks once more attempted this task, and again captured Maltot, this proved too hot and costly to hold, and in the afternoon it was forced to withdraw. Maltot itself being in a hollow, is completely dominated by the Bourguebus ridge on the opposite bank of the River Orne, and on this feature, which was later discovered to be the key to exits from the south-east of Caen as well as the south-west, were sited not only a large number of "flak" guns defending the city, but in addition a most formidable concentration of multi-barrelled mortars. These very effective weapons were grouped together in brigades, several of which were already in action against Second Army and caused probably more trouble and casualties than anything else at the Germans' disposal. At all events, they were now able to achieve with them something dear to the heart of the Staff College student but so difficult to carry out in practice—denying a locality to the enemy through fire-power, and Maltot was that locality.

In consequence of this it was not possible to start Phase 4 of the operation, and there were no further material changes that day, nor indeed during the remainder of the time, now drawing to a close, that 8 Corps was responsible for this sector. On the following morning it was notified that Headquarters 12 Corps which had just arrived in Normandy would take over the area and the troops under command of 8 Corps as soon as "Jupiter" was concluded, and that the Corps would then go into reserve, to re-group and prepare for fresh tasks ahead.

On 11th July the enemy continued to react violently to possession of the ground so far gained by 8 Corps, and staged a number of vicious local counter-attacks, particularly against Hill 112. From prisoners' stories it was plain that the object of containing the German armour on 8 Corps front was succeeding, for although the tired 9 SS Panzer Division had been relieved by 277 Infantry Division on the night 9th-10th July, and had gone back to Villers Bocage for a rest, this formation was hurriedly brought back to restore the situation created by "Jupiter." In addition, elements of 1 SS Panzer Division had been identified on the Corps' extreme east flank around Louvigny, where the confused nature of the battle was a source of some embarrassment to 43 (Wessex) Division, as it was thought that the Canadians had progressed further than in fact they had. However, by nightfall, after a day of heavy and fluctuating fighting, all the positions had been maintained, though at the cost of somewhat heavy casualties, particularly to 43 (Wessex) Division. The final day in the line, 12th July, was uneventful, for activity was much reduced on both sides, and at 0200 hours on 13th July, 12 Corps, commanded by Lieutenant-General N. M. Ritchie, took over the sector and 8 Corps passed into reserve.

Summary 1st—12th July

Thus ended the first series of battles in which 8 Corps had taken part, and the results as a whole were by no means discouraging. In retrospect, they seem, of course, more spectacular and can be evaluated at their true worth, but at the time the precarious condition in which the enemy was beginning to find himself was fully apparent only to to his field commanders, especially Field-Marshal Rommel, whose appreciation of the situation written on 15th July was pessimistic in the extreme. Here are some relevant extracts:—" The position on the front in Normandy is daily becoming more difficult, and is approaching a serious crisis. No forces worth mentioning can be brought to the Normandy front without weakening that of the Fifteenth Army on the Channel coast or the Mediterranean front in Southern France. But the front of Seventh Army is in urgent need of two fresh divisions as the forces there have been fought to a standstill.

" Our own losses are so high that the fighting strengths of the divisions is sinking very rapidly. 97,000 men lost in action so far; 10,000 reinforcements. 225 tanks destroyed, but only 17 replacements.

" *We must reckon with the fact that the enemy, within a measurable time, will succeed in breaking through our thinly-held front, especially that of Seventh Army* (facing the Americans), *and in thrusting deep into France. Apart from the local reserves of Panzer Group West, which are immediately tied down by the fighting on the front of the Panzer Group* (opposite 8 Corps), *and owing to enemy command of the air, can move only at night, no mobile reserves for defence against such a break through are at the disposal of Seventh Army.*

" The Army is fighting heroically everywhere but the unequal combat is nearing its end. It is, in my opinion, necessary to draw the appropriate conclusions from this situation."

It is clear from this appreciation that Rommel realised the hopelessness of the German position, but his superiors in the High Command as well as his new chief, Field Marshal von Kluge, had as yet no conception of the disaster about to overtake the German forces in Normandy. Indeed, determined and optimistic about the task newly entrusted to him, von Kluge was just making his first inspection of the battlefront, though thereafter his ardour was somewhat dampened.

Preliminary signs, however, that the situation was getting out of control of the Wehrmacht, developed for all to see during the period 1st–12th July. The first was the fact that through lack of success, waning strength, and heavy casualties, the enemy had been forced to pass to the defensive and give up any thought of trying to drive the Allies back into the sea. The second, more significant still, was that, although reinforcements had been produced at last to effect the withdrawal from the line of the precious panzer divisions—now a matter of the utmost urgency—the alternating blows of Second Army had never quite permitted it to take place. Thus 16 G.A.F. Division began to relieve 21 Panzer Division, but the battle for Caen put a stop to this and forced the latter to stay in the line, whilst " Jupiter " kept 10 SS Panzer Division fully occupied and brought 9 SS Panzer Division hurrying back into action in a new sector. Part of 1 SS Panzer Division was identified round Esquay and 2 SS Panzer Division had been moved back to the Cotentin peninsula to counter the American threat there. Of all the SS armour only the remnants of 12 SS Panzer Division resting in the woods north of Falaise were fully disengaged by 12th July when 8 Corps handed over to 12 Corps. The clearest illustration of the strained resources of the enemy has been given by the extraordinary story told by prisoners from 9 SS Panzer Division, who reported that having been relieved by 277 Infantry Division at 0300 hours on Sunday, 10th July, and promised a long rest, they were hurriedly brought back into action against 43 (Wessex) Division around Hill 112 during the evening of Monday, 11th, July, only thirty-six hours later.

As the Commander-in-Chief continued remorselessly to develop operations in the manner he had planned, so an orderly campaign was becoming more and more difficult for the Germans. The policy of containing the Allies had already degenerated into a policy of plugging the gaps created by Allied thrusts, and was shortly to be carried a stage further with the adoption of what might be called "fire brigade tactics"—that is, rushing their better mobile divisions (nearly always the SS) from one side of the front to the other according to where the conflagration seemed at the time most threatening. The first example of this was, of course, the move of 9 SS Panzer Division referred to above, but later operations by 8 Corps entitled "Goodwood" and "Bluecoat" caused many a weary trek to the German tanks to and fro over the River Orne before their final destruction.

Thus generally throughout the Corps, with the exception of the armoured brigade of Guards Armoured Division and 6 Guards Tank Brigade, all the troops had now received their first taste of action and had come through the ordeal of some of the most heavy fighting experienced so far in Normandy (and in fact to be seen during the whole campaign in the West) with flying colours. No one who witnessed it can ever forget the magnificent spirit shown by 15 (Scottish) Division in the attacks around Cheux and St. Mauvieu, nor the gallantry and dash of 11 Armoured Division across the River Odon, whilst in the face of the worst and heaviest blows which the enemy was able to deliver, the Corps as a whole was as steady as a rock. Unfortunately epics have their dark side, and though by comparison with similar battles in the 1914-18 war and the size of 8 Corps, which on the last day of "Jupiter" had risen to over 100,000 strong, the losses in killed, wounded and missing seem reasonably light, in point of fact they amounted to over 7,000 all ranks, in which 15 (Scottish) Division with 2,500 and 43 (Wessex) Division with 2,400 were the principal sufferers.

So far as Corps Headquarters was concerned, the exacting training in England paid a handsome dividend in action, for the machine ran smoothly from the first. There must always be some inevitable changes in routine when a formation headquarters accomplishes the transition from exercises at home to operations in the field, but in the case of 8 Corps they were remarkably few. One of the earliest, however, was an alteration in the set-up of the Command Post itself. Hitherto it had consisted of only the three "G" Branch command vehicles, but now one extra was allotted to the Intelligence section of it, whilst those belonging to the B.G.S. and G.S.O. 2 (Air) were also incorporated, the whole being arranged round a hollow square over which a canvas hood was stretched. The resultant structure, sheltered and well lighted by a Sapper electrical plant, proved almost too comfortable—particularly towards the end of the evening, when the Staff tended generally to congregate and discuss the events of the day. Despite the official information tent carefully maintained a considerable distance away from the Command Post, visitors, in addition, constantly strayed in at all times and were with difficulty persuaded to go. Most interruptions also seemed to come about the time that the B.G.S. settled down to dictate an operation order or when he was trying to hold a telephone conversation with one of the divisions on rather a bad line. Later on, when the cold weather arrived, the introduction of an urn of hot tea or cocoa about ten o'clock each evening provided, if such were needed, an added attraction for those who liked to "coffee-house" and hear the news. There were certainly few dull moments and always plenty of life in the Command Post.

Among the Staff during this time was a shrewd observer in the person of the confidential clerk to the B.G.S., Serjeant Green, who at the end of the war embodied his impressions in a playlet which received a wide circulation amongst delighted members of the Headquarters. In writing it the author must have been inspired, for this small sketch is a most accurate portrayal of life in the Command Post when excitement ran high and work was at full pressure. Let not the reader be deceived by the apparently casual air displayed therein, for if this may have seemed so on the surface, in reality the standard of staff work and the conscientious manner in which subordinate formations were served, established a mutual friendship and confidence possessed by few if any of its rivals on the Western Front, as the permanent divisions, 15 (Scottish), Guards or 11 Armoured Division, would be the first to admit, for they were always happy to return to the fold after service under another corps headquarters.

One other innovation was the introduction of a morning conference at 0900 hours for the whole Staff at which the situation was discussed and the intentions for the day made clear. There is always an insatiable thirst for news during a campaign, and the ease with which false rumours can arise is truly astonishing. The morning conference did much to correct this tendency among the Staff, whilst two other measures were introduced to counteract it amongst the Headquarters personnel generally. The first was regular briefing of the whole Headquarters on the progress of the war by a "G" staff officer; the second was to start a Corps Headquarters news sheet entitled "The White Knight," which appeared every morning with a short account of the previous day's fighting and a résumé of the B.B.C. news as well as perhaps a cartoon or a short topical item. This venture, started and continued to the end of active operations by the Education Officer, Major Tibbits, and his branch, proved highly popular and was soon looked upon as one of the necessities of life on active service.

The national press of Britain and the United States, in the shape of the many correspondents assigned to Normandy, made its appearance at the Headquarters as soon as "Epsom" began and thereafter daily. Following an initial meeting with General O'Connor on the eve of the battle, the correspondents were briefed every morning and afternoon, at first by the B.G.S., but later by the G.S.O.2 (Intelligence)—an onerous duty somewhat relieved by the presence of the field press censors, who could fortunately be relied upon to put a "stop" on any indiscretion. However, good relations always existed between the Press representatives and 8 Corps, and indeed both soon became firm friends. The Allies were extremely lucky in the calibre of their front line reporters, who not only provided a very accurate coverage of events, but, in the words of the Supreme Commander, were "quasi-staff officers," being privy to many secrets and never once betraying their trust. Nothing is so stimulating to the morale of troops as to know that their efforts are followed and understood by their families at home. In this respect, also, the campaign in Normandy may be looked upon as a model.

By the time that 12 Corps assumed responsibility for the sector west of Caen, permitting 8 Corps to go into reserve and plan a yet more ambitious undertaking, it was known that as a headquarters in the field 8 Corps had "made the grade" and was a success.

A fitting summary to the whole of this strenuous period is contained in the following message from the Commander-in-Chief which was issued to all British and American troops on 11th July:—

"To all soldiers of 21 Army Group,

"1. A great deal has happened since my last message to you on 10th June—one month ago; the battle in Normandy has been fierce and hard since then, and much has been achieved.

"2. Our gains have been definite and concrete; and we have held everything we have gained, despite the desperate efforts of the enemy to push us back into the sea.
    On the west flank—Cherbourg.
    On the east flank—Caen.
    And much territory in between.

"And all the time a tremendous struggle with a skilful enemy, whose good fighting qualities and tenacity in battle cannot but attract our admiration. The pace has been hot, and it was clear that someone would have to give ground sooner or later; it was equally clear that the Allied soldiers would see the thing through to the end and would never give up; and so the Germans have been forced to give ground—which is very right and proper.

"3. And to-day, the Allied Armies fighting in Normandy have good grounds for solid satisfaction.

"We have taken over 54,000 prisoners. We have given the enemy forces a tremendous pounding, and we know from prisoners what great losses they have suffered.

"And we have enlarged and extended our lodgement area, and in that area we are very firm and secure, and we are developing our offensive operations in accordance with our plans.

"4. And so, to every Allied soldier in Normandy I say: 'Well done. Well done indeed. You have performed a great task in a manner which is fully in keeping with the great traditions of the fighting stocks from which we all come. And your families and friends in the homeland may well be very proud of their menfolk serving overseas.'

"5. It is the earnest desire of every Allied soldier in Normandy to finish this business off as quickly as possible, and to pull his full weight and do his duty until it is so finished off. That we all know. And I cannot do better than to conclude this message by quoting the favourite prayer of Sir Francis Drake: 'O Lord God, when Thou givest to Thy servants to endeavour any great matter, grant us also to know that it is not the beginning, but the continuing of the same until it be thoroughly finished, which yieldeth the true glory.'

"6. Let us fight on to victory in the spirit of that prayer.

"7. Good luck to each one of you."

          B. L. MONTGOMERY, *General*,
FRANCE.   *Commander-in-Chief*,
11th July, 1944.   21 *Army Group*.

CHAPTER 3
"Goodwood"

Operation "Goodwood" 18th—21st July 1944

THE operation which 8 Corps was now called upon to plan and mount, proved to be, for various reasons, by far the most interesting and spectacular of any undertaken by either side during the struggle in Normandy. It also aroused a certain amount of controversy and misunderstanding at the time due to misconceptions of its aims. The object of this chapter, so far as 8 Corps is concerned, is, therefore, to clear these up in detail, and dispose of them once and for all, in the course of the narrative of these momentous events.

Field-Marshal Montgomery in his book "Normandy to the Baltic" has already dealt with these criticisms in general and no clearer summary exists of the conditions under which Operation "Goodwood" was mounted, than the following quotation from this book:—

"The situation—18th July.

"We were now on the threshold of great events. We were ready to break out of the bridgehead.

"We still firmly retained the initiative. We had prevented the enemy from switching further reinforcements to the western flank and had forced him to commit again the armoured forces he had sought to withdraw into reserve. We had continued to punish the enemy severely and force him into what I call 'wet hen tactics'—rushing to and fro to stem our thrusts and plug the holes in his line.

"The sooner we got going on the western flank the better while the setting for the break-out remained favourable. Apart from the local conditions in Normandy, it seemed impossible that the enemy should continue much longer to anticipate an invasion in the Pas de Calais; however great his anxiety for the safety of the flying bomb sites, he must surely soon give over-riding priority to the Normandy battlefield, and when he took that decision substantial reinforcements would become available from Fifteenth Army.

"I have said how important it was to my plans that, once started, the break-out operation should maintain its momentum. It was therefore essential to ensure that the assault would make a clean break through the enemy defences facing the Americans, and that a corridor would be speedily opened through which armoured forces could be passed into the open country. To make sure of this, it was decided to seek heavy bomber assistance; but because of the weather the operation had to be progressively postponed until 25th July, in order to obtain favourable flying conditions.

"Meanwhile on the eastern flank offensive operations were sustained; by 17th July 8 Corps was ready to begin the offensive east of the Orne.

"The operations of 8 Corps between 18th and 21st July gave rise to a number of misunderstandings at the time. It was a battle for

"GOODWOOD"

MAP II

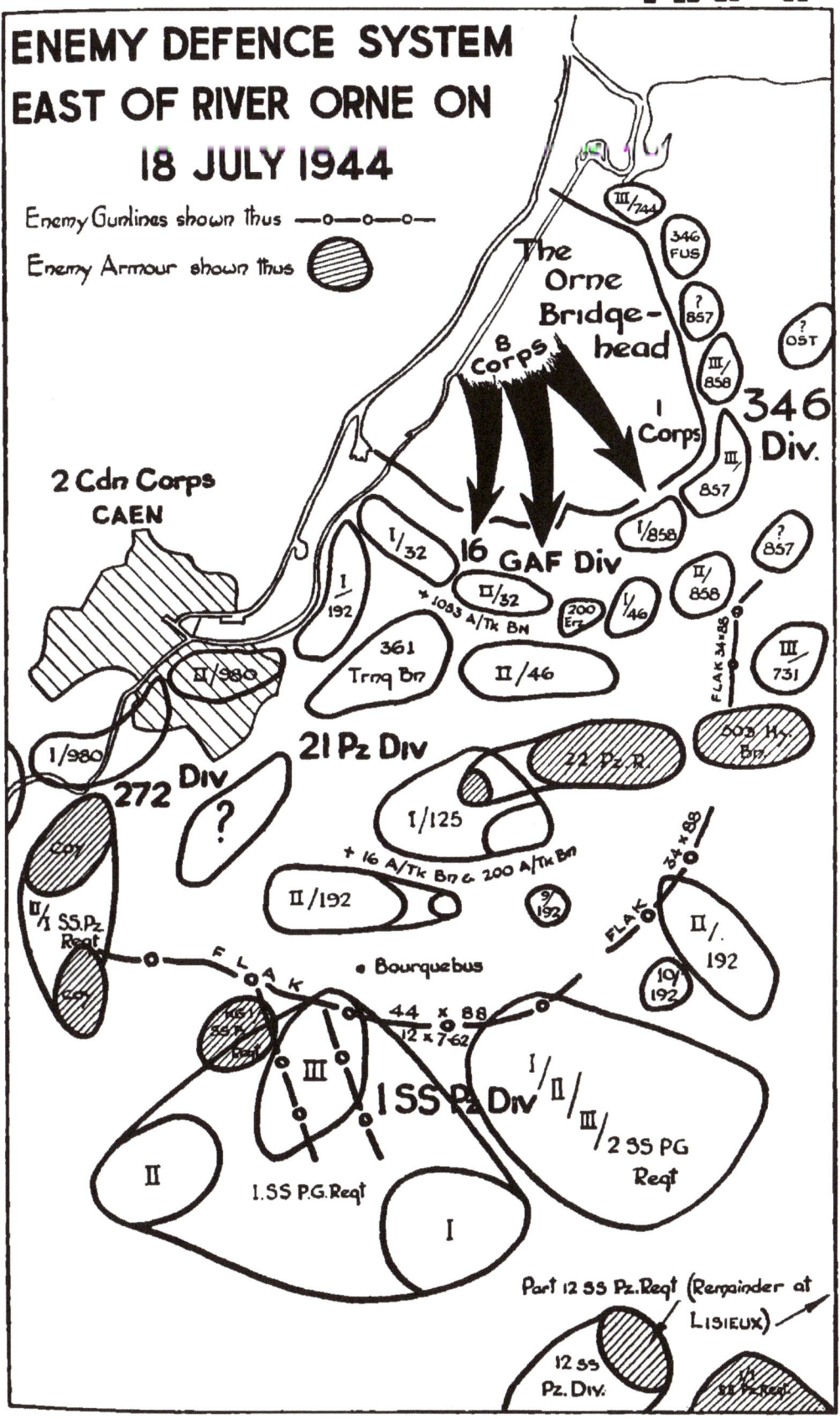

position, which was designed first to bring into play the full effect on the enemy of a direct and powerful threat to Falaise, and the open country to the east of the town, and secondly to secure ground on which major forces could be poised ready to strike out to the south and southeast, when the American break-out forces thrust eastwards to meet them. I now believe that the misconception concerning this operation arose primarily because the forthcoming battle for position was in fact the prelude to operations of wider scope, which when the time came were to form part of the Allied drive to the Seine. Added to this, the break-out operation by First United States Army was, for obvious reasons, being kept a close secret, and since it was clearly time we broke the enemy cordon surrounding us, it was understandable that a major operation of this kind should suggest wider implications than in fact it had."

So much for the general situation obtaining in mid-July on the Western Front. Let us now pass to an examination of the planning and launching of this enterprise.

The hand-over to 12 Corps was settled at a conference presided over by Brigadier Chilton, Chief of Staff of Second Army and held at the Chateau de Lantheuil at 1600 hours on 11th July. Under its arrangements the troops which were now to be controlled by 12 Corps fell into two categories:—

(a) those under command without restriction on their use, of which the principal were:—

15 (Scottish) Division
43 (Wessex) Division
53 (Welsh) Division
31 Tank Brigade (less 141 Royal Armoured Corps)
34 Tank Brigade
4 Armoured Brigade

(b) those formations and units which were to come under command only in the event of emergency, but otherwise to remain under 8 Corps. They were as follows:—

11 Armoured Division—now backing up 53 (Welsh) Division in the Rauray area.
8 A.G.R.A.—in general support of the whole Corps front.
91 Anti-Tank Regiment, R.A.—at the disposal of 12 Corps until 15th July.

The reason for this differentiation was that General Dempsey was anxious to begin organising new operations to be carried out on an Army basis, but did not wish for the moment to unbalance the front by wholesale withdrawals until 12 Corps was firmly in the saddle. Formations and units mentioned in paragraph (b) above were, however, free to plan with Headquarters 8 Corps, and two additional divisions out of the line were also allotted to the Corps in the shape of Guards Armoured Division, now able to collect together as an entity for the first time in Normandy, and 59 (Staffordshire) Infantry Division which was resting and recovering around Ryes after a fiery and exhausting baptism of fire at the capture of Caen.

Preparations began immediately to implement the new plan and at 1000 hours on 13th July General Dempsey visited the Corps Commander to outline the pattern of the forthcoming battles at a meeting at which Lieutenant-General Crocker of 1 Corps and Lieutenant-General Simonds of 2 Canadian Corps were also present. There was already one considerable

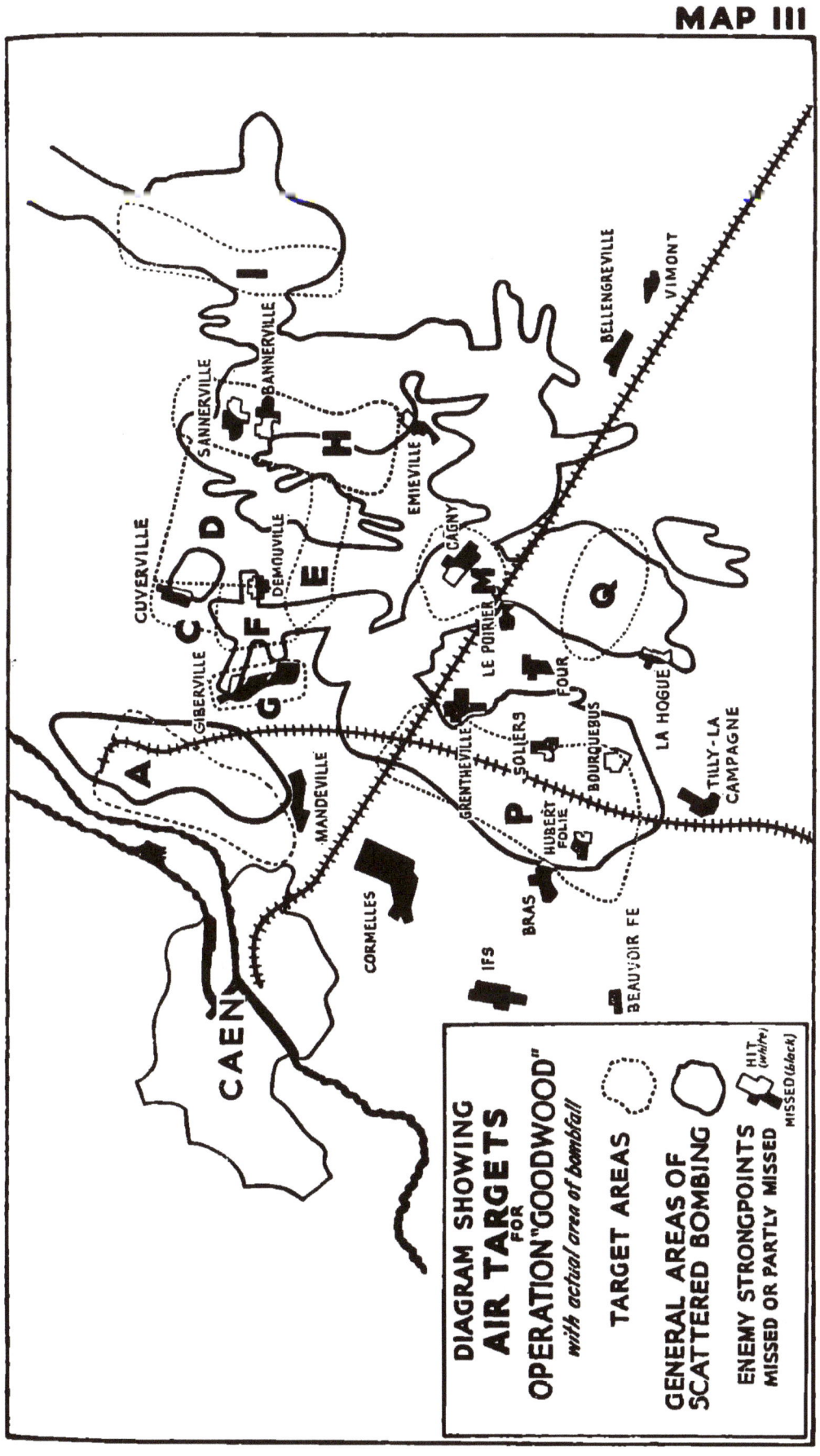

change in the allocation of troops to the Corps, for in place of 59 (Staffordshire) Division, the third division was also to be armoured and proved to be 7 Armoured Division, the original "Desert Rats" now in 8 Corps for the first time. This alteration had been brought about by a directive issued on 10th July by the Commander-in-Chief to his Army Commanders, which included the following instructions to General Dempsey: —

"Second Army will retain the ability to operate with a strong armoured force east of the River Orne in the general area between Caen and Falaise.

"For this purpose a corps of three armoured divisions will be held in reserve, ready to be employed when ordered by me.

"The opportunity for the employment of this corps may be sudden and fleeting. Therefore the study of the problems arising will begin at once."

The basic intention was now to pass these three armoured divisions through the narrow, confined Orne bridgehead east of Caen and so debouch into the open country to the south to carry out the strategic intentions of the Commander-in-Chief already outlined. The broad decisions reached at this conference were confirmed later in the day in an operation instruction from Second Army. This, however, was a preliminary instruction in general terms only, issued to facilitate the necessary detailed planning by the troops involved, in the course of which and before the plan of attack assumed its final form, some alterations were undoubtedly to be expected.

It seems most probable that in this document lies the origin of the misconceptions concerning phases of Operation "Goodwood" which were the cause of the friction between leading members of the Allied High Command, subsequently reported in some highly sensational and totally inaccurate memoirs published in the United States.

The reader need be in no such doubt about the purpose of Operation "Goodwood," for later in this chapter are to be found the directives concerning it of both the Commander-in-Chief and General Dempsey, as well as a detailed account of the actual orders issued from Headquarters 8 Corps. However, before embarking on a study of these, it will be as well to examine the enemy situation obtaining in Normandy by mid-July.

The Enemy Situation by 18th July.

It has been seen how the attacks made during the early part of July by Second Army, had succeeded in keeping the German armoured forces in action on its front despite the arrival of at least three new infantry divisions— one from Holland and the remaining two from Southern France. More such arrivals were however awaited from the south, whilst eventually the German High Command must be expected to make up its mind as to the unlikelihood of a further Allied landing in the Pas de Calais region. This latter decision would then permit the release of the divisions in the Fifteenth German Army to the help of their hard-pressed comrades in the Normandy theatre. The time was, moreover, drawing near when the U.S. forces would be favourably positioned to begin their break-out operations, and as we know from his appreciation of 15th July, Rommel was already apprehensive of this eventuality. Attacks made by 12 and 30 Corps on 15th and 16th July achieved a limited advance, but their main benefit to 8 Corps was that 9 SS and 10 SS Panzer Divisions as well as tanks from 1 SS Panzer Division were all involved in costly actions, resulting, according to prisoners' statements, in a further whittling down of their strength. In the struggle for the possession of Caen on 9th and 10th July, 1 Corps had fought 21 and 12 SS Panzer Divisions, elements of 1 SS Panzer Division and part of the newly arrived 16 G.A.F. Field Division. Thereafter, except for some abortive attacks by 51 (Highland) Division in the Colombelles factory estate to the east of the city on 11th July, this sector had become quiescent, and remained so until "Goodwood" was launched, with 16 G.A.F. Field Division manning it between Vaucelles and Touffreville, to the north of which 346 Infantry Division was responsible. The enemy during this week, therefore, seized the opportunity to effect the withdrawal (except for one small battle group) of 21 Panzer Division from the line, and in addition, of the elements of 1 SS Panzer Division holding the front astride the Orne between Vaucelles and Louvigny, thus effecting a local improvement in the desperate overall situation in which he found himself. The latter manœuvre was unknown at the time to Second Army owing to the absence of any identifications from this area, though the arrival at the front of the relieving formation, 272 Infantry Division, from the Mediterranean coast was suspected. When by 17th July the attacks of 12 Corps slackened around Maltot and Hill 112, 272 Infantry Division was able to extend westwards and relieve 9 SS Panzer Division. The tactical picture from the point of view of armoured reserves was, therefore, far more favourable to the enemy on 18th July than it had been when 8 Corps handed over to 12 Corps a week previously, for now 21 Panzer, 1, 9 and 12 SS Panzer Divisions were all uncommitted, and significantly enough three of these were positioned east of the River Orne. Despite the local disengagement of this armour, the Commander-in-Chief's efforts to hold it on the British front were still proving successful.

Except for the arrival of 272 Infantry Division in the line, the general disposition of the enemy panzer divisions was known, as the following extract from the 8 Corps Planning Intelligence Summary No. 1 issued on 15th July shows clearly:—

"East of the River Orne the only panzer formations now known to be present are:—

1. *21 Panzer Division.*

This is mainly in the area of Argences, though elements are again in the line around Caen (Battle Group 'Luck'). Tank strength of this division may be reckoned approximately 45-50 tanks (with probably also 35 assault guns).

2. *1 SS Panzer Division (Adolf Hitler).*

This division is not so easy to locate. Part of its infantry is around Louvigny, its artillery is south of Fleury-sur-Orne, but the location of its tanks, which number approximately 100, is not known for certainty. They may, however, be around in the St. Andre-sur-Orne area.

3. *12 SS Panzer Division (Hitler Jugend)*

After its strenuous operations lasting from early in the campaign until last week, the remnants of this division were relieved and are now thought to be concentrated just south of the junction between the Rivers Orne and Laize. This division (about 50 tanks and some 7,000 men) is resting but well placed to reinforce east of the Orne or west of the Laize in the event of a threat to Bourguebus from the north-east.

Of new arrivals there is as yet no sign in the immediate vicinity of the Second Army sector, but reports indicate a movement over the River Seine which is probably bringing by easy stages an infantry formation into our area. There is a reasonably good field to choose from but at the moment the favourites are 16 G.A.F. Field Division and 89

Infantry Division. It may be as well, therefore, to expect elements of one of these."

Strengths in detail of these divisions were estimated as follows:—

	1 SS Panzer Division (Adolf Hitler)	12 SS Panzer Division (Hitler Jugend)	21 Panzer Division
Equivalent full battalions	5	2	2+
Total personnel	15,000	7,000	8,000
Field and Medium Artillery	40-50	20+	25
Assault Guns	?	Nil	35
Anti-Tank Guns over 5 cm. calibre and 8.8 flak guns	75	50	35-40

Certain other formations and units were also known to be present and of these the following were the most important:—

(a) 101 Heavy Tank Battalion with 20-25 Panther and Tiger tanks.

(b) 7 Werfer Brigade equipped with 15 and 21 cm. multi-barrelled mortars.

(c) A large but unspecified number of flak guns belonging to G.A.F. and Army units.

In addition to the above information, excellent photographic coverage permitted the issue on 17th July of defence overprints of the entire area over which "Goodwood" was expected to be fought. These overprints revealed a mass of enemy defences stretching southwards and extending over the whole front, as well as a large number of gun and nebelwerfer positions, particularly along the Bourguebus ridge south of Caen. It was obvious, therefore, that the 8 Corps attack would have to reckon with a very strong enemy defensive position sited in considerable depth. Nor was the strength of the German gun positions minimised or underestimated, for the following counter-battery appreciation by Brigadier Matthew was prepared for the Corps Commander on 15th July:—

"1. In coastal area Franceville and Cabourg there are guns which can be dealt with by the Navy. These guns are capable of being turned round into the bridgehead but are not sited primarily for this task.

2. Three groups of enemy guns estimated at 12-24 are in the areas:—
    (a) Broucourt
    (b) Savare
    (c) Janville

As these guns are out of medium and field range they can only be dealt with by fighter bombers.

3. In the areas to be dealt with by heavy bombers there are about 40 guns which will be covered and neutralised by the heavy bombers.

In the area north of the railway Caen-Vimont there are up to 90 guns which will have to be dealt with by counter-battery bombardment.

4. South-west of the railway Caen-Vimont and north of east-west grid line 62 there are estimated not to be more than 20 guns which can be seen from Caen and can be observed by Air O.P.s.

5. South of grid line 62 westward to the Orne and south to east-west grid line 55 there are a large number of guns probably totalling not more than 100. The front edge of the woods west and east of

Garcelles-Secqueville and to the north of them appears to be the main gun area with battle positions in this area. *This area will require a heavy counter-battery effort and is getting towards the extreme range of our medium guns. I anticipate that in this area the armour will meet with considerable gun opposition which it will be difficult to neutralise.*

6. Between the River Orne and River Laize there are possibly about 10 heavy guns which might be turned round after some time to meet our attacks."

A considerable amount of information on the layout of the German forces was thus available before the battle, but there was never any doubt among those who took part in planning this operation that the task set 8 Corps of breaking through a series of defence lines sited in depth, supported by very considerable artillery and possessing a mobile counter-attack force of between 200-250 tanks, would prove difficult indeed, and incurred considerable risks.

The true nature of the German defences between the Rivers Orne and Dives made them, however, formidable in the extreme, since for reasons which, unfortunately, could not be known to the Allies, they were even stronger and more deeply echeloned than was realised.

The strategic significance of the Caen area to the Germans has already been explained as due to their misconception of the manner in which they considered the Commander-in-Chief proposed to develop the campaign. Lieutenant-General Speidel in the report of Army Group "B" to the Fuehrer's Headquarters for the week ending 16th July, thus had the following comments to make:—

"The British Second Army has not achieved its aim of breaking through and operating in the open country after the occupation of Caen. The attack was not followed up on account of heavy losses. However, re-grouping and preparation on an increasing scale were observed towards the end of the week. The well-known operational intentions of the Montgomery Army Group still appear to exist. The British Second Army is closely concentrated in the area of Caen and to the south-west, and will carry out the thrust across the Orne towards Paris. *The local attacks on 15th July between Maltot and Vendes may be the prelude to the large-scale attack which is expected from the evening of the 17th for making a break-through across the Orne.*"

Continuing the report with a gross miscalculation of the number of Allied divisions still waiting to cross over from the United Kingdom to Normandy (estimating 56 against an actual 10 at that time in England), General Speidel reveals that fear of a second landing in the Pas de Calais region, at this late juncture still dominated the strategic appreciation of the German High Command in the West. It was the foundation of the importance that the enemy attached to the Caen area, for by stopping a break-out toward Paris he believed that he was compelling the Allies to postpone their second landing.

Quite apart from the strategic significance of this region, its tactical importance had been apparent to the enemy long before "D" Day. In fact, the Germans had always regarded the gap between the Orne and the Dives as the most vulnerable sector of Western Normandy. From documents and interrogation it was later discovered that they assumed that any landings west of the Seine would be astride the Orne beween Bayeux and Trouville, and that, in this event, the fairly open corridor leading into the Falaise plain would be in the middle of any bridgehead. West of the Orne and east of Dives they reasoned that the rugged nature of the terrain would preclude large-scale armoured operations, but in the open country between the two rivers lay the natural path into the central Normandy plain. Thus in manœuvres held prior to the Allied invasion all German defensive plans had been based on the necessity of blocking this area, and it was realised that the key to its defence was the Bourguebus ridge and the high ground to the south of it. Brigadefuehrer Meyer, commander of 12 SS Panzer Division, reported that he had carried out exercises based on holding this area as far back as 1942 with 1 SS Panzer Division, and also in 1944 with 12 SS Panzer Division.

This pre-"D" Day appreciation hardened into a conviction after the start of "Overlord." To Field-Marshal Rommel the Bourguebus position was all-important, for by holding it he could block an attack both through Caen and from the Orne bridgehead established by 6 Airborne Division. As early as 1st July, therefore, he gave permission to the local corps commander, Sepp Dietrich, to withdraw from the city, if necessary, in order to establish an adequate defence along the Bourguebus ridge. Though this permission was at once countermanded on the orders of Hitler, it clearly shows the trend of Rommel's thinking. The fall of Caen, therefore, in no wise disrupted the enemy's organised defence of this zone. Indeed, it enabled Dietrich rather to strengthen it, for he could at last concentrate on essentials. Moreover, first with the remnants of 12 SS Panzer Division and later with 21 Panzer and 1 SS Panzer Divisions, he was now able also to build reserve positions, appreciating that a thrust in the direction of Falaise would be the next Allied move. Three new defence lines were prepared to protect the approaches to Falaise, and there were thus four belts of enemy defences, in all, in this sector.

The first was that of the "expendable infantry," which was intended to take the shock of any artillery bombardment or air bombing. This was garrisoned on the enemy right flank—the entrance to the tank run—from Touffreville to Colombelles by 16 G.A.F. Field Division supported by a General Headquarters anti-tank battalion. The river front from Colombelles through Vaucelles and across the Orne to Louvigny was held by the lately arrived 272 Infantry Division, and behind these two formations, in immediate tactical reserve, were positioned all the tanks and half the infantry of 21 Panzer Division reinforced by 503 Heavy Tank Battalion with its 36 "Tigers." This force was deployed in a counter-attack role in the triangle formed by the two railways and the River Dives. Beyond the second railway lay the next defensive zone designed to frustrate any further progress by armour which might both penetrate the forward defence zone and brush aside the immediate tactical reserves. The defence of this area, south of the Caen-Vimont railway, was based on the series of mutually supporting villages—Grentheville, Soliers, Four, Bras, Hubert-Folie, Bourguebus, Frenouville and Le Poirier—in each of which there was approximately one company of infantry (now averaging 40-60 men), and between three and five anti-tank guns—either of 75 or 88 mm. calibre. In these villages were thus scattered the guns of two anti-tank battalions, so that it was almost impossible for armour to move through this area without coming under anti-tank fire from two or three quarters.

South of this second defence zone and running roughly along the crest of the ridge between Hubert-Folie and Andre-sur-Orne, through Tilly la Campagne and La Hogue and round to the woods east of La Hogue, the enemy had forty-four 88 mm. flak guns and twelve of 3.7 inch calibre. An extension of this gun line ran north of the Caen-Vimont railway to beyond Troarn and in that sector there were another thirty-four 88 mm. flak guns, all of which, like those along the Bourguebus ridge, were sited in a dual-purpose role. In addition to these flak guns the enemy had another 60 to 80 artillery pieces between Troarn and the Orne. Almost as important as the artillery, however, were the two and a half brigades of nebelwerfers which were east of the Orne—some 270 nebelwerfers in all, or more than 1,000 barrels from which to bring down mortar fire on the area between the two rivers.

The next defence locality was organised around the Bourguebus ridge itself, the guns there being protected from ground attack by the infantry of 1 SS Panzer Division, whose six panzer grenadier battalions were deployed to hold the string of villages and woods between Fontenay-le-Marmion and the Caen-Vimont railway. These six battalions thus provided a third defensive zone to be penetrated before the British armour could make any clean break-through, whilst south of it Dietrich had in mobile reserve the Panther tank battalion of 1 SS Panzer Division consisting of 50-60 runners, and two battle groups of 12 SS Panzer Division, each with a battalion of infantry and a company of Mark IV tanks.

In all these defences the only element the enemy lacked was minefields. In view of the importance he attached to this sector it is surprising that he did not attempt to lay mines in general along the front—a comparatively easy task, if any had been procurable. Before "D" Day, however, all available mines were laid on, or near, the beaches, and after 6th June, Allied air attack so disorganised German communications that there was no chance of moving up from Verdun the millions that were stored there in the engineer dumps.

Although there were no minefields to be negotiated, the problem of getting through the defences was, however, formidable enough, for in order to penetrate into open country, where it could engage enemy tanks in a running fight, the British armour thus had to break through ten miles of heavily defended positions.

The enemy defence system as outlined here can be appreciated at its true extent from Map No. II.

General Situation in the Orne Bridgehead and Topography of the Area

A bridgehead over the River Orne had been established by 6 Airborne Division during the night 5th-6th June, in advance of the "D" Day landings. From the outset it had proved a great irritant to the Germans, and they had made repeated attempts to wipe it out. However the airborne troops had stood firm, being subsequently joined in their defence by 51 (Highland) Division, so that for some time past the positions east of the Orne had become too strong to suffer elimination at the hands of the enemy. Lately the bridgehead had not seen any major effort, for Second Army had been content merely to hold the ground already won and to repel attacks, and this policy of defence had included laying minefields which were to prove a source of great embarrassment to 8 Corps in the course of mounting and launching "Goodwood." For the moment, therefore, the area, save for a little shelling and mortaring, was quiet, and the troops in it were suffering almost as much discomfort from the mosquitoes, of which there was a plague in the low-lying flooded valley of the Dives, as from the enemy. 51 (Highland) Division on 11th July had, it is true, made some abortive attacks in the Colombelles factory area but these were simply to contain 21 Panzer Division and were only local in scope. Nevertheless, had it been possible to gain possession of these enormous factories with their high chimneys commanding such excellent observation over the Corps concentration area, much useful information would later, without doubt, have been denied to the enemy.

So far as the type of country is concerned over which 8 Corps was to fight, on the main axis of advance southwards from the river Orne, it consists of fairly open agricultural land studded with a number of compact stone built villages surrounded by orchards which are mostly enclosed with stout fences or lines of tall trees. Between the villages the ground is completely open with no banks or hedges and very few fences.

The only other obstacles on the front were the two railways, Caen-Troarn and Caen-Vimont. The first is a single line and for a large part of its length on both sides it has six feet high embankments, which during the battle were found to be impassable to wheeled vehicles. The second railway, Caen-Vimont, runs alternatively along an embankment or through a deep cutting and in each case the banks are ten feet or more high and, except in a few places, considerable obstacles to tanks.

The lie of the ground was, to say the least, distinctly unfavourable to the attacking side, for it rises gently southwards from Colombelles-Sainte Honorine-Escoville, in a series of minor undulations up to the Bourguebus ridge and thence to the woods and hamlets of Tilly la Campagne-Garcelles Secqueville-Secqueville la Campagne. This elevated ground affords complete observation over almost the entire area of the advance, whilst the defenders had the benefit of long fields of fire and facilities for concealed movement in the woods and villages, of which they did not fail to take full advantage. Whilst therefore the country generally was by no means as enclosed as that fought over in "Epsom," it still gave the enemy plenty of cover, particularly in the vicinity of the villages, enabling him to site his anti-tank weapons in cleverly hidden positions from which full use could be made of their superior range.

The numerous villages, too, provide a series of mutually supporting strong points not more than 1,500 yards apart, which if garrisoned with resolute troops make a perfect natural defence line. The enemy therefore was not slow to adapt these as the backbone of his second defence zone. Had the bombing programme laid on in conjunction with the ground attack, neutralised all these localities as the Corps Commander requested, it would have been a considerable help, for thereby an appreciable difference would have been made to the number of tank casualties sustained by 8 Corps on 18th and 19th July. However, as will be shown later, some of these targets were missed, causing far-reaching repercussions. Moreover at this season of the year the intervening cornfields were naturally shoulder high with crops, so that during the battle this also helped to conceal enemy movements and such field defences or gun positions as were in the open.

Outside this centre area, which by the nature of the flanking terrain was thus the inescapable axis of advance for the armour as it began to debouch from the bridgehead, on the left, within a few thousand yards in the early stages of attack and immediately adjacent to it in the latter stages, lie the wooded heights of the Bois de Bavent and the bocage country extending from Touffreville to Frenouville. All this left flank remained in enemy hands during the early part of the advance, and in some cases was not wholly cleared until the afternoon of 19th July. Similarly the factory areas of Mondeville and Commelles, which restricted manœuvre on the left flank, were not taken until quite late in the operation.

The setting for Operation "Goodwood" thus overwhelmingly favoured the defence.

The Objects and Plan of Operation "Goodwood" and Problems arising therefrom

Following the conference of senior officers at Creully on the morning of Friday, 14th July, detailed planning was at once begun by the staffs of Corps Headquarters and the three divisions. For mounting an ambitious undertaking of this nature very little time indeed was left and in particular the staff officers of Q (Movements) and Provost branches were destined to to be virtually swamped in the next three days organising one of the most difficult troop concentrations which any formation of Second Army was ever called upon to carry through during the whole of the campaign in North-West Europe.

Early on 15th July General Dempsey visited General O'Connor and handed him a copy of a document modestly entitled "Notes on Second Army Operations 16th-18th July," but which in reality was a personal directive from the Commander-in-Chief on the aims and conduct of the forthcoming battle written in his usual terse and succinct style.

Here is what it said:

"NOTES ON SECOND ARMY OPERATIONS
16th July-18th July

1. *Object of this operation.*

   To engage the German armour in battle and 'write it down' to such an extent that it is of no further value to the Germans as a basis of the battle.

   To gain a good bridgehead over the River Orne through Caen, and thus to improve our positions on the eastern flank.

   Generally to destroy German equipment and personnel.

2. *Affect of this operation on the Allied policy.*

   We require the whole of the Cherbourg and Brittany peninsulas.

   A victory on the eastern flank will help us to gain what we want on the western flank.

   But the eastern flank is a bastion on which the whole future of the campaign in North West Europe depends; it must remain a firm bastion; if it became unstable the operations on the western flank would cease.

   Therefore, while taking advantage of every opportunity to destroy the enemy, we must be very careful to maintain our own balance and ensure a firm base.

3. *The enemy.*

   There are a lot of enemy divisions in the area south-east of Caen:

21 Panzer Division.	16 G.A.F. Field Division.
1 SS Panzer Division.	272 Infantry Division.
12 SS Panzer Division.	

   Another one is coming and will be here this week-end.

4. *Operations of 12 Corps and Canadian Corps—16th and 17th July.*

Advantage must be taken of these to make the Germans think we are going to break out across the Orne between Caen and Amaye.

5. *Initial Operations 8 Corps.*

The three armoured divisions will be required to dominate the area Bourguebus-Vimont-Bretteville, and to fight and destroy the enemy.

But armoured cars should push far to the south towards Falaise, and spread alarm and despondency, and discover 'the form.'

6. *2 Canadian Corps.*

While para 5 is going on, the Canadians must capture Vaucelles, get through communications and establish themselves in a very firm bridgehead on the general line Fleury-Cormelles-Mondeville.

7. *Later Operations 8 Corps.*

When 6 is done, then 8 Corps can 'crack about' as the situation demands.

But not before 6 is done.

8. *To sum up for 8 Corps.*

Para 5.
Para 7.

Finally.

Para 6 is vital.

B. L. MONTGOMERY.
15-7-44"

This document provides the answer to any ill-informed criticism of the subsequent development of operations in Normandy, for it shows quite clearly the aims and intentions of General Montgomery. Above all, it proves that there was never any question of a headlong gallop off "into the blue" by three armoured divisions without, it be noted, any infantry formations supporting them and before the capture of Vaucelles provided, in any event, the firm base permitting such an undertaking to be launched. In paragraph 5 the ultimate positioning of the British armour was laid down as the general area Bourguebus-Vimont-Bretteville, and here the mass of the enemy panzer forces was to be contained and destroyed. With what success this was in fact accomplished will be apparent later.

By the end of the day the 8 Corps plan was firm, and at 0300 hours on 16th July the Corps operation instruction was issued to all taking part. In this instruction the Corps intention is laid down as follows:—

"On 18th July, 8 Corps will debouch from the existing bridgehead east of the River Orne with a view to:

(a) Dominating the area Bourguebus-Vimont-Bretteville-sur-Laize.

(b) Destroying any enemy armour or other forces encountered en route to and in this area.

(c) If conditions are favourable, subsequently exploiting to the south."

As a final clarification of the Second Army plan, General Dempsey issued on 17th July the following summary of it to all corps commanders:—

"SECOND ARMY OPERATIONS

Commencing on 18th July

West of the Orne.

1. 12 Corps will hold the whole of the commanding ground on the general line Evrecy-Esquay-Eterville. They will establish a force on the spur south-east of Evrecy and develop a strong threat on the axis Evrecy-Amaye.

They will do all they can to lead the enemy to believe that Second Army intends to cross the River Orne on their front.

2. 30 Corps will improve their positions on the front Vendes-Noyers-Missy, and operate with light forces in the direction of Villers Bocage. Their operation will be designed to draw enemy reserves into the thick country on their front and to contain them there.

East of the Orne.

3. 1 Corps will establish 3 Division in the area Bivres-Troarn-St. Pair-Emieville-Touffreville, and will hold this area against enemy attack from east and south-east.

1 Corps will also occupy and hold the villages of Cuverville and Demouville.

Patrolling and exploitation will be carried out to the east and north-east of 3 Division area, but main bodies will not be moved from this area without reference to me.

4. 8 Corps will establish armoured divisions in the areas:—
   (a) Vimont.
   (b) Garcelles-Secqueville.
   (c) Hubert-Folie-Verrieres.

The task of these three divisions will be to get their main bodies so established that there can be no enemy penetration through the ring, to destroy all enemy troop concentrations and installations in the area; to defeat enemy armour which may be brought against them.

Vigorous patrolling and exploitation will be carried out to the east and south-east to the line of the Dives—to the south in the direction of Falaise—to the south-west as far as the River Orne at Thury Harcourt.

Main bodies of the three divisions will not be moved from areas (a), (b) and (c) without reference to me.

5. 2 Canadian Corps will capture and hold Vaucelles and Giberville with one division and build bridges over River Orne at Caen. This is a vital part of the whole Army operations.

They will be prepared, on instructions from me, to advance their front to the line Fleury-Cormelles and may start to employ another division for this task.

Their operation of expanding the Caen bridgehead will include a junction of their forces east and west of the River Orne on the line Eterville-Fleury.

M. C. DEMPSEY,
Lieutenant-General,
Commander, Second Army."

17th July, 44.

This instruction shows that the Army Commander was even more cautious than the Commander-in-Chief as to the development of Operation "Goodwood," for in it the armoured divisions are ordered to be positioned in three areas from which they may not be moved without his permission.

So much, therefore, for any wild talk about the failure to capture Falaise.

The Army Commander's personal instruction also provides a neat and concise summary of the complementary activities of the neighbouring 1 Corps and the newly activated 2 Canadian Corps. As well as the tasks mentioned, however, these corps were to provide a firm base for 8 Corps generally, both in the Orne bridgehead and the city of Caen, and also much valuable artillery support in the early stages of the operation. In addition 1 Corps, as will be recounted later, had great responsibilities in setting the stage for the break-out and assisting 8 Corps in its passage through the bridgehead territory.

The Corps Commander's Problems

There were three main problems which influenced the Corps Commander in planning "Goodwood."

(a) Security of preparation in order to obtain some element of surprise.

(b) The fact that the size of the Orne bridgehead ordained that the break-out must be made on a long narrow front by one armoured division only.

(c) As a result of the foregoing sub-paragraph (b) air support was vital, and therefore the operation was contingent on weather permitting this to be given.

(a) *Security.*

Security was obviously of the first importance if the necessary preparations were to be concealed from the enemy. This was most difficult, for the retention of the Colombelles factory area permitted observation by the enemy over a considerable area of the Orne bridgehead, and in particular of traffic moving across the Caen Canal and River Orne. The movement of transport was not in itself a danger, for the whole bridgehead was a teaming mass of vehicles in motion, both by day and by night. The important point was to conceal the movement of armour from west to east, and the solution here was to move the tanks at night only, and not until the last minute. However, the necessary construction of additional heavy bridges over these two waterways undoubtedly caused suspicion to the enemy in advance, whilst the opposing corps commander, Sepp Dietrich, afterwards stated that by employing a trick he had learned in Russia, of pressing his ear to the ground, he had been able to detect the move of the armour concentrating, before, in fact, any crossed over into the Orne bridgehead. This assertion may seem far-fetched, but the inhabitants of Caen provide some supporting evidence. The Caen region has a formation of cavernous limestone, and in the cliffs overlooking the Orne to the south of the city, there are caves and subterranean passages which run for hundreds of yards into the rock. Frenchmen, who took shelter in these caves during the battles raging round about, later told interrogators that at night they always knew when large British tank movements were taking place, for like Sepp Dietrich, they heard the ominous rumbling. This, of course, was unknown to Second Army at the time, but as a further effort to obtain surprise in mounting this operation a deception plan was organised to give the impression that 8 Corps would be passed through a gap in the sector held by 12 Corps to the west of the River Orne. In the event Sepp Dietrich did in fact anticipate that the major thrust would come from this direction, but he also feared one over the Dives against Lisieux, and on the afternoon of 17th July sent a battle group including all the " Panther " tanks of 12 SS Division to the vicinity of this town.

One other disquieting factor was that during the week-end preceding the attack, for once the German Air Force was in action, since their reconnaissance planes were extremely active east of the Orne. Air photographs must, therefore, have confirmed ground observation reports of new bridges over the river and canal and the improvements to the traffic routes.

(b) *The Orne Bridgehead.*

The restricted nature of this bridgehead did not permit more than one of the armoured divisions to be passed into it either on the grounds of security or accommodation before the break out began and thereby made more room. Because of this factor, 8 Corps was forced to advance one division up, and it was therefore clear that one armoured brigade only could be produced on the ground at " H " hour. Had it been possible to assemble two armoured brigades on the start line, an advance on a two brigade front would still have been impossible since the gaps to be created in the British minefields would not allow the passage of more than one armoured *regiment* at a time. The initial manner of the debouchment of 8 Corps was thus enforced by conditions which it was impossible to alter.

(c) *Air Support.*

The whole of the operation was dependent upon air support. This, in turn, hinged upon the weather, and a final decision as to whether the R.A.F. could co-operate or not could only be made a few hours before the battle was due to start. It was not possible to delay concentration of the armour until this decision was given, and this meant that plans had to be made to conceal this so that the element of surprise, upon which the success of the venture so largely depended, would not be sacrificed in the event of postponement. Had the operation been put off, it was arranged that Guards Armoured Division and 7 Armoured Division should disperse their vehicles west of the river in an area already so crowded with transport that their presence was unlikely to be noticed. 11 Armoured Division, although east of the river, had a reasonable amount of cover to protect its own transport from view.

Composition of 8 Corps on 18th July

Operation " Goodwood " enabled 8 Corps to be constituted for the first time in action as a completely armoured corps. Three armoured divisions were allotted to the Corps to carry out the difficult task of breaking out of the Orne bridgehead, as well as three armoured car regiments with which to reconnoitre deep into enemy territory. Among these, the Corps was delighted to welcome back 2 Household Cavalry Regiment, commanded by Lieutenant-Colonel Henry Abel Smith—which had trained so long and happily with Corps Headquarters in England.

The composition and command set-up of 8 Corps at 0600 hours 18th July was, therefore, as follows:—

Formations	Strength	
	Officers	Other Ranks
Headquarters 8 Corps and 8 Corps Troops	594	9,417
Guards Armoured Division	771	14,838
7 Armoured Division	783	14,400
11 Armoured Division	741	13,648
8 A.G.R.A.	305	6,311
	3,194	58,614

It will be seen that the size of the Corps troops had increased considerably, but this arose through the fact that all rear echelons had now arrived in the theatre from England, whilst additional allocations of engineers and pioneers made by Second Army for the operation swelled the total. The divisions, too, despite the hard fighting in which 7 and 11 Armoured Divisions had already been involved, were now practically at full strength again.

The 8 Corps Plan for Operation "Goodwood"

Following the initial air bombardment, it was decided that 8 Corps would advance, "one division up," in the order:—

    11 Armoured Division
    Guards Armoured Division
    7 Armoured Division

The shape of the Orne bridgehead having determined the manner of the Corps break-out, it became a question of the utmost urgency to ensure thereafter as fast a build up of armour on the battlefield as possible, in conformity, of course, with the air bombing programme. Calculations of the relevant factors showed that the following timings might reasonably be expected, assuming "H" hour to be 0745 hours:

(1) The leading tanks of the first brigade (29 Armoured Brigade) would arrive at Cagny at approximately 0900 hours, where the bombing programme would enforce a short halt before the advance could be resumed.

(2) Two armoured regiments of Guards Armoured Division would start to cross the Orne bridges at 0745 hours, would be clear of them by 0915 hours and should thus be in the vicinity of Cagny by 1030 hours, with the third armoured regiment arriving by midday.

(3) The move forward of 7 Armoured Division being phased back one hour, and using only one bridge, tanks of this division would move off at 0845 hours and be arriving around Cagny from approximately 1115 hours until 1400 hours.

This time-table indicated, therefore, a continual flow of armour into the Cagny area from 0900 hours to 1400 hours.

Divisional tasks were laid down as follows:

(a) *11 Armoured Division.*

    At "H" hour 11 Armoured Division with under command:—

        Inns of Court Regiment
        One squadron of 22 Dragoons (flail tanks)

was ordered to break out on the front of 51 (Highland) Division, through gaps in the minefield already constructed under the supervision of 1 Corps, and initially to occupy the villages of Cuverville and Demouville. Thence the division was to continue on, crossing the Caen-Vimont railway between Grentheville and Cagny, and finally occupy firmly the general area Bras-Roquancourt-Fontenay le Marmion-Beauvoir Ferme. One armoured regiment was to be detached in the vicinity of Cagny in order to prevent any interference by the enemy from the direction of Vimont, but otherwise 11 Armoured Division had no responsibilities for the left flank, except for its own protection. The main task of the division was to destroy any German forces that it encountered, but once its objective had been secured then certain patrolling tasks were to be undertaken towards St. Andre-sur-Orne, Bretteville-sur-Laize and along the main road to Thury Harcourt, in order, as opportunity offered, to gain contact with other formations including 2 Canadian Corps to the north.

(b) *Guards Armoured Division.*

Guards Armoured Division with under command:—
  Two squadrons 2 Household Cavalry
  One squadron 22 Dragoons

had the task of moving in rear of 11 Armoured Division as far as Cagny where it was first to relieve the armoured regiment containing this village and then swing left to establish a firm base in Vimont.

Again the main task of this division was to destroy any enemy forces encountered but in this case also it was to protect the left flank of the Corps.

Once Vimont was captured and held, liaison was to be made with 7 Armoured Division and patrols sent out towards Argences, Mezidon, Emieville and St. Pierre du Souquet.

(c) *7 Armoured Division.*

The action of 7 Armoured Division depended largely on the progress of the two divisions in front of it. Following Guards Armoured Division and crossing the railway west of Cagny, it was to be ready to support 11 Armoured Division if required, but finally to position itself around La Hogue-Garcelles Secqueville, with patrols out towards St. Sylvain, Langanverie and Cintheaux.

Artillery Support

The fire plan for the support of the attack was most complicated and involved the integration of tasks among the artillery of the three corps participating, 1, 8 and 2 Canadian Corps. The whole of this, together with the allocation of A.G.R.A. resources, was the responsibility of Brigadier Matthew, and he evolved a detailed plan to cover each phase of the operation, of which the following is a summary:—

Phase 1.

Up to an hour and a half before "H" hour (and during the heavy bombing) all guns were available to fire an anti-tank counter battery programme on located enemy positions.

Phase 2.

During the hour and a half preceding "H" hour all guns were to fire a counter-battery programme organised by 1 Corps.

Phase 3.

At "H" hour the move forward of 11 Armoured Division was to be supported by a rolling barrage as far as the Caen-Vimont railway, whilst barrages and concentrations preceded the advance of 3 British Division and

3 Canadian Division on the flanks. Counter-battery fire was to be continued as long as required while the armour was advancing, and in addition to two field regiments in direct support of each armoured division, there were a number of regiments available to bring down fire on various targets as the leading troops called for them to be shelled.

Owing to the small area and crowded nature of the bridgehead east of the River Orne, most of the guns had to be sited to the west of the river, and this had the effect of reducing very appreciably the distance over which they could give support to the armour. Thus at a very early stage in planning it became apparent that full artillery assistance could be provided up to the foot of the Bourguebus ridge only, but that beyond this a delay would be inevitable until medium regiments could be brought forward, a difficult task since they had to be phased in with the mass of traffic which had to cross the Orne bridges with the three armoured divisions.

The alternative to this delay was to support the final phase of the operation, i.e., the advance to the area Bourguebus-Vimont-Bretteville-sur-Laize, by air bombardment, and this solution was decided upon, though as will be seen later, Fate was to will otherwise.

In all for Operation "Goodwood" the following artillery was made available:—

Nineteen field regiments	=	456 guns
Thirteen medium regiments	=	208 "
Three heavy regiments	=	48 "
Two heavy anti-aircraft regiments	=	48 "
A total of		760 guns

The allotment of ammunition laid down was:—

Field Artillery	500 rounds per gun
Medium artillery	300 " " "
Heavy artillery	150 " " "

In addition to the land artillery, three ships of the Royal Navy anchored off the coast were also co-opted into supporting the attack by dealing with the coastal guns in the vicinity of Franceville and Cabourg.

They were:—

H.M.S. Roberts with two 15-inch guns
H.M.S. Mauritius with twelve 6-inch guns.
H.M.S. Enterprise with seven 6-inch guns.

R. E. Tasks and Plans

The R.E. tasks arising during the preparations for mounting Operation "Goodwood" and the subsequent battle were very considerable, and fell under four main headings:—

(a) Development of routes for the concentration, and later build-up during the battle, both up to the start line and beyond, and the maintenance of these routes.

(b) Construction of extra bridges over the River Orne and Caen Canal.

(c) Clearing the British defensive minefields at the confines of the Orne bridgehead, so that unrestricted movement of all vehicles across the start line would be assured.

(d) Tasks arising during the progress of the action, particularly the quick passage of the armour across obstacles in the line of advance.

(a) *Route Developments.*

Three routes were considered necessary for the eastwards move of the armour, and each had to be duplicated on account of the tracked vehicle element. In some places these routes forward existed already, but a large amount of high speed work by R.E. units was required from 13th July onwards, so that six might be completed and ready by last light on 16th July when the concentration of the Corps east of the River Orne was due to begin. This task proved enormous and beyond the powers of the combined Sapper resources of Second Army and 1 and 8 Corps. Recourse had therefore to be made to borrowing the engineers of the attacking formations, including those of at least one of the armoured formations, 11 Armoured Division, which forward of the river assisted in constructing the remaining routes under the supervision of 1 Corps.

Maintenance of these routes was also a particular problem to be faced until the capture of Vaucelles permitted the main Caen-Falaise road to be used; this was undertaken by 1 Corps as far as the road Ste. Honorine-Escoville, after which each corps was responsible within its own boundaries. In the early stages this involved considerable detailed planning on the part of 11 Armoured Division to ensure the rapid development of one wheeled route forward, unimpeded by any bomb damage and ready for early use by the supply echelons.

(b) *Bridging.*

The River Orne and the Caen Canal run side by side within a few yards of each other and thus provide a double water obstacle. Existing road bridges over them between Benouville and Ranville had already been captured intact by 6 Airborne Division on "D" Day, but these now required strengthening in view of the amount of heavy traffic which would pass over them. In addition, however, two new pairs of bridges required to be built, and the construction of these was carried out by 1 Corps. By the time the concentration of 8 Corps began, therefore, there were three separate Class 40 bridges over the canal and river, each being served by one pair of wheeled and tracked routes from the west and leading down to the start line. These were felt to be the minimum necessary for the preliminary concentration and launching operations, whilst additional bridges would still have to be built at the earliest opportunity. 1 Corps, therefore, was ordered to provide two extra crossings, one further north and one south of those already existing, by 2359 hours on "D" Day—18th July. 2 Canadian Corps also projected two or three bridges over the River Orne between Caen and Vaucelles as soon as the situation permitted, so that 1 and 8 Corps would then have the exclusive use of those to the north.

(c) *Minefield Clearance.*

After the original establishment of the Orne bridgehead, it had been the policy to hold the ground won east of the River Orne against any enemy armoured attack, with the maximum use of wire and mines. As a result there was a thickly sown defensive minefield across the whole of the front east of the river, and most careful arrangements were therefore necessary to ensure the attacking troops and vehicles passed through without any hold-up.

1 Corps was again made responsible for supervising this task, which was given to 51 (Highland) Division aided by one field company from 3 British Division. It proved in the event, however, to be unusually difficult for a variety of reasons, the chief of which were that the minefield records were out of date and unreliable on account of heavy shelling by the enemy having detonated and displaced a large number of mines. Moreover, the minefield had for the most part been laid in standing corn or potato patches which made its location difficult, and this was further complicated by the fact that anti-personnel mines had been added at a later date, thus making the clearing operations slower and more unpleasant.

The first attempt to take up the mines on the night 15th-16th July was not successful, and as a result it was decided to open up exits using the normal gapping drill without any reference to records. This was carried out on the night 16th-17th July, when fourteen gaps were made and wired off. On the following night four extra gaps were created and the whole area clearly marked with white tape and signposted at the request of Major-General Roberts, commanding 11 Armoured Division. These gaps were sufficient to allow the passage of one armoured regiment at a time, but no more.

It is of interest to note, and some indication of the magnitude of the task, that when "Goodwood" was over and mine clearance could be tackled by day, it took three field companies five days to lift all the mines on the front of 51 (Highland) Division.

The R.E. preparations required for Operation "Goodwood" were therefore far greater than in any previous or subsequent operation in Normandy, and were successfully carried out in a minimum of time, which reflected great credit on the Sappers.

Air Support

Operation "Goodwood" was to be assisted by an air effort on a larger scale than anything hitherto staged in direct support of ground forces, and the whole operation was made entirely dependant upon it. Thus, in the event of there being no air support available on the day in question, the attack would inevitably be postponed. This produced a number of problems and restrictions during the planning period, and certain counter-plans had to be allowed for in case there should be any delay. The main disadvantage was that it could not be known until only a very short while beforehand whether the state of the weather would permit flying, and thus the necessary preliminary concentrations of tanks and vehicles might become known to the enemy, unless they were very quickly dispersed—a difficult task under the circumstances.

The plan to employ such a large air force did not at first meet general approval. Previous experiences at Cassino in Italy and ten days earlier at Caen had been disappointing, for enemy opposition had not been eliminated whilst our own troops had been hampered by cratering and roads blocked by debris. However, the Commander-in-Chief requested General Eisenhower to agree to it and in addition to ask for assistance from the independent R.A.F. Bomber Command of Air Chief Marshal Sir Arthur Harris, which was duly forthcoming It was thus finally settled on the highest level that the R.A.F. could, and would, provide the support asked for. Now, however, Corps Headquarters was to feel the lack of its air adviser, for no senior R.A.F. officer was available to assist in choosing the targets to be bombed or the timing of the attacks. Everything had to be arranged with Headquarters Second Army, whence the G.S.O.1 (Intelligence) accompanied by the A.O.C. 83 Group R.A.F. flew to England for the necessary joint planning at the Headquarters of R.A.F. Bomber Command.

The target areas finally chosen for medium and heavy night bombers (Lancasters and Halifaxes) and heavy day bombers (Flying Fortresses) are shown on the attached Map No. III, the number of aircraft taking part together with the timings laid down for the attacks being as follows:—

Time of attack	Number and type of aircraft	Targets	Type of bombs
0545-0630	1,056 heavy night bombers (R.A.F. Bomber Command).	A. H. M.	H.E.
0700-0745	482 medium bombers (9 U.S.A.A.F.)	U.D.E.F. and G.	Fragmentation
0830-0900	539 heavy day bombers (8 U.S.A.A.F.)	I. P. Q.	Fragmentation

In addition to the above, 83 Group R.A.F. operating with Second Army, also agreed to undertake any other requirements. These included attacks on:—

(a) Enemy defended localities at Le Mesnil Frementel, Frenouville, Grentheville and Garcelles Secqueville.

(b) Enemy gun areas marked O, J and U on the map.

(c) Enemy reserve areas around Fleury-sur-Orne, Clinchamps-sur-Orne and Vimont-Argences.

(d) Interference with any enemy movement west from Vimont-Argences.

(e) Armed reconnaissance of the battlefield area and normal impromptu direct air support, as called for by the troops on the ground.

The principle guiding the selection of all these targets was the progressive neutralisation of enemy positions. Thus first the sides of the corridor down which 8 Corps was to advance were to be attacked. As a result enemy positions in and along this area would be destroyed and the armour would consequently not be held up by them. Secondly, the strongpoint of Cagny and enemy gun areas in I, P and Q on the map were to be dealt with, and in both these series of targets great care was taken to ensure that no cratering might result anywhere in the path of the tanks. Lastly, the remaining targets, which were the responsibility of 83 Group R.A.F., were on the confines of the battle area except for the two strong points of Le Mesnil Frementel and Garcelles Secqueville.

One further complication was caused by this bombing programme to the forces on the ground. The R.A.F. required to be assured that no troops were within:—

(a) 2,000 yards of H.E. bomb targets, or

(b) 2,500 yards of areas of fragmentation bombing.

Finally, no troops unless dug in, were to be anywhere within 3,000 yards of any target area. This necessitated a slight withdrawal to a safe area by 154

Infantry Brigade and 152 Infantry Brigade, both of 51 (Highland) Division, together with part of 185 Infantry Brigade of 3 British Division, which was awkward and inconvenient but had to be accepted.

It will be noted that there was no bombing in the afternoon by the heavy bombers. General O'Connor, from the outset, had been most anxious to obtain a second heavy bombing effort at approximately 1500 hours on the day of the offensive, at which time it was estimated that the leading armour would be in a position to move forward to its final objectives. Thus in the minutes of the conference held by the Corps Commander at 1800 hours on 16th July, item 7 records the decision to hold the armour of 11 Armoured Division in the Cagny area until the second heavy bombing ceased, and then to direct it on to the Bourguebus to cause maximum destruction to the enemy. It was also known that at this point the limit of range of the medium artillery was being reached. Unfortunately, for reasons which were beyond the control of Corps Headquarters, the heavy bombers could not again be made available at this time.

Concentration before the Battle

It has already been pointed out that when the concentration for this operation was ordered, the armoured divisions allotted to 8 Corps were widely dispersed. Thus 11 Armoured Division was half-way between Caen and Bayeux; Guards Armoured Division was two miles east of Bayeux, and 7 Armoured Division was disposed around Tilly-sur-Seulles. The problem was now to move these formations across the lines of communication of Second Army to a battlefield east of the River Orne, undetected by the enemy and with as little inconvenience as possible to the troops in action.

A most careful concentration plan was therefore drawn up under the aegis of Second Army, and a special Corps Traffic Office, working directly under the orders of the B.G.S., was established to ensure that it was carried out. Working this out was a considerable feat, for many different and, indeed, opposing factors had to be considered, among which the chief were:—

(a) Traffic congestion throughout the bridgehead was very great and only a limited number of west to east tracks existed.

(b) Three bridges only would be available over the River Orne and Caen Canal.

(c) All three armoured divisions required to cross the maintenance routes of 2 Canadian Corps and 1 Corps.

(d) The move eastwards of the tanks had to be concealed from the enemy's air reconnaissance, and, in the vicinity of the bridgehead, from ground observation in addition.

(e) The bridgehead east of the river was very small and permitted only a small portion of 8 Corps in the area before the battle started. The flow of traffic up to and across the start line once action had begun had therefore to be carefully controlled and as rapid as possible.

The Plan for Traffic Control

Three routes for wheeled vehicles with affiliated routes for tracks were used for the move of the Corps, and from 2100 hours on 16th July, when the concentration began, until 7 Armoured Division arrived east of the river (expected to be late on 18th July) these were reserved for 8 Corps west to east traffic only, and the movement was organised as follows:—

| | West of River Orne | | Bridge | East of River Orne |
	Wheels	Tracks		Wheels and Tracks
Route	A	Rat	York	Palm
,,	B	Cat	Euston	Holly
,,	C	Calf	London	Briar

Block timings were allotted to formations on each route and the subsequent moves co-ordinated by the Corps Traffic Office situated about 4,000 yards west of the River Orne on Route B. So far as the "bridge area" was concerned this was the responsibility of Lieutenant-Colonel G. P. H. Fitzgerald, A.P.M. 8 Corps. He stationed a traffic officer at each pair of bridges and at control points along the road Hermanville-Benville, and touch was kept between them and the Traffic Office by wireless and telephone. As the latter also had lines to the Corps Command Post, and the Headquarters of Guards and 7 Armoured Divisions, it was thus possible to call parties forward as necessary. The traffic officers also organised "sidings," in which traffic could be held in the case of any sudden change in the order of march.

It is not proposed to go into all the details of the move up of the armoured divisions, but, in short, after the passage and staging in the Orne bridgehead of 11 Armoured Division, the plan was for Guards and 7 Armoured Division each to be positioned along these routes, with the head of their armoured brigades by the morning of 18th July, a short distance west of the Orne bridges, and able at "H" hour and "H" plus 60 minutes respectively, to begin crossing them. 7 Armoured Division was phased back one hour to permit the passage of two Canadian infantry brigades destined for the attack on Colombelles.

The concentration of 11 Armoured Division in the bridgehead area was conducted on the following lines. On Sunday night, 16th-17th July, 159 Infantry Brigade Group and the headquarters of both the Division and 29 Armoured Brigade were passed east of the Orne. On the succeeding night, 17th-18th July, 91 Anti-Tank Regiment R.A., 2 Northamptonshire Yeomanry and the Inns of Court Regiment crossed, using two bridges during the early part of the night and one bridge from 0100-0500 hours on 18th July. This method was adopted in order to achieve surprise, so that the first party which went over on Sunday night consisted entirely of wheeled vehicles and could move without making undue noise, whilst the second party composed solely of tracked vehicles, was held back until the last possible moment, thereby minimising the enemy's chance of quick reaction to the operation.

In the event, the very elaborate concentration proceeded without a hitch, and a total of over 6,000 vehicles and tanks flowed over the bridges on 18th July at the rate of between 150 and 200 vehicles per hour for each bridge.

The magnitude of the task of introducing and, above all, concealing yet another formation east of the Orne can best be visualised by a glance at Maps II and III where its extent is shown. The impossibility of passing any additional troops into this area is only too clear.

Finally Corps Headquarters itself moved from the Lantheuil woods to a site adjacent to the main Courseulles-Caen road at Beny-sur-Mer, a convenient site for a move down through Caen and Vaucelles if future events necessitated it.

18th July—The Battle

By the early hours of 18th July, the stage was set for the great venture to begin. 29 Armoured Brigade followed by 2 Northamptonshire Yeomanry had successfully negotiated the Orne bridges in the dark (the crossing being perhaps slightly accelerated by enemy shelling) and moved down towards the limits of the bridgehead. During this time the necessary additional gaps in the minefields were being blown and the whole forward area sign-posted and marked out with white tape, to ensure as easy a passage as possible for the tanks.

Meanwhile at 0145 hours information was received at Corps Headquarters from Headquarters Second Army that Operation "Goodwood" would take place as arranged on 18th July, "H" hour being confirmed as 0745 hours.

The morning dawned bright and clear, a happy augury both to the air forces and the troops on the ground, and punctually at 0545 hours the heavy bombers of the R.A.F. Bomber Command appeared. For the next forty-five minutes a seemingly endless stream of Lancasters and Halifaxes, 1,056 in all, pounded the woods and villages to the east of the Corps axis of advance, and on the other side, the factory district of Colombelles and Mondeville, which were the Canadian objectives. The following broadcast which was given on the evening of the first day by the B.B.C. commentator, Chester Wilmot, gives a dramatic description of events leading up to the battle and this opening phase:—

"The Germans were fooled because we used, as our jumping-off place, ground that had lain fallow from a military point of view since 'D' Day. On that day the 6 Airborne Division seized the bridges over the Orne between Caen and the sea, and they gained a small bridgehead—about four miles long and two miles deep—on the eastern bank.

"Last Friday I paid a casual visit to the original bridgehead. The front was just as quiet as it had been for weeks, but at once I saw signs that it wouldn't remain quiet—bulldozers were cutting new tracks for tanks— Sappers were putting in two new Bailey bridges . . . infantry of a British division were moving in small scattered groups along the lanes and through the cornfields . . . and then I saw several armoured vehicles which had been fighting elsewhere. Those signs were enough—so I stayed in the bridgehead east of the Orne all the week-end.

" By day there was little sign of increased traffic on the roads, but each night the bridges were alive with transport that came across by dark and was hidden before dawn under trees and beside hedges. Several times on Sunday German reconnaissance planes came over ; the ack-ack boys drove them off, but we wondered how much they'd seen, how much their spotters could see from the top of the Colombelles factory chimneys that looked right down upon the river and our bridges.

" Then on Sunday evening one of our photo-recce Spitfires was shot down in German territory. Was the camera intact? Might the Germans get the films and see that it had been photographing the area behind Caen? We must stop them. Orders were flashed to the artillery to shell the area where the 'Spit' had crashed. Mustangs came over and poured incendiary bullets into the same area. But we looked in vain for the smoke signal that would mean the plane and its photographs were burning. We wondered how much the enemy knew.

"That night our armoured forces began to cross the bridges—from last light they came rumbling over in a steady stream—armoured command trucks, scout cars, half-tracks, jeeps, supply trucks, self-propelled guns. Twice during the night German planes swept in to take flashlight photographs. We wondered how much they could see. The same thing happened the next night—Monday night—the night before the attack, for then the tanks came over. By dawn they were in position . . . but by dawn it didn't matter whether or not the Germans knew they'd come. By then it was too late—the bombing had begun.

"In the half-light I stood on a hill on the east bank of the Orne, looking down on an open field at the foot of the hill. I could see the camouflaged shapes of tanks, hundreds of them—tanks that hadn't been there the night before, but now they were assembling to attack. And in the distance there was the sole surviving chimney of the great steel factory at Colombelles and the towers and buildings of the suburbs of Caen that the Germans still held.

"Then I turned and looked out to sea . . . the Lancasters and Halifaxes were beginning to darken the northern sky . . . they came over the horizon in a black swarm. The markers dropped their target indicators and in a few seconds bombs were cascading down on the steel factory and the suburbs of Caen . . . and on the German strongpoints on either flank of the line along which our tanks were to advance.

"For a while the flak was thick . . . but every minute it got less as our field-gunners found their targets—the German ack-ack positions—pin-pointed for them by spotting planes—little Austers—which seemed to be worming their way in between the very sticks of bombs, searching for the flak positions that dared to fire.

"For forty-five minutes the procession of bombers came on unbroken, and when they'd gone, the thunder of the guns swelled up and filled the air, as the artillery carried on the bombardment.

"In the field below the tanks were moving forward towards their start line—on the crest of a rise about two miles from me the bombardment drowned the rumble of their tanks, for now the Navy joined in and huge shells were crumping down on German guns, which our field pieces couldn't reach."

The first attack was followed at 0700 hours by a second, this time by 482 medium bombers from 9 U.S.A.A.F. In this case fragmentation bombs were used on the villages of Cuverville and Demouville, and on the general area over which the armour was due to advance, from approximately Cuverville-Touffreville as far as a line 1,000 yards south of the Caen-Troarn road. This attack also lasted forty-five minutes and during it 29 Armoured Brigade began to move out of the concentration area through the gaps in the minefields, and down to the start line. The leading company was 3 Royal Tank Regiment which had under command one motor company from 8 Rifle Brigade, one self-propelled battery from 13 Regiment R.H.A., one squadron of flail tanks from 22 Dragoons and one troop of assault engineers from 26 Assault Squadron, R.E. It was followed by the remainder of the brigade in the order:—

    Tac Headquarters 29 Armoured Brigade.

    2 Fife and Forfar Yeomanry, with a company from 8 Rifle Brigade and a battery from 13 Regiment R.H.A.

    23 Hussars.

    8 Rifle Brigade, less three companies.

Meanwhile 159 Infantry Brigade was also getting into position ready to attack Demouville and Cuverville on the right of the advance of 29 Armoured Brigade.

Promptly at 0745 hours the guns opened up and 11 Armoured Division moved forward across the start line, heartened and encouraged by the devastating rain of bombs and the equally impressive artillery bombardment. Eight field regiments put down a rolling barrage in front of the tanks whilst two field, six medium and two heavy regiments fired concentrations on the flanks, particularly on the villages Cuverville, Demouville and Liberville. South of the railway leading from Caen, the strong points of Cagny and Emieville were also heavily shelled, while three additional heavy regiments carried out harassing fire on targets as far south as Garcelles Secqueville and Secqueville la Campagne with the object of dealing with the movement of any enemy reserves.

During the early stages of the advance the third wave of the air support programme started and from 0800 hours for about half an hour, 539 Flying Fortresses of 8 U.S.A.A.F. dropped fragmentation bombs on enemy gun position around Bourguebus and Troarn. This completed the heavy bombing effort, and henceforth only the tactical air force operating with Second Army, was available for direct support on call through A.S.S.U. (air support signals unit) channels. In passing, it is of interest to note that although over 2,000 planes were flown over from England for this operation, only 25 were lost —all from anti-aircraft fire, for no German aircraft ventured to put in an appearance.

Meanwhile the armour was pushing on, and by 0830 hours all three regiments of 29 Armoured Brigade were clear of the minefields. For the first mile thereafter little opposition was experienced, since the enemy troops were too stunned by the shattering bombing to put up much resistance. Soon large numbers of Germans had been captured, some still in their dug-outs and all white and shaken from their experience of Allied air power. Most of these troops did not actually surrender but had to be rounded up, sitting dazed and listless in their slit trenches and not attempting to fire their weapons. The bulk proved to be from 16 G.A.F. Division but, later in the day, it was satisfactory to observe among the prisoners a considerable number from units of the redoubtable 21 Panzer Division.

The first slight opposition was encountered by 3 Royal Tank Regiment from the orchards south-east of Cuverville, where an enemy infantry platoon and two anti-tank guns were quickly knocked out. At 0830 hours the barrage had reached the end of the first phase—a line 300 yards south of the Caen-Troarn railway, and here a pause of twenty minutes was made in order to enable the second armoured regiment, 2 Fife and Forfar Yeomanry, to come up on the left of 3 Royal Tank Regiment and the advance thus to be continued " two up." The railway was not a serious tank obstacle but it caused some slight delay, and not all the tanks of the second regiment were over it before the guns began firing once again at 0850 hours, and the advance was resumed. During this phase, both regiments found increasing difficulty in keeping up with the barrage owing to the danger of the leading armour getting out of supporting distance of their reserve squadrons which were still trying to cross the railway. However, opposition from the Germans in this area was not heavy, for here also, they were still dazed. Much equipment was found abandoned and several hundreds of non-protesting enemy rounded up.

The infantry, too, was making good progress, and at 0835 hours 3 Monmouthshire Regiment entered Cuverville, which was completely cleared by 1030 hours. Likewise, 1 Herefordshire Regiment seized the orchards southeast of this village, and was firmly established in them by 1015 hours. The next village, Demouville, was, however, discovered by a patrol from the Inns of Court Regiment to be still firmly held by the enemy, and it became a question of relieving the troops in Cuverville in order that they might attack this strong-point, since there was as yet no other infantry available, save for 4 King's Shropshire Light Infantry, which was held as a reserve for any emergency.

Soon after 0900 hours the artillery barrage ceased as arranged, and thereafter fire support was available on call, though in actual fact field regiments by now were reaching their maximum range. Nevertheless the armoured regiments pushed on, and by 0935 hours their leading squadrons were across the second railway line—that running from Caen to Vimont. This proved to be a somewhat tougher obstacle than the first, but no undue delay was encountered. 3 Royal Tank Regiment, in reaching this area, had passed to the west of the heavily bombed village of Le Mesnil Frementel without meeting opposition, but 2 Fife and Forfar Yeomanry, advancing to the east of it, came under considerable anti-tank fire from the equally heavily bombed enemy strong-point of Cagny, which seemed surprising, but was to be explained later. At about the same time, 23 Hussars crossing the first railway, was engaged by enemy tanks coming from Emieville. The enemy was thus beginning to join battle.

As soon as 3 Royal Tank Regiment crossed the second railway, stiff resistance was encountered on the right in Grentheville, but by 1010 hours this had been by-passed to the west, and the regiment had reached the vicinity of Soliers, where 2 Fife and Forfar Yeomanry had already come up against strong defences, coupled with anti-tank gun fire from the adjacent village of Four. Behind this leading armour, the company of 8 Rifle Brigade accompanying it, was kept very fully occupied mopping up the localities so far overrun, notably Grentheville, and it was apparent that with the ending of the barrage, opposition was henceforth going to be stiffer and the advance correspondingly slower. Self-propelled guns and "Panther" tanks were next seen in the Bourguebus area and heavy fire experienced from the western end of Frenouville. From now on and for the remainder of the morning, although further progress was made by 29 Armoured Brigade, it was much more limited in scope and at the cost of increasing tank casualties. While the enemy garrisons in Soliers and Four were being kept occupied, a troop of tanks from 2 Fife and Forfar Yeomanry succeeded at about 1115 hours in reaching the road leading eastwards from the very strongly defended village of Bourguebus, where it was finally held. This proved in fact to be the southernmost limit of advance achieved by the Corps in the whole operation, though Bourguebus itself was taken two days later.

At the same time that this infiltration forward between Soliers and Four was taking place, 3 Royal Tank Regiment moved down the near side of the railway running southwards and was able to cross over 500 yards south-west of Soliers. The leading squadron then began to advance up the hill towards Hubert-Folie but almost immediately came under heavy fire from enemy tanks and anti-tank guns in this village and on both sides of it. Artillery concentrations were called for, and as a result some tanks were able to get across the road to Bourguebus, whilst a section of carriers from 8 Rifle Brigade actually drove through Hubert-Folie itself.

In the rear of the leading armour, meanwhile, 8 Rifle Brigade and further back still, 159 Infantry Brigade, were clearing and organising the ground won. Thus Le Mesnil Frementel was occupied and established as a firm base against a possible armoured counter attack, without any great trouble, producing in so doing a bag of nearly 150 prisoners. Though mortaring and shelling of Cuverville caused some delay in the relief there of 3 Monmouthshire Regiment by 7 Argyll and Sutherland Highlanders, by midday this had been completed and Demouville was ripe for attack.

During these operations by 11 Armoured Division, Guards and 7 Armoured Divisions had also begun their allotted tasks. So far as the Guards were concerned, in the early stages there had been some time lost in getting over the River Orne, but this had been more than made up and by 0945 hours the head of 5 Guards Armoured Brigade was halted some 500 yards behind the tail of 29 Armoured Brigade in the vicinity of Demouville. From there the advance was resumed "two up," with 2 Armoured Grenadier Guards directed on Cagny and 2 Armoured Coldstream Guards by-passing this village to the north and making for Vimont. 2 Recce Welsh Guards was positioned behind these two regiments and 2 Armoured Irish Guards brought up the rear as brigade reserve. As in the case of 29 Armoured Brigade, an infantry company from 1 Motorised Grenadier Guards was allotted to each armoured regiment.

At approximately 1000 hours 5 Guards Armoured Brigade was instructed to press on as soon as possible in order to come up on the left flank of 29 Armoured Brigade and so reduce enemy pressure from the east. By 1045 hours leading elements of the brigade were about 1,000 yards west of Emieville, and a short while later on the northern outskirts of Cagny. Enemy anti-tank guns, again notwithstanding the bombing, were very active in both these villages, and as a result the Guards suffered casualties and were unable to make any further progress. It was therefore decided to disengage from these unpleasant areas and to advance on Vimont, skirting Cagny to the west and south. This hold-up inevitably had its repercussions further back on the deployment of the remainder of the Corps, notably on 7 Armoured Division which by this time was half across the Orne bridges with its leading troops, 5 Royal Tank Regiment, just east of Cuverville. There the latter was held up on the right by 2 Northamptonshire Yeomanry assisting 159 Infantry Brigade, and on the left by the tail of 5 Guards Armoured Brigade.

Elsewhere, in 1 Corps sector, satisfactory progress had been made by 3 British Division in reducing the villages of Touffreville and Sannerville and clearing the wooded area in the triangle of roads south-east of Escoville. 2 Canadian Corps, too, had occupied a large part of the Colombelles factory district against moderate opposition.

Taking into consideration all the varying factors, operations had up till now developed according to plan, and could be regarded as satisfactory. Thus at midday Second Army was able to issue the following situation report:—

> "At dawn probably the heaviest and most concentrated air assault ever launched in support of a military operation took place. Over 1,500 heavy bombers and nearly 600 mediums blasted a gap 7,000 yards wide through which a powerful armoured and infantry attack was launched. At 0745 hours, 8 Corps, with one armoured division up, attacked southwards with infantry of 2 Canadian Corps and 1 Corps attacking on each flank. The armoured division moved very fast, and was followed rapidly by two more. By midday, strong armoured formations of 8 Corps had advanced nearly seven miles to the south and had broken through the main German defences. The infantry on either flank were engaged in mopping up the Colombelles factory and the villages between Caen and Troarn. 83 Group P.A.F., with the assistance

of units of 9 U.S.A.A.F., gave magnificent support throughout the morning, attacking in particular gun positions and movement in the battle area."

This report exhibits great optimism, but unfortunately at the time that it was being penned the situation was changing, for the losses being sustained by the tanks proved in no uncertain fashion that, far from a break-through of the main enemy defences having taken place, the German defenders in areas over-run but not yet mopped up were fast recovering from the stupor occasioned by the bombing attacks. Moreover, the penetration of over seven miles achieved by 11 Armoured Division had not failed to stimulate the inevitable enemy counter measures, which by noon were beginning to be felt at their full effect. If the left flank at the start had seemed the more troublesome, by midday most danger, without doubt, came on the right and centre of the advance from the area of the Bourguebus ridge, which completely dominated the ground over-run by the armour. At this juncture, too, the chain of enemy strong points in the shape of the villages of Soliers, Bras, Hubert Folie, Four and Bourguebus by-passed by the armour, but not reduced, since sufficient infantry was not yet available, gathered heart from the delay imposed on the British tanks and began to inflict considerable casualties on them in their exposed positions in open country. Roving bands of enemy tanks, mainly "Panthers," and self-propelled guns started to appear working in troops of two or three, or even on occasion singly, and making effective use of their superior range from positions cleverly concealed among the débris of the bomb-smashed villages or the occasional clump of trees. Thus, to quote only the experience of one armoured regiment between 1130 hours and midday: "2 Fife and Forfar Yeomanry reported a 'Panther' on the left flank beyond Four and heavy fire from enemy tanks and guns in Frenouville which had pinned down its left squadron. It was ordered to try to disengage from Frenouville, which would be dealt with by 5 Guards Armoured Brigade, and to push on past Bourguebus towards Tilly la Campagne. This, however, was not possible, and 2 Fife and Forfar Yeomanry continued to report determined opposition by enemy tanks, four of which were moving south-east from Frenouville, four were camouflaged in a position 1,000 yards south-east of Bourguebus, while a little later four 'Panthers' moved into Bourguebus from the south-east, followed 15 minutes later by eight more tanks thought to be 'Tigers.' In the face of all this opposition, 2 Fife and Forfar Yeomanry found it quite impossible to advance any further south from its present position." Of the original 50 tanks of this regiment by the end of this particular action only 18 were mustered. A similar tale was to be told by 3 Royal Tank Regiment on the right, but 23 Hussars attempting to screen Cagny and Four from positions slightly to the west, suffered somewhat fewer losses, though these were indeed heavy enough.

Thus by midday 29 Armoured Brigade having advanced nearly 12,000 yards from the start line was halted, counter-attacked and firmly held by enemy tanks and anti-tank guns, sited either on commanding ground or in mutually supporting strong points which had escaped the effects of the preliminary air and artillery bombardments. The answer, in fact, both to the successful early break-out and subsequent slow-down and halting of the armour, is provided by an examination of the results of the bombing. Let us therefore now turn to this.

From the enemy point of view the morning had proved a difficult one, for the Allied bombing effort provided, while it lasted, problems which were quite beyond the power of the German High Command to solve. Reading captured records, it is clear that from the foremost enemy positions down to the first railway leading from Caen to Troarn the defences were effectively neutralised even though no H.E. bombs were used. The bombing was sufficiently accurate and intense to keep the Germans quiet, and the armour seemed to them to arrive "before the dust had settled." It seems from the German evidence that fragmentation bombing can secure effective neutralisation if the ground forces can follow up within an hour to an hour and a half, and in a letter on 21st July to the Fuehrer, Field-Marshal von Kluge wrote the following vivid description of the results of this bombing of his troops:—

> "My discussion yesterday with the commanders of the formations in the Caen sector has afforded regrettable evidence that, in face of the enemy's complete command of the air, there is no way by which we can find a strategy which will counter-balance its actually annihilating effect unless we give up the field of battle. Whole armoured formations allotted to the counter-attack were caught in bomb-carpets of the greatest intensity, so that they could be got out of the torn-up ground only by prolonged effort and in some cases only by dragging them out. The actual result was that they arrived too late.
>
> The psychological effect of such a mass of bombs coming down with all the power of elemental nature on the fighting troops, especially the infantry, is a factor which has to be given especially serious consideration. It is immaterial whether such a bomb carpet catches good troops or bad, they are more or less annihilated. If that occurs frequently, then the power of endurance of the forces is put to the highest test. In fact it becomes dormant and dies."

This summing-up by von Kluge explains why 29 Armoured Brigade was able to penetrate through the expendable infantry and through the immediate armoured reserves down to the second railway with little or no trouble. The "Mark IV" tanks of 21 Panzer Division were never brought effectively into action during the morning and one company of 503 Heavy Tank Battalion in Emieville was badly hit by the H.E. bombardment of the R.A.F. At least four of its "Tiger" tanks were put out of action and others were immobilised for a considerable time because of the difficulty of negotiating the heavily cratered ground. Sufficient tanks of this battalion, however, did survive and, moving round the flank of the bombed area were able to establish themselves in Cagny, which had also been a target for Bomber Command and had been squarely hit. The infantry there had been severely shaken and was only able to offer light resistance when attacked by Guards Armoured Division later in the evening of 18th July. There would, indeed, have been little trouble from Cagny at all, had not this company of "Tigers" been able to move in there during the morning, for it was these tanks which caused such trouble to 29 Armoured Brigade when it tried to push south from the second railway.

It has been pointed out that every village along the axis of advance was strongly held by infantry and anti-tank guns. The bombing programme had provided for most of them to be hit with fragmentation bombs, and the general pattern of this bombing was good, but owing to some extraordinary bad luck, certain vital areas were missed. In the case of Grentheville for example, the western half of the village was hit, but the eastern flank was almost untouched. In Soliers the same thing happened; 3 Royal Tank Regiment passing west of the village got through unscathed, but 2 Fife and Forfar Yeomanry trying to by-pass the village to the east, came under the heavy fire referred to above, from defences which the bombing had missed. On the other flank of the penetration, in both Frenouville and La Hogue the reverse occurred, it was the eastern half of each village that was hit, and the defences on the western fringe from which the attacking armour could be engaged, somehow survived.

The result was that as 29 Armoured Brigade pushed south-westwards from the Caen-Vimont railway, it ran into an area which had vital spots unneutralised by the bombing and beyond the range of the supporting guns, and the delay imposed by the anti-tank defences in these villages gave the enemy time to move into the battle the tanks of 1 SS Panzer Division.

The problem of dealing with these villages was, moreover, complicated by the intensity of the fire which the enemy was able to bring down from his array of flak and field artillery and nebelwerfers on the Bourguebus ridge and in the woods east of La Hogue. This gun area had not been touched by the bombing and its infantry positions, held by the six battalions of 1 SS Panzer Division, were similarly intact.

These infantry battalions did not attempt to counter-attack or even to move forward during 18th July, but stayed firmly in their positions between the River Laize and Vimont. However, the "Panther" battalion of 1 SS Panzer Division, which had been stationed around Rouvres, moved through these infantry positions during the morning, and was in a position to engage the leading tanks of 29 Armoured Brigade about noon, while the British armour was still heavily involved in dealing with the infantry and anti-tank guns in the villages between Bourguebus and the Caen-Vimont railway. 1 SS Panzer Division had actually been alerted on the afternoon of 17th July but, because the direction of the main thrust was not known, its "Panther" battalion was not moved forward. On the morning of 18th July, however, when the pattern of the bombing revealed the general intention, Sepp Dietrich ordered Brigadefuehrer Wisch, commanding the division, to send his "Panther" battalion to the Bourguebus area. The Germans evidently did not expect this battalion to become involved too early, and just after midday, when Wisch discovered that British tanks had almost reached Bourguebus, he ordered his armour back behind the infantry positions of 1 SS Panzer Division. This order was, in fact, intercepted over the wireless by the 2 Canadian Corps Special Wireless Section, together with the reply to Wisch, which stated that the withdrawal of these tanks could not take place, since they were already too heavily engaged. They were, moreover, by this time being so harassed by Typhoons that their freedom of tactical manœuvre was strictly limited. It was, unfortunately, their dominating position and superior range which counted most.

The arrival of the "Panthers" from 1 SS Panzer Division at a moment when the foremost elements of 8 Corps had smashed through the first belt of enemy defences, penetrated, but not subdued the second, and had yet to come up against the third and fourth, marked however, the end of the period of swift advance by the British armour, which by early afternoon had suffered heavy losses. Nevertheless 29 Armoured Brigade stood firm, and though the tanks which had succeeded in crossing the Hubert-Folie-Bourguebus-La Hogue road had either been knocked out or forced to withdraw, a strong counter attack by "Panthers," supported by self-propelled guns from Le Poirier, Four Soliers, Bourguebus, Bras, Hubert Folie and Cormelles, on 2 Fife and Forfar Yeomanry and 3 Royal Tank Regiment at 1300 hours was decisively repulsed with the aid of 23 Hussars and rocket-carrying Typhoon aircraft, and a number of "Panthers" were destroyed. At the same time Grentheville was beginning to be cleared, yielding many prisoners from 21 Panzer Division and also some nebelwerfers intact.

It was now clear that new measures would have to be undertaken, if the divisional objectives were to be achieved, and the Corps Commander therefore held a conference with the commanders of 7 and 11 Armoured Divisions, as a result of which a plan was made to continue the thrust towards Hubert-Folie, La Hogue and the Bourguebus ridge by both 29 and 22 Armoured Brigades, the latter now to come up on the right of the advance. Had this increased armoured strength been brought to bear it is possible that the enemy might have been forced off the greatly-desired Bourguebus feature, but so much depended on getting 7 Armoured Division quickly through the corridor and movement here was becoming increasingly difficult owing to opposition on the flanks, particularly to the east.

The clearance of this flank by 3 British Division had been held up owing to an error in bombing. The R.A.F. had been asked to attack Touffreville, Sannerville and Banneville, and to use H.E., since cratering was acceptable in this area, but on account of the danger to British troops, Bomber Command decided not to take Touffreville as an aiming point. The result was that this village was not hit at all, and when 3 British Division attacked, there was a hard fight, and armour which by-passed it had considerable trouble with craters south of the village. Thus the enemy in Sannerville and Banneville had time to recover from the shock of the bombing and the "Tigers" of 503 Tank Battalion were able to move west to Cagny. These tanks—together with the 88 mm. guns in this area— now established an anti-tank screen on this flank from La Hogue, through Frenouville, to Emieville and Troarn.

Although throughout the day 1 Corps generally made progress, it could by no means be described as speedy, whilst on the opposite flank Demouville was not finally reduced by 3 Monmouthshire Regiment and 2 Northamptonshire Yeomanry until 1530 hours, nor Giberville taken by the Canadians until later in the afternoon. 22 Armoured Brigade of 7 Armoured Division was, therefore, much held up, and did not, in fact, begin to deploy on the right of 29 Armoured Brigade until the early evening.

Meanwhile, when the new plan began to be implemented it was found that 2 Fife and Forfar Yeomanry, in view of the aggressive intentions of the enemy, was not strong enough to permit 23 Hussars to move over to the right and, with 3 Royal Tank Regiment, to attack Hubert Folie and Bourguebus astride the railway, since thereby the centre of the front would be exposed. At 1425 hours this fact was reported to Headquarters 29 Armoured Brigade, and twenty minutes later a renewed counter-attack by enemy armour in some strength caused fresh casualties both to 23 Hussars and 2 Fife and Forfar Yeomanry. Nor was 3 Royal Tank Regiment in any better situation, for in its uncomfortable position overlooked from both the south and west it was now also subjected to a sharp counter-attack from both Hubert Folie and Bourguebus, lost several more tanks, and by 1530 hours had been forced to withdraw some 500 yards to a position west of Soliers, where it was told to hang on as long as possible. At about this time, too, the remnants of 2 Fife and Forfar Yeomanry were withdrawn north of the Caen-Vimont railway to reorganise.

The enemy was therefore temporarily in the ascendant, and in order to meet this threat from the south-east 2 Northamptonshire Yeomanry was placed under command of 29 Armoured Brigade and ordered up to the vicinity of Brigade Tac Headquarters at the railway bridge north-west of Grentheville, where two troops of 119/75 Anti-Tank Battery were also deployed in defensive positions.

Rocket Typhoons during this time carried out extensive attacks on enemy armour in the Bourguebus area, but despite these (which must have caused considerable damage and casualties) 3 Royal Tank Regiment continued to be heavily engaged, beating off tank attacks at 1545 and 1615 hours. This regiment managed, however, to hold its ground west of Soliers in spite of losses, and claimed to have knocked out several "Panthers."

About 1670 hours reports were received of a large body of enemy tanks— 20-30 in all—moving towards the battlefield from Secqueville-la-Campagne, whilst at the same time others were reported to be withdrawing from Soliers and La Hogue to the east. Some form of concentration was presumably being attempted, for patrols from the Inns of Court Regiment reported that La Hogue was thereby lightly held by infantry only, whilst Bourguebus, badly damaged by the Typhoon attacks, was apparently clear. However, the situation at 1720 hours was unchanged for the enemy still held on firmly to the Bras-Hubert Folie-Bourguebus feature, and had managed to infiltrate a few tanks into Soliers, whilst the positions of 29 Armoured Brigade had not been materially altered—3 Royal Tank Regiment being mainly between Bras and Soliers with some elements forward nearly to Hubert Folie; 23 Hussars in an area between Grentheville, Le Poirier and Four, and 2 Northamptonshire Yeomanry, which had now arrived, had one squadron held up 1,000 yards in front of Bras and along the Caen-Vimont railway at a point where the embankment is about 15 feet high.

The situation with 29 Armoured Brigade depleted in strength and on ground dominated by the enemy was, if not precarious, at least difficult, and at all costs it was necessary now to bring up infantry to establish a firm base for the armour. Accordingly 159 Infantry Brigade handed over Demouville to 51 (Highland) Division and moved forward to establish a firm position around Le Mesnil Frementel, which by 1945 hours had been accomplished.

While 29 Armoured Brigade was undergoing this fiery ordeal, Guards Armoured Division could hardly be said to be faring better. In the early afternoon, 1 Armoured Coldstream Guards had managed to skirt the south-western edge of Cagny and was pushing on towards Frenouville and Le Poirier, but its companions in 5 Guards Armoured Brigade were unable to make similar progress, and had been held on the northern outskirts of the village and about half a mile to the east of it. Heavy fighting went on all afternoon, but towards 1800 hours the Grenadiers had succeeded in entering Cagny, closely followed by two battalions of 32 Guards Brigade. By 1930 hours this troublesome strongpoint had been cleared and a large number of prisoners taken, again mainly from 16 G.A.F. Division and 21 Panzer Division, but including a few from 12 SS Panzer Division. Meanwhile, 1 Armoured Coldstream Guards attempted to capture Le Poirier, but was beaten back, and the regiment was finally halted close to the railway and due south of Cagny, by heavy anti-tank fire from Frenouville and the woods to the north-east. No further advance was made, and when darkness fell it was apparent that Guards Armoured Division was facing a strong anti-tank screen. Upon the subsequent interrogation of the enemy commanders in this sector, the story which emerged of the German efforts to hold Guards Armoured Division is interesting, and illustrative of how narrow was the margin for success with which either side had to contend during "Goodwood." It has been seen how, except for one company, the "Tiger" tanks of 503 Heavy Tank Battalion had survived the early morning bombing. These tanks had thereafter first moved into Cagny, but later been withdrawn, and in conjunction with the 88 mm. flak guns already in the area, had established an anti-tank screen which stretched from La Hogue northwards to Frenouville and thence further north still to Emieville and Troarn. It was this which was now proving a stumbling block to the Guards, though actually the multiple gunfire pouring from it made the enemy appear stronger on the ground than in reality he was. By day the "Tigers" and the 88 mm. guns were able to command the area and destroy any British tank which ventured to come within range, but by night it might have been quite another story, for the Germans were so short of infantry that once Cagny was taken, a gap existed in their defences, and there was little to prevent a thrust, under cover of darkness, from reaching Vimont. This opportunity naturally could not be known to Guards Armoured Division nor, for that matter, had it sufficient infantry for this purpose. The fact remains, however, that Sepp Dietrich was so uncertain of the whole situation on his right flank that when 12 SS Panzer Division was moved into the vicinity of Argences during the evening of 18th July, it was organised into battle groups holding the commanding ground *east* of the River Nuance. Not for another twenty-four hours was this division brought forward to provide adequate infantry support for the gun-line already established.

Towards 1800 hours 22 Armoured Brigade had begun to appear on the scene between 5 Guards Armoured Brigade and 29 Armoured Brigade, with 5 Royal Tank Regiment leading and directed on La Hogue via Four. 29 Armoured Brigade was ordered to conform with this move, but 3 Royal Tank Regiment, now its most forward unit, was by this time running short of ammunition, and since no echelon vehicles could be brought up to replenish the tanks, it was impossible to advance any further. Nor was 23 Hussars on the right any happier, for in the face of counter-attack by tanks, by 1900 hours almost the whole of this regiment had been forced north of the Caen-Vimont railway, whilst more enemy armour had infiltrated back into Soliers. The situation was thus becoming more threatening still. The surviving tanks of 2 Fife and Forfar Yeomanry, by now reorganised, were accordingly assembled immediately to the east of Tac Headquarters 29 Armoured Brigade, and a heavy concentration of all guns within range put down on to Soliers. In spite of this, within an hour, yet another sortie from here by a combined force of "Tigers" and "Panthers" had to be halted by 3 Royal Tank Regiment, as was a further attempt about 2145 hours. This latter effort was led by a Sherman, presumably captured in one of the earlier battles, but the manœuvre was unsuccessful, for it was the first to be destroyed, quickly followed by several more "Panthers," and the remnants then withdrew southwards. Only one further sally was made, at about 2240 hours, in the late dusk, but the visibility by then was very poor and the enemy did not press his attack.

By 2300 hours the front generally was quiet, and all three divisions began to organise their positions for the night, as well as to take stock of the battle so far. It had proved a hard and exhausting experience, particularly for 11 Armoured Division, for when the tank casualties came to be reckoned, the full severity of the struggle could be appreciated, since it was found to have suffered a loss of no less than 126 tanks of all types, practically half its total fighting strength, whilst Guards Armoured Division had also had over 60 knocked out. Many of these, it is true, were successfully recovered and in action again on the morrow, and it was heartening to know that casualties in men had been comparatively light. The following figures were actually reported for the fighting of 18th July, which shows that in comparison with the Odon fighting the rate was much lower.

	Casualties of all types
Guards Armoured Division	137
7 Armoured Division	48
11 Armoured Division	336
	521

The losses inflicted on the enemy, too, were by no means to be discounted, for many had perished in the bombing and the heavy fighting throughout the day, whilst over twelve hundred prisoners had passed through the Corps cage by nightfall. Much enemy armour had likewise ended its career on the battlefield.

8 Corps was still, however, in a most exposed position, still in a re-entrant, and still entirely dependant on the Orne bridges for supply, a fact which had not escaped the enemy. As a result, a fresh tribulation was in store for the Corps, for at 2330 hours the Luftwaffe carried out a sharp attack on the bridges and, preceded by flares, dropped a heavy concentration of bombs aimed at the troops in transit. No damage was sustained either by the Orne bridges or 131 Infantry Brigade of 7 Armoured Division which was crossing them at the time, but the echelons of 29 Armoured Brigade assembled to the east received a large number of casualties, particularly among the replacement tank crews who, having already had the good fortune to survive when their tanks had been knocked out in action earlier in the day, now had the bad luck to suffer more in this rear area than in the armoured battle from which they had emerged unscathed. Main Headquarters 11 Armoured Division, which had reorganised in its original bridgehead location, also had some killed and wounded in this raid and the main wireless link to Corps Headquarters was destroyed, being temporarily replaced by the Corps Commander's "charger" tank from his mobile Tac Headquarters on loan until a new R/T link could be provided. After this, however, there was peace, no more incidents took place in the hours of darkness, and the three armoured divisions were able to complete their final preparations for a renewal of the struggle on the morrow.

The enemy, too, was not idle, and if he had scant idea of the happenings on his right flank, at least he was fully in the picture as to what was going on elsewhere, and acted accordingly. It was the limit of the 8 Corps penetration which received the most attention, for against this, the panzer grenadiers of 1 SS Panzer Division hitherto positioned holding the line Fontenay-le-Marmion-Garcelles Secqueville-Chicheboville, were moved to take over the defence of the chain of village strongpoints around Bourguebus, relieving the elements of 21 Panzer Division which by now had been fought to a standstill. Thus by the morning of 19th July the villages of Bras, Hubert Folie, Bourguebus, Soliers, Four and La Hogue were all garrisoned not by the tired remnants of the previous day's fighting, but by fresh SS troops with tanks in close support.

On the fronts of 1 Corps and 2 Canadian Corps, during the afternoon and evening, a further degree of progress was made, though it could not be called either fast or entirely as planned, for the enemy resisted tenaciously wherever attacked. 3 British Division continued to drive towards Troarn, but the country was very difficult and though fighting lasted into the early hours of 19th July, at 0145 hours the nearest troops were still three or four hundred yards from the town, whilst further north 51 (Highland) Division was held up in the woods east of Touffreville. On the opposite flank, 3 Canadian Division after some heavy engagements had cleared practically the whole of the Colombelles factory area, and 2 Canadian Division had established a small bridgehead over the River Orne in Vaucelles itself, to the west of which it was attacking Louvigny.

Second Army was therefore able to issue the following less exuberant but more balanced summary of operations during the afternoon and up to midnight of the first day of " Goodwood " : —

> "During the afternoon, our rapid advance of the morning was slowed up by stiffening enemy opposition and the need for moving forward infantry units to assist the armour. The air forces continued to give magnificent support for the remainder of the day, a record number of sorties being flown. Infantry had got a small bridgehead over the River Orne in Faubourg-de-Vaucelles, were attacking Louvigny, and were clearing the factory area. A heavy counter attack on Giberville was beaten off, and approximately 500 prisoners captured. Enemy counter attacks with tanks developed against our own armour, which had been forced to take up positions in the area Bras-Bourguebus-Grentheville. A strong anti-tank screen between Frenouville and Emieville halted the armoured thrust in the direction of Vimont. The infantry on the left were established as far south as Cuillerville. The drive towards Troarn continues."

19th July

The Corps intention for 19th July was in no wise changed, for it was clearly impossible to stay in the awkward and exposed salient so far achieved. At all costs the commanding ground before which 8 Corps was spread as in a diorama must be occupied, Vaucelles captured, and the pocket of enemy liquidated which was still holding out in the triangle between Louvigny, Colombelles and Bourguebus. The plan remained, therefore, for the armoured divisions to push on to their objectives, whilst 2 Canadian Corps opened the routes from Caen through the suburbs on the east bank of the Orne, and 1 Corps continued operations against Troarn.

The morning dawned dull and overcast and at 0600 hours 2 Northamptonshire Yeomanry began to reconnoitre south along the line of the railway, but the guns along the Bourguebus were as wakeful and watchful as hitherto and repulsed the attempt. Shortly afterwards a fairly sharp counter attack was launched against 3 Royal Tank Regiment from the region of Bras and Hubert Folie, and as a result this regiment was withdrawn to a position between the railway and the Caen-Vimont road. Following this, however, there were no incidents of any importance for some time, though there were several reports of the Germans digging-in. It appeared that the enemy was not offensively inclined, but that he intended to cling on firmly in his prepared positions and resist any further expansion southwards.

So far as the armoured divisions were concerned, General Roberts of 11 Armoured Division had early informed his neighbour, 7 Armoured Division, that the reorganisation necessary in 29 Armoured Brigade would prevent much in the way of offensive action being undertaken for the first few hours of daylight, and in fact along the central front little took place other than extensive probing and reconnaissance. At this juncture, in view of the reports of generally renewed enemy strength, the fact that German reserves were not only intact but probably increased by the arrival in the Falaise area of an additional panzer division, and as air photographs taken from 16th July onwards had shown the development of a new defensive system ahead between Laize le Val and Roquancourt, the Corps Commander decided that before there was any question of a resumption of the general drive to the south, it was first necessary to capture the string of village strongpoints and above all the dominating Bourguebus ridge.

At 1200 hours General O'Connor held a conference at Tac Headquarters 11 Armoured Division and issued orders on the basis of a revised plan, the gist of which was:

(a) At 1600 hours 11 Armoured Division would undertake the difficult task of reducing Bras on its eminence, despite the line of 88 mm. guns backing it, and thereafter its satellite village, Hubert Folie.

(b) Guards Armoured Division was to attack Le Poirier at 1700 hours, and exploit towards Frenouville but not to attempt further operations towards Vimont.

(c) At 1700 hours the comparatively fresh 7 Armoured Division had the major rôle of completing the capture of Soliers and then advancing against Four and Bourguebus. Subsequently, if conditions were favourable, exploitation towards Verrieres would be attempted.

All these attacks were to have full artillery support.

While these moves were in progress, the ground over-run would be cleared of any remaining enemy pockets and contact established with the Canadian troops on the right as soon as they had taken Vaucelles. In this manner the whole corner position of Second Army would be, to use a favourite phrase of the Commander-in-Chief, "tidied up," and become a firm base for whatever further operations might be contemplated in this sector.

This three-pronged drive was completely successful, though as might be expected, Bourguebus proved the toughest nut to crack, and was not ultimately entered until the following morning. However, 2 Northamptonshire Yeomanry moved off from south of Cormelles at 1600 hours, supported by 8 Rifle Brigade and twenty minutes later, after a sharp preliminary artillery bombardment, the leading tanks had arrived at the western outskirts of Bras, where heavy fire from the south-west, which caused some considerable casualties, held them up. Accordingly, 3 Royal Tank Regiment, which was waiting for the fall of Bras before beginning its own assault on Hubert Folie, was ordered to attack from the east. This manœuvre took the enemy by surprise, for by 1640 hours it had pierced the defences, the village was entered and by 1710 hours the armour had passed right through to make contact with 2 Northamptonshire Yeomanry on the south-west side. Bras had been strongly held by at least a battalion of SS infantry from 1 SS Panzer Division, well dug-in and reinforced by anti-tank guns. Moreover, these troops were entirely fresh, for during the night they had relieved the tired and depleted panzer grenadiers of 21 Panzer Division and, as might be expected of soldiers of the Fuehrer's bodyguard, they fought bravely. However, owing to the speed with which 8 Rifle Brigade followed 3 Royal Tank Regiment into the village, they had little time to collect themselves. Some came out of their slit trenches with grenades in their hands and were rapidly dealt with; elsewhere inside the built-up area there were still machine gun posts and snipers holding out, and they, too, were speedily mopped up; a mass effort to escape to the south-west by some 50-100 Germans provided a good shoot both to the troops beating the village and to 3 Royal Tank Regiment on the outskirts. By 1800 hours, only forty-five minutes after the riflemen had entered it, Bras was reported clear of enemy, very few of whom can have succeeded in escaping. This little action is not only almost of textbook perfection, but the prize thereby won was of the utmost importance to the Corps. One entire battalion of 1 SS Panzer Grenadier Regiment had been utterly destroyed at small cost, but more important still, a vital link in the chain of enemy fortified villages dominating the area occupied by 8 Corps had been seized, for Bras is situated on a spur overlooking the whole of the north-east, and its capture was the first step towards neutralising the value of the Bourguebus ridge to the enemy. The Army Commander directed, in view of its importance, that it was to be firmly held against possible counter attack, pending arrangements to be made for 2 Canadian Corps to take it over, and 159 Infantry Brigade, which was in process of moving up towards the area, was ordered to provide the garrison. Finally, about 1800 hours, 3 Monmouthshire Regiment arrived, and relieved 8 Rifle Brigade inside this village.

Meanwhile, no time was being lost, for 2 Northamptonshire Yeomanry moved forward at 1810 hours against Hubert Folie under supporting fire from field and medium guns. Shortly after the attack started, a report was received which stated that 22 Armoured Brigade had already occupied this place, and a halt was called to verify the truth of this. By 1830 hours the information had been proved to be false, but during this period enemy " Tiger " tanks had inflicted several new losses on the already weak squadrons of this regiment, and it was therefore decided, that 2 Fife and Forfar Yeomanry should now carry out this operation. At 2000 hours, preceded by a ten-minute barrage, and themselves heavily mortared and shelled en route, tanks of this unit, followed by a company from 8 Rifle Brigade, advanced against Hubert Folie and entered it against light opposition at 2035 hours. They were joined there at 2145 hours by 4 King's Shropshire Light Infantry from 159 Infantry Brigade, the remaining battalion of which was also brought into a reserve position behind Bras and Hubert Folie, where, in conjunction with 23 Hussars, effective support could be provided against any enemy counter measures. It was now possible to withdraw the remaining regiments of 29 Armoured Brigade from the line and to concentrate them for the night north of Grentheville. Continuously in action as the spearhead of the whole operation from the very start, the brigade was by now very tired, and if 19th July had not been so costly as the previous day, nevertheless 65 tanks had been knocked out in the fighting, and of these 37 belonged to 2 Northamptonshire Yeomanry. The participation of 29 Armoured Brigade in " Goodwood " proved, however, now to be at an end, for at the moment when withdrawal of its units from the line had been completed, information was received from Second Army that the area held by 11 Armoured Division was to be taken over on the following day by Canadian infantry, and 29 Armoured Brigade would then pass into reserve. This was, in fact, the first move of a progressive take over by infantry from the armour of 8 Corps.

Elsewhere on the Corps front satisfactory progress had also been made. Guards Armoured Division was holding a difficult sector, for early morning reconnaissance confirmed previous reports of the strength of the enemy position east of Cagny. 1 Armoured Coldstream Guards and 2 Armoured Irish Guards by midday had not been able to advance in the direction of Emieville or along the railway towards Frenouville, so that an infantry attack was made by 3 Irish Guards from 32 Guards Brigade in Cagny, supported by 2 Armoured Grenadier Guards and this achieved a limited advance, clearing the orchards north-east of Frenouville in so doing. This was, however, all that could be done, for east of this position the enemy gun line was too strong to be pierced. Later in the afternoon 1 Welsh Guards attacked Le Poirier, which was still holding out, though virtually surrounded, and after sharp fighting, by 1800 hours had subdued it. During the remaining hours of daylight several prowling "Panther" tanks were destroyed, but otherwise the enemy was content to remain in possession of his main position, into which, by now, the infantry of 12 SS Panzer Division had been moved as a reinforcement. No further incidents took place that night. Guards Armoured Division remained firmly in position around Cagny, and an attack on Frenouville, with air support, was planned for the first light on 20th July.

For 7 Armoured Division, 19th July was really the first time that its full strength could be employed in the operation, for it was not until dawn on this day that its last units had crossed over the River Orne and were getting clear of the bridgehead area. 131 Infantry Brigade was early ordered to move forward to the area of Demouville, but was dogged, as hitherto, by traffic congestion, and could only make slow progress. However, by 1100 hours, 1/5 Queen's Royal Regiment was immediately north of Cuverville and by this time General Erskine, commanding the division, had decided to make Grentheville a firm base for 22 Armoured Brigade, the leading tanks of which were now in action against Soliers and Four. These villages were still firmly and indeed aggressively held, for just after 0700 hours a sharp sortie on 5 Royal Tank Regiment by "Tigers" from Four had to be beaten off, whilst "Panthers" to the east also gave considerable trouble during the morning. In addition, there was heavy enemy shelling generally, and all efforts to enter Four were unsuccessful. Against Soliers, however, matters progressed better and by 1120 hours one squadron of tanks had succeeded in getting through the defences, and together with a company from 1 Rifle Brigade was engaged in mopping up inside the built-up area.

After the midday conference held by the Corps Commander at Tac Headquarters 11 Armoured Division, the task of 7 Armoured Division was slightly altered, and the main effort was now directed against Bourguebus, which had proved so tough a proposition on the previous day. During the early afternoon, therefore, a certain amount of reorganisation was undertaken, and by "H" Hour—1700 hours—all was ready for a resumption of the offensive. 5 Royal Tank Regiment, using Soliers as a base, moved south against Bourguebus, starting well against moderate opposition. Enemy resistance soon stiffened, but by 1840 hours one squadron had reached the outskirts, where a mixed force of "Panthers" and "Tigers" caused much trouble (though it lost a satisfactory number of tanks in the process) as did supporting fire from La Hogue and the woods to the south. By 2040 hours Bourguebus had been invested on three sides, but the enemy to the south-east in La Hogue was a great nuisance, though after an air "strike" was put in at 2155 hours this sector quietened down considerably. As a result of this attack, 5 Royal Tank Regiment was able to get within 200 yards of the Bourguebus-La Hogue road about half-way between the two villages, but failed to capture Bourguebus itself.

Meanwhile, 1 Royal Tank Regiment, assisted by a company of 1 Rifle Brigade, by 2100 hours had finally succeeded after heavy fighting in taking Four.

The ground fighting generally over the area of operations was hampered by the unusual phenomenon of a "circus" of about 30 enemy fighter-bombers, which was active south and east of Caen during the afternoon and evening. A number of air attacks were made, including one on Headquarters 159 Infantry Brigade, which was machine-gunned by 18 Messerschmitts. Fortunately very little success attended any of these raids.

Thus by last light all objectives set for the day by General O'Connor had been achieved, with the exception of one village—Bourguebus—which, however, was virtually encircled and in any case at long last effectively neutralised. Although only a short advance had been made on the Corps front, the ground was of great tactical importance, and the situation of 8 Corps at last light was considerably improved when compared with that obtaining at the start of the day. The positions won had, however, entailed heavy fighting, and even during the morning, when the reorganisation and "sorting out" process was in hand, there was a steady toll of casualties in men and tanks, though happily not on the scale of the previous day. The figures reported (which included some "left over" from 18th July) were:—

Guards Armoured Division	33
7 Armoured Division	67
11 Armoured Division	399
	499

From the German point of view, losses had remained high, for the ground gained continued to yield a most satisfactory bag of enemy prisoners. During the day another 1,000 passed through the Corps cage, making a total so far of 47 officers and 2,138 other ranks for Operation "Goodwood," whilst at least 60 enemy tanks were known to have been knocked out in the course of the fighting as well as a large number of guns of all calibres. The capture of a strength return of 1 SS Panzer Grenadier Regiment provided most cheering and significant confirmation of the progressive whittling down of enemy resources, for in this the effective battle strength was shown to be down to nearly 37 per cent. of its establishment. It was felt that if this state of affairs existed already in the crack "Adolf Hitler" SS Division, what must be the fate of lesser favoured formations?

On the front of 2 Canadian Corps, the capture of Vaucelles and the push along the east bank of the River Orne, resulting in a link-up with 11 Armoured Division, had provided the most substantial progress achieved elsewhere, for 1 Corps was still almost stalled in its drive on Troarn. The following summary of operations during 19th July issued by Second Army soon after midnight reflects the condition now generally felt, as a result of the changed character of the fighting and also, perhaps unconsciously, foreshadows the withdrawal of the armoured corps, 8 Corps, from further battle east of the River Orne:—

"Our position south of Caen was greatly strengthened to-day by the capture of Vaucelles from the east and north, and the establishment of a strong infantry bridgehead south of the town. Bridges were built in Caen and routes through Vaucelles were completed. The armour fought all the morning against strongly defended villages, where enemy tanks, anti-tank guns, and infantry resisted fiercely. Progress was slow. On the east, after fierce fighting all the morning, our troops were on the outskirts of Troarn, but not in the town.

The bridgehead south of Caen was extended and our position strengthened after heavy fighting during the afternoon. Infantry attacking along the east bank of the River Orne captured the high ground overlooking St. Andre-sur-Orne. A line of village strongpoints had held up our armour all the morning, but during the afternoon six of these were captured by armoured formations with infantry leading.

Enemy anti-tank guns and tanks in carefully selected ground has resulted in slow progress by armoured formations and forced their infantry into the lead."

20th July

The date, 20th July, is one which will long be remembered in German history, for on it occurred the first open manifestation of opposition by Germans to the policy of their Fuehrer. This took the form of an attempt to seize power by a dissident section of the Officer Corps through the agency of a military revolt in the capital city of Berlin. Although unsuccessful at the time, its immediate repercussions were widespread, affecting leading commanders on all the far-flung battlefronts, and in the end it proved fatally weakening.

In contrast with the momentous events taking place in Germany, 20th July on the battlefield south of Caen was almost quiet, for both sides were largely consolidating their positions, though 8 Corps made a number of local advances. It was clear, however, that the maximum value had now been extracted from Operation "Goodwood," and that any further advance south would primarily be an infantry task, for each successive batch of air photographs showed increasing activity behind the forward enemy positions. The already formidable defences through which 8 Corps had broken were being duplicated further south, and if the ground was not so favourable to the enemy as the commanding heights around Bourguebus, nevertheless its very flatness at least ensured that his always highly successful 88 mm. guns would continue to be able to exploit their markedly superior range. There was also much digging by infantry to be observed up to several miles to the south, and reports from patrols, O.P.s and forward troops, as well as from prisoners, corroborated the evidence of the air photographs that the enemy was building up in considerable strength in front of the Corps position.

The Corps intentions for the day were:—

(a) To complete the capture of Bourguebus.

(b) To hold the present positions with two infantry brigades forward, backed up by a third, together with one armoured brigade and divisional artillery in support.

The remaining two armoured brigades were to rest.

At first light 5 Royal Tank Regiment renewed the assault on Bourguebus and, after a spirited encounter with a "Tiger" tank which was destroyed, entered the village. This was found to be deserted except for some abandoned "Panther" tanks, and infantry was therefore immediately brought up to garrison it. At about this time 4 County of London Yeomanry succeeded in getting forward between Bras and Hubert Folie, cutting the main Caen-Falaise road in the process, and carried out a successful minor mopping up operation in the neighbourhood of Beauvoir Ferme by 1000 hours, engaging a force of about eight "Mark IV." enemy tanks in so doing. This managed to slip away over the hill, but the Corps artillery was called on, and as a result the medium guns had a most successful shoot, knocking out all eight. In addition, 4 County of London Yeomanry had a bag of nearly 100 prisoners from 1 SS Panzer Division, four nebelwerfers, one 88 mm. and one 75 mm. self-propelled gun, all intact, and two "Tiger" and seven other tanks of various types knocked out. It was a most heartening beginning to the day.

Whilst this activity was in progress, the relief of 159 Infantry Brigade on the right was also going on, a counter-attack by seven Tigers on Bras being beaten off with loss of three in the process. The relief by the Canadians being complete by midday, 159 Infantry Brigade then took up positions in reserve and came under temporary command of 7 Armoured Division. 29 Armoured Brigade, of course, was already concentrated in a reserve position west of Grentheville and was not affected by any of these moves.

In the sector of Guards Armoured Division at 0545 hours after a preliminary "strike" by the R.A.F., 5 Coldstream Guards and 1 Welsh Guards supported by artillery, attacked Frenouville, from whence so much opposition had been offered on the previous afternoon, and this time occupied it without difficulty. At 1115 hours the enemy thought to make a counter-attack, but his forming-up positions in the woods to the south-east were scattered by gun fire and at the same time 2 Armoured Recce Welsh Guards shot up six "Panthers" south-west of Emieville. After this there is nothing of importance to record and thus, albeit unspectacular, the morning was useful, for the Corps positions had been improved without cost and something over 20 enemy tanks destroyed in so doing.

In view of the changed character of the situation, a continuation of the present action was no longer profitable on a long term basis for armoured divisions, and the Army Commander therefore decided to withdraw 8 Corps by degrees from the line, with the intention once again of employing it in operations elsewhere—though where, at the moment, was not apparent. As if to confirm this decision, the elements now intervened and from 1600 hours onwards torrential rain turned the hitherto dusty arena into a swampy morass, completely halting all movement, except on metalled roads. Indeed so heavy and prolonged was the downpour that some tanks of 7 Armoured Division became bogged and General Erskine gave orders that, if necessary, these were to be fought as pill boxes. Any further armoured warfare east of the River Orne was, however, in any case, out of the question, and Operation "Goodwood" was thus at an end. There remained only to carry out the routine reliefs and regrouping—temporarily suspended during the storm—before the Corps was able to pass into reserve and concentrate for fresh tasks ahead.

2 Canadian Corps was now instructed by General Dempsey to assume command progressively over the major part of the front of 8 Corps, whilst 1 Corps took over the sector held by Guards Armoured Division, and at 1000 hours on 21st July, 8 Corps ceased to have responsibility for any section of the front. For the moment, however, it held a reserve commitment to provide any assistance necessary for 2 Canadian Corps, though this was not in fact to be called upon.

Summary of Operations 18th-21st July

Operation "Goodwood" was an interesting battle from many points of view. In the first phase and as far approximately as the Cagny area, it was hoped to rush the armour through at the highest possible speed whilst the enemy was still under the influence of the air and artillery bombardments. Subsequently, as distances increased, it was realised that the divisions would become more dependant on their own weapons and each tactical situation would thus have to be dealt with individually as it arose. The form in which these divisions had to be launched into action, however, against the deeply echeloned and resolutely manned German defence zone, held under practically ideal conditions for the defenders, made the accomplishment of the Corps intention laid down an extremely difficult, not to say hazardous, undertaking. Nevertheless, that it was in so large a measure successful, is an achievement of which 8 Corps can be justly proud. The three problems which had faced the Corps at the outset, namely:—

(a) Security in order to win surprise,

(b) The successful deployment of the Corps from the confined Orne bridgehead, and

(c) obtaining the degree of air support vital for the launching and carrying through of the operation.

had all been subsequently answered, though where the solution was not one hundred per cent. complete was either not the responsibility of 8 Corps, or arose from advantages enjoyed by the enemy through the accident of dominating ground. It is obvious that any effort to achieve an armoured break-out east of Caen was completely subordinate to these factors, and therefore any plan was largely predetermined. Let us, however, examine the solutions provided by 8 Corps in the light of the evidence concerning them.

(a) *The Element of Surprise.*

It is clear that a break out in the vicinity of Caen was no surprise to the German High Command which had always expected something of the sort, for both von Rundstedt and Rommel regarded the eastern end of the Allied foothold in Normandy as the " schwerpunkt " area for the combined British, Canadian and American forces. Hitler indeed, for this very reason, had repeatedly demanded that the Orne bridgehead be eliminated. As early as 2nd July General Speidel in his weekly review of the situation had reported to Berlin: "A resumption of the enemy attack may be reckoned with . . . *and various signs seem to indicate that the area east of the Orne will also be involved.*" This appreciation held firm throughout the next two weeks, and the attempt to deceive the Germans with the diversionary attacks carried out by 12 Corps west of the River Orne on 15th-16th July failed completely, for on 17th July, as we have seen, Speidel again reported to the Fuehrer's Headquarters that Second Army could be expected to launch a major offensive from the evening of 17th July, an exceedingly accurate forecast in the event. Whatever the source of this information—whether through Sepp Dietrich pressing his ear to the ground or through intelligent observation of the Orne bridgehead from the tall chimneys in the Colombelles factory estate, the fact remains that the enemy undoubtedly anticipated the attack by 8 Corps. All troops around Caen were alerted early in the afternoon of 17th July and warned to expect an attack that night. Strategic surprise was thus impossible to obtain and was not achieved. Tactical surprise, on the other hand, was undoubtedly gained. Sepp Dietrich, as we know, expected a major effort across the Orne from *west* of Caen, together with, possibly, a subsidiary thrust out of the Orne bridgehead towards the east. None of the opposing enemy commanders, however, foresaw that the major attack would drive south from this confined area—probably no one considered it possible. The armoured reserve for Dietrich's right flank was thus wrongly positioned around Lisieux, instead of being much further west, where it had later to be brought. Under the circumstances, therefore, the efforts to hide the direction from which the main attack would be delivered were successful, and the elaborate and irksome security precautions taken by the Corps to avoid drawing attention to its masses of armour, amply repaid themselves. Had tactical surprise not been achieved, " Goodwood " would have been a failure from the start.

(b) *The Debouchment from the Bridgehead.*

The shape and size of the Orne bridgehead having determined the manner of the advance out of it, the actual performance by the leading armoured division and its immediate successor was astonishingly smooth and rapid. Thereafter, the congestion of traffic, inevitable if any hold-up occurred forward, greatly impeded the advance of the third armoured division, so that the weight of its tanks could not be brought to bear at the time and place desired, and resulted in heavy additional burdens falling on 11 Armoured Division. However, the reputation for dash and skill possessed by this division was fully upheld, for any less well-trained or well-led formation would certainly have failed to make the striking seven mile advance in so short a time, and might well have had great difficulty in achieving a fraction of that distance. The Corps Commander had also been most anxious for the tanks to be accompanied by infantry in armoured carriers, but unfortunately none were available. The appreciable effect which this would have had on the battle can be realised from the great success attending their use by the Canadians in Operation "Totalise."

(c) *Air Support.*

This is a thorny subject, and it is difficult to resist the temptation to be wise after the event. There is no doubt that the support provided by the Allied air forces in Operation "Goodwood" was magnificent—that cannot be gainsaid. Combined with the more accurate fire power of the artillery, it was decisive in helping the Corps forward from the bridgehead. Map No. 111 proves, however, that air bombardment can never be completely reliable for the large number of enemy strongpoints and defences missed in the preliminary bombing, produced repercussions later in the day which could reasonably have been expected never to arise. Like the dragon's teeth of old, they sprang to life unheralded. In point of fact, Sepp Dietrich had expected that the overwhelming Allied air power would be used to blast a breach in his defences by means of a bomb carpet, and had prepared his troops accordingly. Hence the depth of ten miles in his positions, hence the four defensive zones, hence the dug-outs ten feet below ground and the extra strong protection around his guns. Not that these measures sufficed, however, for so devastating were the bombs that when they hit a target squarely the concussion alone overwhelmed the defenders. Von Kluge's letter to the Fuehrer of 21st July is evidence enough of this. Once the strongpoints came to life again amongst the armour, however, they were able to impose a fatal delay. This in all probability would have been rectified if the afternoon bombing of the Bourguebus ridge had been carried out as the Corps Commander requested. Without it, the depleted strength of 29 Armoured Brigade was too weak to rush its formidable defences, whilst the lapse of time from the actual bombing of this area early in the morning until the tanks arrived was sufficient to allow the German garrison to recover from its effects—particularly in the untouched villages of Bras and Hubert Folie, and the equally fortunate gun area adjacent. One big lesson of the operation was that an air bombardment must be followed up by ground troops within an hour or at the most an hour and a half. However, in this case it was not possible, since there could be no second air attack. Decisive results might have been obtained if at first light on 19th July a similar air effort on the same scale as the previous day, had been employed against the Bourguebus position, at that time freshly garrisoned by troops which were not yet firmly established, and a penetration southwards and out into open country would have resulted. But no such repetition of the air programme could be provided. To plan an enterprise of that nature takes time, and the Allied heavy bombers were already standing by again for the main break-out attack by the Americans west of St. Lo, due to start on 20th July, but destined to be delayed until 25th July on account of the bad weather.

Results of Operation "Goodwood"

In two days' fierce fighting 8 Corps had advanced over seven miles to the south on a front six miles wide, thereby enabling 2 Canadian Corps to capture the large built-up area of Vaucelles and to exploit to Fleury-sur-Orne and Ifs. 1 Corps, too, was greatly assisted in the capture of Touffreville, Sammerville and Cuillerville. Over 2,500 prisoners had been taken and upwards of a hundred enemy tanks destroyed. Above all, the enemy had suffered a severe set-back in the sector in which he was most sensitive to attack, for his whole defensive position hinged upon Caen, and was henceforth irretrievably weakened. 21 Army Group, on the other hand, had now gained sufficient elbow room to permit the Canadians to organise their brilliant Operation "Totalise," which ultimately was to drive the German Army out of the Caen plain and into the bloody holocaust of the Falaise "pocket."

So far as the general difficulties of mounting the attack were concerned, these had been overcome in a quite masterly fashion, and very material results achieved, happily at a low cost in lives. The prodigality in the expenditure of tanks in which the Allies had such overwhelming numerical superiority was more than justified by results.

Once again, however, the jealously guarded secret object of attracting the German armour, as in the Odon fighting, was the major factor in the Commander-in-Chief's plan, and the true measure of Operation "Goodwood" is strikingly revealed in examining how far this was achieved. If a tabulated list is prepared showing the comparative build-up of panzer divisions on the British and American fronts in Normandy up to 25th July, the figures reveal the complete success of the overall Allied strategy in the Battle of Normandy.

Here is the answer:—

	Enemy Strength opposite U.S. Armies (Sector: Caumont—Cotentin)			Enemy Strength opposite British and Canadian Armies (Sector: Caumont—Caen)		
	Panzer Divisions	Tanks *	Infantry Battalions	Panzer Divisions	Tanks *	Infantry Battalions
15 June,	½	70	63	4	520	43
25 June,	1	190	87	5	530	49
30 June,	½	140	63	7½	725	64
5 July,	½	215	63	7½	690	64
10 July,	2½	240	72	5½	560	65
15 July,	2½	240	78	5½	580	68
20 July,	2	190	82	7	720	71
25 July,	2	190	85	7	750	92

* *Includes Corps tank battalions.*

The delay caused by bad weather in beginning the American break-out attempt, putting it back from 20th July until 25th July, thus served a good purpose, for it enabled the Germans to complete the counter-measures which had been forced upon them by the launching of "Goodwood," and these counter-measures greatly improved American prospects. Before this operation Rommel had been preparing to strengthen his reserves opposite the

First U.S. Army sector. 2 Panzer Division was about to be withdrawn from Caumont into reserve south of St. Lo, and 116 Panzer Division was *en route* from Amiens to the area west of St. Lo. "Goodwood" acted like a magnet, and drew both these armoured formations to the south-east of Caen, where they were joined by a battle group of 9 SS Panzer Division. Thus on 25th July, when the U.S. attack began, on the British front there were seven panzer divisions and four independent heavy tank battalions. Of these, and not counting the battle group of 9 SS Panzer Division, no less than five were marshalled against 8 Corps. Facing the Americans, however, there were only two panzer divisions and no heavy tanks at all. Had it not been for the battles east of the River Orne, therefore, there would have been at least four panzer divisions facing the First U.S. Army on 25th July. Instead, the enemy was caught off balance, with insufficient strength to halt this latest Allied thrust, and before he could adjust the disposition of his armour the Americans had broken through beyond recall.

The last word and the best comment on 8 Corps' operations lies, however, with the enemy Supreme Commander, Field-Marshal von Kluge. According to his Chief of Staff, General Blumentritt, the optimism with which he had come to Normandy not three weeks earlier had vanished before the end of "Goodwood," and he realised that the Battle of Normandy was irrevocably lost. He at last shared the now wounded Rommel's views on the situation, accepted his extremely pessimistic appreciation of future events, and finally found the courage to forward it to Hitler with a covering letter on 21st July, the concluding paragraph of which ran as follows:—

> "I came here with the fixed determination of making effective your order to stand fast at any price. But now I have seen by experience that this price must be paid by the slow but sure annihilation of the force. In spite of intense efforts the moment has drawn near when the front, already so heavily strained, will break. And once the enemy is in open country an orderly command will hardly be practicable in view of the insufficient mobility of our own troops. I consider it my duty to bring these conclusions to your notice in good time, My Fuehrer. We shall fight on—in fact, my last word to the conference of commanders south of Caen was:
>
>> 'We shall hold out, and if no expedient improves our position fundamentally, we must die honourably on the battlefield!'"

From the evidence of General Blumentritt it appears that von Kluge was brought to this defeatist conclusion primarily by the results of Operation "Goodwood."

CHAPTER 4

"Bluecoat"

Operation "Bluecoat" and the End of the Normandy Campaign

THE withdrawal of the Corps into reserve on 21st July caused a certain amount of speculation, especially among the junior members of the Headquarters staff, as to the next scene of operations, for it was difficult to see where for the moment 8 Corps could be employed. It was now, moreover, a headquarters without troops, for Guards Armoured Division remained east of the River Orne in 1 Corps, whilst 7 Armoured Division had passed to 2 Canadian Corps. Even the faithful 11 Armoured Division was temporarily under command of 12 Corps and conducting experiments with "artificial moonlight," a recent and successful innovation in the use of searchlights for night operations. Not only were there, therefore, no troops to command, but with the introduction of 2 Canadian Corps south of Caen, the whole Second Army line was adequately manned, and there did not seem any great prospect of 8 Corps returning to the fray until there was some considerable change in the situation. In the meantime the opportunities existed for occasional visits to other parts of the front—including the American zone, and the appearance of cars bearing the sign of the "White Knight" in such widely separated spots as Cherbourg and Caen must have caused some slight bewilderment to the enemy intelligence service. "Swanning" is an expressive word for it covers a multitude of sins and is probably the best term to denote this development of the campaign. Not that it was confined to 8 Corps, for if "to swan" be translated as "to wander at will," then it is an instinct inherent in every being. At all events, so far as Normandy was concerned, those, being new to campaigning, who had never tasted it before, now awoke to its delights and for a few days the Headquarters wore a strangely deserted air. The weather cleared somewhat, too, and sea bathing brought a welcome relief from first the dust (Normandy and dust will ever be synonymous) and latterly the mud in which everything seemed to get enveloped.

The break, welcome as it was, did not, however, last for long. At the beginning of the following week some preliminary instructions were given by Second Army for 8 Corps to be prepared to carry out an attack in the extreme west of the British sector. This locality had only just been taken over by Second Army, since from the early days of the invasion it had formed part of the American bridgehead. It had, in fact, been captured by 5 Corps of First U.S. Army about a week after "D" Day in conformity with the first thrust by 7 Armoured Division towards the nearby town of Villers Bocage. Little activity had taken place here subsequently, for against the American area as a whole the Germans had never made a concentrated effort, considering it, as their records reveal, the base for Allied operations, whose springboard and danger threat emanated from around Caen. Whatever forces the enemy kept in the Cotentin peninsula, though too weak and scattered to make a prolonged resistance, were primarily employed defensively around certain nodal points such as Carentan, St. Lo and Valognes. Elsewhere in the U.S. sector the front was allowed to become static. This of course fitted in perfectly with the Commander-in-Chief's plans since their west flank was to be the point of major effort for the American forces. South of Caumont, therefore, from the middle of June, 1 U.S. Infantry Division, one of the original assault formations, had faced in conjunction with 30 Corps the German 2 Panzer Division. The Americans began however to feel the need for additional infantry while mounting their major attack south of St. Lo, and accordingly asked Second Army to extend its boundary westwards and thereby relieve 1 U.S. Infantry Division. General Dempsey agreed and on 22nd July, 15 (Scottish) Infantry Division, now rested and recovered from the heavy Odon fighting, moved in and took over a sector astride Caumont. This resulted in 30 Corps holding a lengthy and awkward front, and the Army Commander therefore proposed once again to commit 8 Corps in this area in an attack which was tentatively planned for Wednesday, 2nd August. Preliminary steps were in hand to prepare for this, but events moved more rapidly than expected and the Commander-in-Chief decided that the moment was opportune for intervention by 8 Corps at an earlier date. On the morning of Friday, 28th July, he countermanded the existing arrangements and ordered that 8 Corps should attack at first light on Sunday morning, 30th July. The news reached Corps Headquarters early in the afternoon of the same day and caused considerable excitement, for the task of preparation seemed superhuman and more than could be done in the bare thirty-six hours available. Not only was Corps Headquarters itself at the east end of the Allied bridgehead, and near the concentration area of 11 Armoured Division, but Guards Armoured Division was across the River Orne on call to 2 Canadian Corps whilst 8 A.G.R.A. still had guns actually deployed in action in this neighbourhood. The one saving grace was that the infantry division making the initial attack, 15 (Scottish) Division, was an old and trusted friend and moreover was already in situ, conversant both with the terrain and the enemy holding it. Once again, therefore, 8 Corps was called upon to organise and carry out a most complicated operation at extremely short notice, in the knowledge that any failure would have serious repercussions on what were undoubtedly destined to be the final battles of the Normandy campaign, as a brief glance at the general situation obtaining at that time will show.

The General Situation on 25th July

By 25th July, 1944, scarcely seven weeks after the landings in Normandy, the necessary conditions for the break out from the Allied bridgehead had been created. The hard and often disappointing fighting was at last about to pay a dividend that would fire the imagination of the entire world and come within an ace of bringing the entire Hitlerite edifice crumbling down into ruin. In the course of this account, frequent reference has been made to the strategy laid down for "Overlord" by General Montgomery. It will perhaps be useful at this juncture to refer to the remarkable map he issued prior to the invasion to all corps headquarters in order to illustrate the basic plan for the battle of Normandy. This shews by a series of phase lines the possible degree of advance to be expected by the Allies at certain given dates. More particularly it indicates, though very roughly, the wide turning movement, based on the Allied eastern flank as a pivot, which was to begin south of St. Lo. The timing of the early phase lines, of course, was not to be adhered to for a variety of reasons, but it is satisfactory to note that the ultimate line up of the British, Canadian and American Armies along the Rivers Seine and Loire, due by D plus 90, was in fact achieved by D plus 75—fifteen days in advance of the target date.

However by 28th July the American thrust had only been in progress some forty-eight hours and though it was going well it had not yet assumed

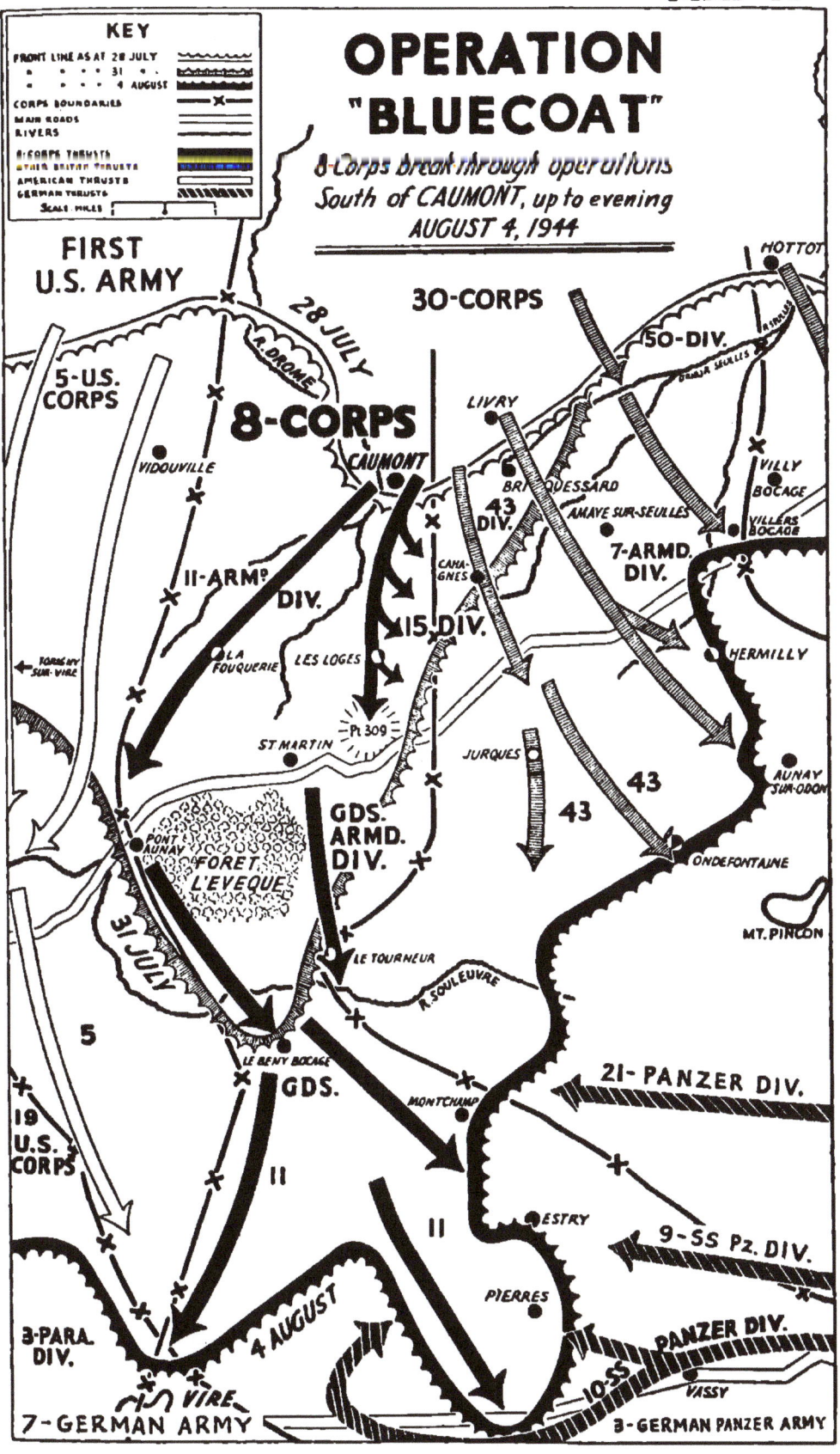

the proportions of a break-out. Meanwhile, at the same time that these operations were in progress, far away to the east of the river, 2 Canadian Corps had also begun an attack along the Caen—Falaise road, to which the enemy reacted very strongly employing a force which included no less than four panzer divisions to stem it. As always, the Germans miscalculated the area of the real "schwerpunkt," even though on this occasion the deduction was hardly difficult for them, for not only had the U.S. sector been building up for this operation for some considerable time, but the latter had also gone off to a false start on 24th July, when two thousand aircraft having taken off from England for the preliminary air bombardment, found on arrival over the target area, that heavy cloud restricted their visibility, and the majority had to return to base with their bomb loads intact. This alone might have revealed both the intentions and the frontage of the actual attack, but the prompt start within a few hours of the Canadian attack east of the Orne doubtless allayed any suspicions. It was only a question of time, however, before the German High Command would realise the mistake and seek to remedy its dispositions, by transferring panzer formations to the west of the Normandy front. The situation is perhaps best summarised by the following paragraph from the book "Normandy to the Baltic."

> "The enemy had very powerful forces in the Orne sector; there were six panzer and SS panzer divisions on the Second Army front, all of which were east of Noyers. West of that place there was no German armour facing the British, and therefore the situation was favourable for delivering a very heavy blow on the right wing of Second Army in the Caumont sector. If we could regroup speedily and launch a thrust in strength southwards from the Caumont area directed on Foret l'Eveque and Beny Bocage, and ultimately to Vire, the effect would be to get behind the German forces which had been swung back to face west by the American break-through; any attempt by the enemy to pivot on the River Vire or in the area between Torigny and Caumont would thus be frustrated, as we should knock away the hinge. I, therefore, ordered Second British Army to regroup in order to deliver a strong offensive on these lines; not less than six divisions were to be employed, and the operation was to proceed with all possible speed. In the meantime, First Canadian Army and the remainder of Second Army were to maintain the maximum offensive activity on the rest of the front in order to pin the enemy opposition and wear it down."

General Dempsey, on receipt of these urgent instructions, proceeded at once to organise a major offensive, to which he gave the name of "Bluecoat," and in which the principal rôle was to be taken by 8 Corps. The general idea was explained by his Chief of Staff, Brigadier Chilton, at a conference held at 1645 hours at Second Army Headquarters at Creully, for the plan decided upon by the Army Commander involved considerable regrouping throughout the British and Canadian forces, and the tasks set were three in number:—

(a) To retain enemy armoured formations on the British and Canadian fronts, thereby minimising any possible pressure against the Americans.

(b) To prevent the enemy from hinging his forces on the high ground in the area Mont Pincon-Bois du Homme. (Point 309.)

(c) To retain a firm and unshakeable hold on the Caen pivot.

As a result of tasks (a) and (b) the operations of First U.S. Army which aimed at breaking through the German defences were directly assisted, whilst at the same time the destruction of the German armies west of the River Seine was hastened and assured. As for the latter eventuality, the writing on the wall was plain for all to see, except apparently their Fuehrer, as an examination of the enemy situation will reveal.

The Enemy Situation by the End of July

By the end of the month the German High Command in France had at long last made up its mind that a second Allied invasion in the Pas de Calais was not likely, for we find in General Speidel's customary and meticulous report to Berlin the following gem:—

> "A second large-scale landing on the west coast of Europe appears to be increasingly improbable, for one further American and also a Canadian Army Headquarters have been transferred to Normandy, and two army groups have probably been formed."

For once he was quite correct in all his deductions, though it would have been cold comfort to the Germans to have known it. With losses totalling upwards of 150,000 men, and replacements of approximately one-tenth of that amount, the unfortunate Field-Marshal von Kluge was at his wit's end to know what to do. In fact, he was exactly in the position of a competent but colourless chess-player, who, at the end of a game with a master exponent, finds himself reduced to moving pawns until his opponent feels disposed to administer the *coup de grâce*. SS Colonel-General Paul Hausser, who since the time of the Odon battles had succeeded the deceased General Dollmann in command of the Seventh German Army holding the front from Caumont westwards, like Rommel had written on 19th July an appreciation of the situation facing his troops. His conclusions were equally gloomy, but, being a practical man, he included certain proposals to his superiors for remedying matters. This report reached von Kluge just prior to the American offensive, and, though there was no time to act upon it, some marginal comments he made to the principal demands by Hausser are interesting, for they illustrate the desperate plight to which the enemy potential had been reduced, as well as the Supreme Commander's own belief that the main battle area was, and would remain, on the eastern flank.

Here are Hausser's demands and von Kluge's replies:—

Hausser asked for:	Von Kluge noted:
1. A mobile formation at full strength as Army reserve. (Seventh Army was reduced to three battalions of infantry for use as a strategic reserve.)	1. Panzer Lehr Division is to be relieved in 14 days by 363 Infantry Division, now marching up. 2 Panzer Division is being relieved by 326 Infantry Division, but *may be needed in the main battle area at Caen*.
2. A steady flow of reinforcements—two march battalions per division per month.	2. Impossible at present, according to OKH's latest declaration (Hitler's Headquarters as Commander-in-Chief of the Army).
3. One or two werfer brigades, heavy artillery and replacements of field artillery, machine guns, etc.	3. 7, 8 and 9 Werfer Brigades *are occupied in the main battle area at Caen*.

4. Increased supplies of ammunition and fuel, and protection of supply routes against air attack, especially the Loire bridges.	4. Supplies have been asked for but are not to be expected to this extent.
5. Protection of troops against fighter-bomber attacks and air attack generally, by stray fighter thrusts by the Luftwaffe.	5. Resistance (*sic*) has been tried, but it is not very successful.

A final summing-up of the German chances in Normandy occurs in the same report by General Speidel quoted earlier in this section, than which no better illustration exists of a gambler's last throw. Here it is:—

"Army Group B will endeavour to prevent a break-through by *recklessly exposing* the fronts which are *not* being attacked."

To such a pass had the once mighty German Army been brought by the intuition of its Fuehrer.

Twenty-four hours after this report had been written, 8 Corps had broken through Seventh Army in its new attack south of Caumont and turned the whole German position to the east.

South of Caumont the enemy front was held by 326 Infantry Division, a formation of good quality formed late in 1942 in Westphalia, but subsequently removed to France, where its final station before being ordered to Normandy, had been around St. Omer. It was the first of the Pas de Calais divisions of the Fifteenth German Army to confront Second Army, for it had relieved 2 Panzer Division about a week previously, and was now firmly in position with two regiments, 751 and 752 Grenadier Regiments, deployed in the line and the third, 753 Grenadier Regiment, in reserve. The sector for which this division was responsible was an extended one, stretching for some nine miles from north-west of Villers Bocage as far as the River Drome. The position was, however, considered to be fully developed with minefields and wire thickening up the defence system, whilst the division itself was believed to consist of some eight or nine battalions of infantry with a large assortment of supporting weapons—some forty-eight field or medium guns, nine assault guns, twenty-four close support infantry guns, twenty-one anti-tank guns of over 5 cm. calibre and more than seventy mortars. No armoured reserves were known to be available as backing for the enemy infantry, but the presence of 654 Anti-Tank Battalion, a G.H.Q. unit with some thirty 88 mm. anti-tank guns mounted on "Panther" chassis, and allotted to 47 Panzer Corps (which controlled 326 Infantry Division) was suspected, and rightly so in the event. Morale, too, was reckoned to be good, but the German High Command did not leave much to chance here, for it was later discovered that on the orders of the divisional commander, Lieutenant-General Viktor von Drabich-Waechter, every soldier received a "pep" talk before going into the line, in which the following points were stressed with typical Teutonic thoroughness and entire disregard for truth:—

"(a) You are relieving a SS formation in a quiet sector.

(b) You will be opposed by troops of the 5 U.S. Infantry Division (*sic*) who have suffered fairly severe casualties.

(c) There is no armour against you.

(d) The enemy will drop, or fire over, leaflets. No one below the rank of major will pick them up. These leaflets invite you to desert, and enjoy the amenities of British prisoner of war camps. Remember that if you do, you will be taken to England and run the risk of death by V1. After that you will be shipped to the United States or Canada for life-long labour. Or you may be exchanged for a British or American paratroop (of which we have captured thousands) tried by court-martial and shot. In any case, your families will suffer in consequence, exclusion from the German ' Volksgemeinschaft ' being the least of their resulting troubles."

After perusal of these charming and characteristic thoughts, let us pass to an examination of the ground over which Operation " Bluecoat " was to take 8 Corps and the measures necessary for mounting this operation.

The Terrain for Operation " Bluecoat "

It will be remembered, from an earlier chapter, how at Sandhutton or Worth Priory, the attention of the Corps Commander, when using the sand models of Normandy, had always been drawn towards the wedge of high ground, which jutted out west of the River Orne, and to its two pronounced and dominating peaks, Mont Pincon and Point 309. No one, however, could have foreseen at the time that the fortunes of war would lead the Corps to fight in this region its most successful and decisive action.

It was against the second of these two features, Point 309, that 8 Corps was now to be launched from a start line running just south of Caumont. This little town stands on a hill, which gives good observation over the area of advance, but the whole is completely dominated by Point 309 from which even better general observation of the battlefield was possible.

The country itself is the closest " bocage " type at its fullest flower, for it abounds in orchards and small fields surrounded by banks three or four feet high, often surmounted by thick hedges. A series of pronounced ridges extend to the south across the axis of advance, whilst numerous streams in many places constitute tank obstacles owing to their width, depth or marshy approaches. Good metalled roads are few and far between, and apart from the one leading southwards from Caumont to St. Martin des Besaces, which is just wide enough for two-way traffic, there is little else except narrow farm tracks and by-roads, always tortuous and often running between high banks and hedges, as in Devonshire. The area contains no places of any size, though there are a few villages and isolated farm houses.

It will be evident, therefore, that movement in such country is bound to be difficult and slow, hampering the bringing-up of reserves, restricting the cross-country performance of tanks, carriers and other vehicles, and hindering supply and replenishment. Moreover, despite the existence of certain viewpoints, the close nature of the country prevents detailed ground observation and thus the accurate locating of opposition.

To sum up, the ground over which 8 Corps was now to operate was, as usual, strongly in favour of the defence and lent itself well to the defensive use of mines and other artificial obstacles in addition to any natural restrictions it imposed on the attackers. A glance at any layered map of this region is sufficient to illustrated the hazards to be expected in operations, particularly with tanks, in " bocage " country.

The Preliminary Concentration for Operation " Bluecoat "

At the afternoon conference held by Brigadier Chilton at Creully on 28th July, the intentions of the Army Commander had been elaborated. In particular, the regrouping of British formations necessary for the varying rôles assigned them, was revealed, and as a result, 8 Corps found itself reconstituted in its original form with the formations with which it had trained so long. This in itself was a happy augury, for it meant that with so little time available, at all events none would be lost in getting to know newcomers, since all formations had long been accustomed to working together.

The main task remained, however, to organise the complicated moves necessary to concentrate the Corps behind 15 (Scottish) Division and ready to move forward when desired. In connection with this concentration, it was obvious that the security factor was of considerable importance, for if full advantage were to be gained from an attack at the western end of the Second Army sector, the necessary preliminary steps must remain undetected by the enemy, as otherwise he would position his panzer formations to meet it. Exceptional measures were, therefore, taken to ensure that news did not leak out beforehand and, especially, that the move of the armour remained secret. This time, fortunately, there was neither a Sepp Dietrich on the opposing side nor limestone caves to act as sounding boards for the enemy, but this notwithstanding the following precautions were carried out:—

(a) The "White Knight" sign was removed from vehicles and personnel of Corps Headquarters, and the normal signing of approaches to the headquarters was not used until after the battle had started.

(b) All formations observed wireless silence from the time they began to concentrate until three hours before "H" hour.

(c) Only the guns of 15 (Scottish) Division were allowed to register, and no increase in Air O.P. activity was permitted.

(d) The moves of 6 Guards Tank Brigade and the majority of 11 Armoured Division were made under cover of darkness.

(e) Second Army organised a deception plan involving the use of wireless and dummy tanks.

In spite of all these efforts, it was later disquieting to discover that the intention to attack in this area was known in advance by the enemy. It arose through the capture of a patrol in the vicinity of Sept Vents, a hamlet one mile south-west of Caumont, during the early evening of 29th July. Fortunately very little information can have been possessed at that time by the patrol concerning "Bluecoat," and what little it had, was probably unwittingly revealed to a skilled interrogator. At all events the following order was discovered two days later in the files of one of the battalion headquarters which had been over-run:

"II Battalion 752 Grenadier Regiment   Battle Headquarters.
   (G Operations)   29th July, 1944

Subject:—Increased state of preparation and alarm.

For to-night, 29th-30th July, a special degree of watch is ordered.
From statements of prisoners the enemy will attack our positions to-morrow morning, 30th July, at 0400 hours.

(Signed) STATKOWSKI,

Battalion Commander."

Prisoners from 326 Infantry Division confirmed this surprising news, but stated that they were nearly always expecting an attack of some nature, though not by tanks as the country was so unsuitable, and therefore, no extra precautions had been taken. Thus, fortunately for 8 Corps, the Germans do not appear to have realised either the magnitude of the offensive about to burst upon them or to anticipate the use of large armoured forces in connection with it.

The problem therefore involved in assembling 8 Corps around Caumont was difficult, and since Sunday, 30th July, was "D" Day, it had to be solved in a hurry. Most of the formations concerned had to cross the maintenance routes of corps already in action, but once again Second Army Headquarters co-ordinated all movement and ensured a smooth passage for every unit according to the following programme:—

Night 28th-29th July.

6 Guards Tank Brigade	Bayeux area to Caumont area to come under command 15 (Scottish) Division. (18 miles.)
8 A.G.R.A.	Giberville (east of River Orne) to area south of Bayeux. (30 miles.)
11 Armoured Division	Area northwest of Caen to area Caumont (behind 8 A.G.R.A.—move completed 1600 hours, 29th July). (25 miles.)

29th July.

Headquarters 8 Corps	Beny-sur-Mer (8 miles north of Caen)-Noron la Poterie. (20 miles.)
2 Household Cavalry Regiment	Beny-sur-Mer-Caumont (same area as 11 Armoured Division). (26 miles.)
1 Lothians	Crepon (8 miles north-east of Bayeux) -Caumont (same area as 11 Armoured Division). (25 miles.)
8 A.G.R.A.	South of Bayeux—area north of Caumont. (16 miles.)

30th July.

Guards Armoured Division	East of River Orne—area north of Caumont. (45 miles.)

The distances shown in brackets are conservative estimates but the strain imposed on all troops, especially the tank crews, can be imagined, when it is realised that as the head of the Corps was launching its attack, the tail element was still east of the River Orne, nearly fifty miles away. 11 Armoured Division, in fact, only arrived in its new area a few hours before the battle was due to start, after a long and tiring march.

Composition of 8 Corps on 30th July

FORMATION	STRENGTH	
	Officers	*Other Ranks*
Headquarters 8 Corps and Corps troops	596	10,883
Guards Armoured Division	730	13,650
11 Armoured Division	715	13,788
15 (Scottish) Division	829	16,141
6 Guards Tank Brigade	199	3,904
8 A.G.R.A.	214	4,643
2 Household Cavalry Regiment	58	738
Inns of Court Regiment	55	765
	3,396	61,512

8 Corps Intention and Plan

The Corps intention for Operation "Bluecoat" as laid down in 8 Corps Operation Instruction No. 6, signed by the B.G.S. at 0100 hours on 29th July, was as follows:—

"On Sunday, 30th July, 8 Corps will establish itself in the area of the high ground around La Bergerie Ferme (Point 309) with a view to:—

    (a) protecting the right flank of 30 Corps

    (b) a subsequent exploitation towards Point Aunay."

The plan, briefly, was to begin the move southwards from the Caumont area, after preliminary air and artillery bombardment on a two divisional front with 11 Armoured Division on the right, and 15 (Scottish) Division, reinforced with 6 Guards Tank Brigade, on the left. The main resistance was expected to occur in the path of the Scots, and their advance was, therefore, organised on the "leapfrog" principle and carefully divided into four phases:—

Phase 1. Capture of the village of Sept Vents and the wooded area around Lutain.

Phase 2. Capture of the high ground immediately south-east of Les Loges.

Phase 3. Capture of Point 309—the main objective.

and finally—

Phase 4. Pushing forward patrols to the River Souleuvre and on the right to make contact with 11 Armoured Division in the Foret l'Eveque.

In view of the speed with which this venture had to be organised and to make sure that all ranks among the Scots were clear about its importance, the Corps Commander addressed the following letter to Major-General MacMillan, commanding 15 (Scottish) Division:—

"You are again being asked to carry out an operation of the greatest importance.

As you know, the break-through on the American front has been most successful, and their armoured troops and infantry formations are striking southwards and westwards.

The enemy is doing everything in his power to restrict the area of penetration by the Americans, but to do this successfully he must hinge his forces on some important feature of the ground, holding fast to this position, and being prepared to give ground slowly on his left flank.

From a study of the map, the high ground east and west of the Bois du Homme seems well suited for the purpose, although there is no evidence yet to indicate his intentions, but it is most important for the success of the operations in Normandy that he should be prevented from doing this.

Obviously, the earlier the operation can take place, the more far-reaching will be the results to the Americans.

From the point of view of timing of an operation of this sort, there are always two methods to be considered. The first—an attempt to rush the enemy defences before he is properly established. This has obvious advantages, but also the disadvantages which must always be present if the operations are prepared at short notice. The second—a more methodical advance with probably more efficient fire support, but with the disadvantage that it allows the enemy more time to bring up reinforcements.

After consideration of the above, and in view of the vital importance of the operation to the whole Allied plan, the Commander-in-Chief has decided that it is to be undertaken at the earliest possible moment.

I fully realise how much is being asked of you, and what difficulties you will have to contend with, but I am sure they will be overcome in the same way as they have been overcome in the past. You have, in my opinion, the finest fighting record of any division in Normandy, and I do not feel that this task will be in any way beyond your powers.

Will you please explain the situation to your officers and other ranks so that they may understand the reasons for speed and the vital issues which are at stake.

I know they will respond as they have always done, and I am sure that their success will be the turning point in the campaign.

(Signed) R. N. O'CONNOR,
Lieutenant-General
Commander 8 Corps."

To the west, 11 Armoured Division, organised into two battle groups, was to move down in conformity with the varying bounds of the Scots and thereby to protect their right.

Guards Armoured Division remained in Corps reserve.

So far as the flanks of the Corps were concerned, on one side 8 Corps found itself positioned on the boundary between First U.S. Army and Second Army, whilst on the other lay 30 Corps, which in this battle was also to make a major attack at the same time as 8 Corps, being directed first of all on Mont Pincon and subsequently Le Beny Bocage. The Americans, however, were putting all their strength into the action further west and 5 U.S. Corps on the Corps right was thus not planning to launch a simultaneous offensive.

On the day before the battle, General O'Connor visited the American Corps Commander, Major-General Leonard T. Gerow, at his headquarters, to explain the situation to him, and although there was no question of a joint plan between the two formations, it was arranged that the closest liaison should be kept. General Gerow also promised to follow up any enemy withdrawal on his front until such time as 5 U.S. Corps was pinched out by the advance of its neighbours, 19 U.S. Corps, which as far as could be gathered, was the ultimate American intention in this sector. At the start of "Bluecoat" the forward positions of 5 U.S. Corps would thus still be some distance behind those held by 15 (Scottish) Division, but as the battle progressed the Americans would endeavour to catch up and thereby prevent the right flank of the Corps from becoming exposed. Given reasonable luck, therefore, it was expected that for the first time 8 Corps would not have to conduct operations from a salient, since at the worst, only one flank would be open. Events, however, were to turn out otherwise.

Artillery Support

The fire plan for support of the attack was organised by the C.C.R.A. in his usual comprehensive fashion. All counter-battery tasks within the Corps boundaries were co-ordinated by him, as well as a programme of timed concentrations for Phase 1 of the advance. Apart from this, both divisions were responsible for laying on their own barrages, concentrations and D.F. tasks as the need arose during the advance, and an additional field regiment having been put under command of 11 Armoured Division, both formations started off equally strong in fire power. A great increase in ammunition expenditure was anticipated, and extra allotments of 250 rounds per gun for medium, and no less than 530 for field artillery, were made. Once again the crushing superiority of the British guns was to be drummed into the enemy.

Air Support

"Bluecoat" is an example of an operation planned in conjunction with a large air support programme but not dependent upon it. A fleet of some 1,600 medium and heavy bombers from the R.A.F. Bomber Command and 9 U.S. Air Force was to be employed, of which 700 were used on the front of 30 Corps, and the remainder on that of 8 Corps. The main arrangements were as follows:—

    (a) Heavy and medium bomber attacks on selected area targets.
    (b) Fighter bomber attacks on the fronts of 15 (Scottish) Division and 11 Armoured Division against known mortar and machine gun positions, and also Lutain wood.
    (c) Fighter bomber attacks on opportunity targets,
    (d) Armoured reconnaissance of all approaches to the battle area.

This time, however, there was one big difference from previous air support vouchsafed the Corps. In all previous operations planned and carried out by 8 Corps, a "turnround" or second medium or heavy bomber attack had been requested to beat down enemy reserves and defences in depth, so that the momentum of the advance should in no way be hampered and complete penetration achieved. Thus in Operation "Goodwood" an incalculable effect might have been caused by an afternoon bombing of the Bourguebus position. Unfortunately for one reason or another—shortage of aircraft, commitments elsewhere or simply bad weather, this request had always been refused. On this occasion, however, it was agreed that a second bombing raid should take place in the 8 Corps sector on the Bois du Homme during the afternoon and, as it turned out, this proved to be of decisive importance to the continued smooth advance of the Corps.

Nevertheless, throughout the planning of "Bluecoat" it was very firmly laid down that the operation would be launched regardless of whether air support was possible or not.

Engineer Tasks

There was little time for extensive alterations to routes but bulldozers were soon at work levelling banks, widening verges and straightening awkward corners, and though as a result the swirling dust was enough to choke the unfortunate military policemen directing the convoys, an even flow of traffic was assured. Many of our own mines, too, had to be lifted in the process, for the Sappers had to prepare three routes for both wheeled and tracked vehicles in the 15 (Scottish) Division area and no less than six in that of 11 Armoured Division.

By the late evening of 29th July these hurried preparations had been finished and all troops were in their assembly areas ready for battle on the morrow.

30th July—The Break-through

At dawn on 30th July the weather turned out to be dull and uninviting, for a thick mist covered the ground and heavy clouds obscured the sun. The result was that the air programme had to be somewhat curtailed, though fortunately without serious effect on the development of the action planned for the morning, for in the 8 Corps sector the Scottish attack was to secure the objectives laid down for Phase 1 of the operation before the first air bombing. During the night the two battalions leading the advance, 9 Cameronians and 2 Gordon Highlanders, left their concentration areas and by 0400 hours had "married up" with their respective Churchill tank squadrons from 4 Tank Grenadier Guards, in the forming-up points. Experience during previous fighting in bocage country had fully borne out the value of the fullest co-operation between tanks and infantry and, therefore, the Corps Commander decided that down even to sub-units, infantry and armoured brigades were to be grouped together to give tank units a proportion of infantry and similarly infantry companies a quota of tanks. Thus for Operation "Bluecoat," on the right 11 Armoured Division was organised into two brigade groups,

    (a) 159 Infantry Brigade consisting of two infantry battalions and one armoured regiment,

and (b) 29 Armoured Brigade with two armoured regiments, one motor battalion and one infantry battalion,

whilst on the left of the Corps advance 15 (Scottish) Division received an allotment of one tank battalion from 6 Guards Tank Brigade to each of its three infantry brigades. Later in the course of the action, when Guards Armoured Division entered the battle, it was similarly regrouped, and the wisdom and foresight of this decision was to be demonstrated time and time again in the course of the many isolated actions that were fought during the next two days and also by the situation in which 8 Corps found itself through its advance so far outstripping that of its neighbours.

"H" hour for the attack was 0655 hours and punctually at that time, Cameronians on the right and Gordons on the left, the leading companies crossed the start line, whilst at the same moment a smoke screen was laid by the Corps artillery to mask the forward slopes of Point 309, which overlooked the whole area. Enemy guns and mortars opened up almost immediately, causing a few casualties but counter-battery fire reduced this somewhat, and with the help of tanks, the objectives in Phase 1 were reached soon after 0900 hours. A number of tanks were, however, lost in the process on minefields, notably on one laid between Le Bourg and Sept Vents, where five Churchill tanks were put out of action. Here flails were called in to help and soon swept a path, and no undue delay was suffered. Lutain wood, which had to be captured in this phase, also proved to be a difficult locality, with an obvious attraction for enemy mortars. However, by 1030 hours, the whole area of Sept Vents and Lutain wood was cleared of enemy and quickly organised against possible counter attack, for these were only the forward defences of 326 Infantry Division.

During the latter stages of this fighting, R.A.F. Bomber Command and 9 U.S. Army Air Force had been carrying out their allotted tasks. The cloudy sky had not permitted the fighter bomber operations to take place and of the 693 R.A.F. heavy bombers which arrived over the battlefield from 0730 hours onwards, only some 480 were able to locate their targets in the 30 Corps area and attack them successfully. By 0900 hours, however, the weather had sufficiently improved to allow the medium bombers of 9 U.S. Army Air Force to carry out their full programme in the 8 Corps area, and this, in the unanimous opinion of German soldiers taken prisoner, was devastating in its effect. It was attended, too, by more success in one direction than had been anticipated, for it apparently caught the opposing divisional commander's battle headquarters, killing him and a number of his principal staff officers. This helped to account during the remainder of the day for the very ragged defence put up by the enemy, although, of course, it was unknown at the time to the attackers.

Phase 2 of the advance by 15 (Scottish) Division had been planned to take place once the objectives in the first phase had been mopped up. However, in view of the successful and speedy break-in against the German defences on the Corps front, and while the air was still echoing with the explosions of the air "strike," it was decided to push on with the next part of the battle. The battalions carrying out this new attack were, on the right 10 Highland Light Infantry and on the left 2 Argyll and Sutherland Highlanders, and since it was thought that here the battles might now become fiercer, each unit had a whole tank battalion in support, 4 Tank Coldstream Guards right and 3 Tank Scots Guards left. The way up to the start line was, in fact, found to be extremely awkward, both on account of the German minefields and isolated parties of enemy holding out and still to be eliminated under Phase 1. The right hand armour was, however, able to make better progress. At 0940 hours, therefore, the two leading squadrons of Coldstream tanks were instructed to push on to the second of the objectives set for the day, leaving the infantry to follow up as quickly as possible. Meanwhile on the left, the tanks and infantry had also become separated, the Argylls having first moved forward behind 2 Gordon Highlanders to the foot of Caumont ridge in order to avoid enemy shelling; here the tanks which came under fire as they drove down the forward slope joined them about 0745 hours. Thereafter their joint advance had been slow, and by 0930 hours had only progressed some 400-500 yards after moderately heavy fighting. It was obvious that if any benefit were going to be gained, from both the accompanying barrage and the air bombing, much better speed would have to be made to the start line, and so 3 Tank Scots Guards was ordered to advance, if necessary, unescorted by infantry. Thus at 1105 hours its tanks were across the start line, but the Argylls, held up in the rear, were unable to get moving again before 1230 hours.

Employing the usual bocage tactics of shooting up every hedge and building with machine-gun or H.E. fire, the leading squadrons of Scots Guardsmen quickly progressed about 1,200 yards south of the start line to the area of La Recussoniere, but though they waited for an hour for the Argylls to catch up, it was soon realised that unless the advance were resumed, the opportunity would be given to the enemy to recover from the bombing and to reorganise his defence. Starting off once more across the most difficult tank country, and by-passing such centres of resistance as Les Loges, owing to the absence of the infantry, 3 Tank Scots Guards finally reached the second objective, the ridge called Point 226 south of Les Loges and Hervieux. By 1530 hours this position had been consolidated and half-an-hour later 2 Argyll and Sutherland Highlanders arrived. 3 Tank Scots Guards then asked for permission to proceed with Phase 3, but this had to be refused in view of the disappointing manner in which operations had developed for the neighbouring 30 Corps.

Attacking south in its sector at approximately the same time as 8 Corps, 30 Corps on the left had early come up against a streamlet running through the village of Briquessard, which proved during the morning to be an obstacle more than usually difficult to surmount. While 30 Corps was being checked here, the consequences arising for 8 Corps were serious, for through the rapid and successful advance of 15 (Scottish) Division, the whole of the left flank of the Corps was becoming exposed, and since local enemy reserves in the vicinity had not been dealt with, it was later to be necessary to deploy the Scots so as to hold almost the whole area of their advance as a defence sector facing east and south-east. For the moment, however, it was sufficient to organise the locality around Les Loges and Point 226, which, though by no means precarious, was open to attack from the east, as the Germans were soon to realise. During the early evening the position was heavily shelled, and a formidable local counter-attack by several "Tiger" tanks supported by self-propelled 88 mm. guns was launched against it. Three tanks of 3 Tank Scots Guards were quickly knocked out from a distance, and one of the enemy hidden in the dense vegetation then advanced further in, and with supreme daring shot up eleven more Churchills in the space of a few moments before disappearing once again. It is pleasing to record that this courageous adventurer was mortally stricken by the Scots Guards in the process, for after the battle this well-named "Tiger" was discovered abandoned a short distance away. However, despite so audacious a sally, no ground was recovered by the enemy, and 15 (Scottish) Division remained firmly in possession of its intermediate objective.

Meanwhile, although on the left the original plan had been abandoned, on the right flank of 15 (Scottish) Division all was well, and at 1555 hours the second air attack by medium bombers of the 9 U.S. Army Air Force went in against the reserve positions of 326 Infantry Division on the slopes of Point 309 around La Bergerie Ferme and the western end of the Bois du Homme. General MacMillan was now faced with an awkward problem, for speed being the keynote if full advantage of the effect of the air bombing were to be taken, and the distance up to Point 309 being also considerable, how was he to gain this tremendous natural bastion, before the enemy had time to recover his balance? After consulting Brigadier Verney, commander of 6 Guards Tank Brigade, he decided upon the daring and resolute stroke of despatching a force of tanks without supporting infantry, to seize this feature with the utmost speed, and to follow it with a second wave of armour on this occasion carrying infantry to consolidate the ground won.

This stratagem was outstandingly successful. At 1615 hours Lieutenant-Colonel Sir Walter Barttelot, commanding 4 Tank Coldstream Guards, was ordered over the wireless by Brigadier Verney to carry out this task, and at 1645 hours the advance was organised and ready to start. The battalion moved off, using as its centre line the road leading through La Morichesse and Launay, but stubborn enemy infantry opposition being encountered in the first of these villages, the Commanding Officer decided from then on to travel across country towards the greatly desired objective. The final stages of the advance were through most difficult country, and several of the Churchills became detached and bogged. The enemy was very active, and if his infantrymen went to ground when the British tanks were actually passing them, they were only too happy to spring to life again afterwards and to waylay any straggler. By 1900 hours success had crowned this magnificent run-through, and 4 Tank Coldstream Guards was in complete possession of Point 309, an eminence over 1,000 feet high and dominating its surroundings even more than does the slightly taller Mont Pincon. There is no doubt that the afternoon air "strike" together with the surprising and unexpectedly rapid advance by the armour completely upset German calculations and put an end to any organised defence here; thus was avoided a costly battle, more bloody perhaps than that in which 30 Corps later in the week subdued Mont Pincon. The enemy had evidently withdrawn very recently from these parts, and in the greatest haste, but the lack of infantry and the gathering dusk forbade further exploitation to the south.

Whilst this action was in progress 4 Tank Grenadier Guards had made contact with 2 Glasgow Highlanders, which its tanks were to transport, in the vicinity of the cross-roads north of Hervieux. The Scots were carried as far as La Morichesse, but opposition again arising, the Glasgow Highlanders were forced to dismount and continue on towards the objective on foot, which they reached at 2230 hours, being followed later during the night by 7 Seaforth Highlanders. The danger of an enemy counter-attack dislodging the armour was now past, and 4 Tank Coldstream Guards was thus able to pull back from the summit to leaguer on the reverse slope, whilst the two Scottish battalions—man-handling the anti-tank guns with them, so harsh were the slopes—set-to and consolidated the position.

What of the Corps' western flank whilst this drama was taking place? Here it had been a less spectacular, though equally exhausting and successful performance. At 0700 hours 11 Armoured Division advanced as planned along two routes, in the brigade group formation already described. Although the original intention had been to create a 600-yard gap in any minefield discovered, so great were the number of mines encountered that only with considerable difficulty could the routes themselves be cleared. Apart from this, the right hand move of 11 Armoured Division with 23 Hussars and 3 Monmouthshire Regiment in the lead, progressed steadily in conformity with the advance of the Scots and reached La Morichesse, where 6 Guards Tank Brigade had already experienced trouble earlier in the evening, about 2145 hours. 3 Royal Tank Regiment and 8 Rifle Brigade were now passed through, and in the last light of the day covered another half-mile to the south. On the right route of 11 Armoured Division, 159 Infantry Brigade Group met greater opposition, particularly in the village of Gronay where 1 Herefordshire Regiment was engaged in fierce fighting almost the whole of the day before it was finally cleared. It was not until 1800 hours that 4 King's Shropshire Light Infantry and 2 Fife and Forfar Yeomanry were able to push on and capture La Baissilliere, but from here onwards the pace quickened and when darkness fell 2 Fife and Forfar Yeomanry was due east of Dampierre.

So far as 8 Corps' neighbours were concerned, neither 5 U.S. Corps nor 30 Corps had been able to make more than slight progress in their sectors despite heavy fighting, and nightfall saw the Corps therefore in its usual salient. Nevertheless it was clear that at the end of the first day of Operation "Bluecoat" 8 Corps was in a highly favourable position since there had been a clean break through the positions manned by 326 Infantry Division under almost ideal conditions for defence. This formation had indeed taken a mortal blow, for not only were its commander and principal staff officers dead as a result of the bombing, but many of its units had also suffered heavy losses in the same manner, while already by dusk several hundred prisoners had found their way into the Corps cage. This disorganisation proved useful also on the morrow to 5 U.S. Corps and 30 Corps, for they both discovered that the hitherto stubborn opposition on their respective fronts had collapsed and that they were able to ease forward unchallenged for a considerable distance in the wake of the withdrawing enemy.

It was now a question of how fast the enemy could react to the latest developments, since the menacing nature of the threat to his whole eastern flank could no longer be concealed, following the capture of Point 309, and the complete penetration of Seventh Army's lines. In passing, it is interesting to note that when the 8 Corps break-through took place, advanced American forces attacking further west were approaching Avranches and Villedieu, and as yet had not achieved the complete breach in the German positions which two days later enabled Third U.S. Army to pass mobile formations first into

Brittany and later round to the east. Though 8 Corps had neither the orders to penetrate deep into enemy territory in this fashion, nor the supply build-up to sustain any such widespread foray, it is satisfactory to know that the conditions for such an operation were in fact created in the first two days fighting south of Caumont. The spectacular mobile role, however, in the strategy laid down by the Commander-in-Chief, was reserved for American armoured formations and the British and Canadian armies had in the meantime still to hold the overwhelming might of the enemy. All the various pieces in the jig-saw were nevertheless at last coming together, for now the moment was at hand when the Allied forces would begin their wheel-round on the Caen pivot, face east and drive towards the River Seine, and it remained to be seen what the enemy would or could do to master the situation. 116 Panzer Division from south of Caen had arrived during the afternoon west of Tessy, to bolster up the weakened Seventh Army forces resisting the American drive in that area, and a little later 2 Panzer Division was also identified there after its brief trip over the River Orne.

The question of possible reinforcements was closely tied up with the position east of the Orne, for the German High Command dared not withdraw its panzer formations in too wholesale a fashion from this sector, since a major Allied break-through to the south would trap the entire German forces in Normandy. Apart from 2 and 116 Panzer Divisions, there were however several others still uncommitted here at the moment and it was to be expected that one or more of these would now be switched against 8 Corps. Last light Tac R reported some tank movement north-west of Thury Harcourt, and also a considerable amount of motor and horse-drawn transport moving south towards Aunay-sur-Odon. It appeared that on the front of 30 Corps the enemy was falling back, whilst additional armour was being brought in, which would probably find its way to the 8 Corps front on the morrow.

31st July

While the majority of the Scottish units, having first made secure their newly-won positions, were enjoying a well-earned rest, 15 (Scottish) Reconnaissance Regiment had remained in action after nightfall in order to probe forward of Point 309 and report what degree of enemy resistance might be encountered on the next day. By dawn, it had succeeded in crossing the road leading east from St. Martin des Besaces and was patrolling some distance in the south. St. Martin des Besaces itself, being the junction of four trunk roads, was found to be strongly held; 15 (Scottish) Reconnaissance Regiment was therefore instructed to picket the eastern exits from this village and also to be on the watch for any enemy counter attacks which might be delivered from the left. In the meantime, 11 Armoured Division, which was better placed than 15 (Scottish) Division to continue the advance, had been able to push on throughout the night, and was now ordered to capture St. Martin des Besaces from the west. This task was given to 159 Infantry Brigade, but simultaneously 29 Armoured Brigade was to move forward and cut the main road running westwards to Point Aunay. The night being extremely dark and the country densely wooded, 4 King's Shropshire Light Infantry making its way down towards St. Martin des Besaces faced a difficult problem of control, for in the absence of anything other than the most rudimentary tracks, separate bodies would soon become lost in the cross-country journey, especially if much opposition were offered. By a happy chance, a well-defined but obviously rarely used path was discovered leading through the wood itself and along this the whole battalion passed silently in single file. This can hardly be claimed as normal military procedure, since the smallest riposte from the Germans would have sufficed to cause confusion and prevent the battalion from attaining its objective on time. However, as a gamble, necessary and warranted by the situation, it was justified. Moreover, it was successful, for daybreak found 4 King's Shropshire Light Infantry assembled astride the main road and ready to attack the village from the west in conjunction with 8 Rifle Brigade of 29 Armoured Brigade, which with great perseverance had fought its way in the dark down the Caumont road against considerable resistance, as far as the railway skirting the north of St. Martin des Besaces. The German defenders here were not easily subdued, for heavy fighting went on most of the morning, and though an entry into the market square was achieved by 8 Rifle Brigade supported by 3 Royal Tank Regiment about 1100 hours, the village was not wholly cleared until the afternoon.

By this time, however, the importance of this capture had been quite eclipsed by an unheralded exploit by 2 Household Cavalry (the armoured car regiment operating with 11 Armoured Division) earlier in the morning and which was to have a decisive influence on the development of the offensive. Patrolling in front of the advancing 159 Infantry Brigade, a troop of armoured cars had come upon a track leading through the extensive Forêt l'Eveque which was neither blocked by mines nor defended by Germans. The reason for this oversight became apparent later when an enemy wireless message was intercepted showing that the pathway in question formed the boundary between 326 Infantry Division and 3 Parachute Division, and that both these formations assumed the other to be responsible for it. At all events, the Household Cavalry patrol, whose task was to get forward and if possible to reconnoitre the crossings over the next major natural obstacle, the River Souleuvre, was able to pass along it unchecked, and on emerging from the forest found the important bridge over the river on the main road from St. Lo to Le Beny-Bocage not only unblown but unguarded. This is proof, if such be necessary, of the chaos created in the defences of Seventh Army by the speed of the operations conducted by 8 Corps, for the retention of this river line by German forces was a pre-requisite for stabilising the situation here. Two troops of tanks from 2 Northamptonshire Yeomanry were dispatched down the same forest trail to reinforce the Household Cavalry patrol watching the bridge and after a successful encounter on the way with two enemy self-propelled guns of 654 Anti-tank Battalion, making a belated and ineffective appearance, they reached the vital crossing, which for the next six hours was held by this combined force.

Shortly after learning this excellent news, General O'Connor, at 1400 hours, issued a special directive to the Commander of 11 Armoured Division in the following terms:—

"For the future development of the Allied plan it is important that:—

(a) You capture the high ground round Point Aunay to-night, so that the advance to Etouvy can proceed rapidly to-morrow.

(b) You should occupy to-night Point 204, Point 205 and also the high ground east of Le Beny Bocage about Point 266. The latter point will be occupied to-night in sufficient strength for the bridges over the River Souleuvre to be seized from the south to-morrow morning. 2 Household Cavalry will to-night patrol south with the utmost vigour in the direction of Vire. This task is also essential to the Allied plan."

The issue of these instructions marked a notable departure from the original plan formulated by Second Army for "Bluecoat," since in view of the failure of 30 Corps to achieve an equally satisfactory advance, and on hearing of this latest success by 8 Corps, the Army Commander had decided that the latter was to become the main striking exponent in the operation. He accordingly assigned to it the objective originally allotted to 30 Corps in this area—namely, the commanding heights around Le Beny Bocage. The Allied swing to the east was beginning even earlier and further north than had been anticipated, for 8 Corps was now to converge on to the axis of advance of 30 Corps. Whilst this was a highly satisfactory situation at the time, it was to sow the seeds of a big disappointment in store for the Corps three weeks later.

Soon after 1500 hours, 23 Hussars and 3 Monmouthshire Regiment were passed through St. Martin des Besaces with orders to advance via Point Aunay down to the River Souleuvre and there to cross over, using the bridge captured intact by 2 Household Cavalry. In the U.S. Sector 3 Parachute Division had been withdrawing during the morning and 5 U.S. Corps by this time had, therefore, progressed as far as Point Aunay. Though forewarned of the new plan, unfortunately General Gerow had not been able to prevent a detachment of his troops from attempting to carry out a mission he had earlier given them, of occupying the high ground south-west of La Ferriere. As a result the British and U.S. columns met head-on along the Point Aunay road and some considerable delay was caused before the American troops could move aside. 23 Hussars was thus held up and did not in fact begin to cross the river until 2100 hours, after which contact was resumed with enemy forces. Meanwhile the remainder of 11 Armoured Division followed-up and by last light had reached La Couaille on the right and La Ferriere on the left.

So far as the Germans were concerned, Tac R during the morning had again confirmed the movement on a large scale, of armour westwards from Thury Harcourt towards the Corps front, and it remained to be seen which of the Panzer Divisions east of the river had been given the doubtful honour of meeting the new British thrust. Once more, the use of the roads by day showed the measure of the enemy's desperation, for the R.A.F. was able to inflict great execution among his convoys in the brilliantly clear July weather. The sequel, however, followed in the early evening when the first identification was made by a unit of 15 (Scottish) Division of 2 Armoured Recce Regiment of 21 Panzer Division. Three German soldiers digging-in some distance to the east of Point 309 were captured, and quite confidently declared that their division was the first, but that others would follow. Their morale was high, and quite different from that of prisoners from 326 Infantry Division, an increasing number of whom, during the day, had either given themselves up without a fight or were simply deserters. The advance was, henceforth, to become more difficult, and opposition to stiffen.

Elsewhere, although 30 Corps had succeeded by nightfall in making some progress and was roughly on a line parallel with Hervieux and Dampierre, the long advance of 11 Armoured Division during the day had made 8 Corps more exposed than ever on the left, and it was clearly impossible to withdraw 15 (Scottish) Division from its enforced rôle of flank protection. The Corps Commander therefore decided now to make use of Guards Armoured Division, which had moved into the Caumont area some twenty-four hours earlier, and at 1630 hours orders were given to Major-General Allan Adair, commanding the division, to take up the advance on the left of 11 Armoured Division. By dusk, 5 Guards Armoured Brigade in the lead, had encountered the enemy around Point 238, south-east of St. Martin des Besaces. The general situation by the end of the second day of Operation "Bluecoat" was thus very good. The coup carried out on the previous evening by 6 Guards Tank Brigade of capturing Point 309 had been equalled during the afternoon of 31st July by that of 11 Armoured Division in traversing the extremely difficult Forêt l'Eveque and seizing the crossings over the River Souleuvre. The effect of these on the future of the Normandy campaign was incalculable. Not only had the front of Seventh Army been completely shattered, but in addition the British line was now wheeling east around the very high ground on which the Germans had themselves hoped to pivot. Already too, the object of intercepting enemy armour on its way to the American sector was being achieved. On the debit side, however, was the fact that the Corps was still operating in a pronounced salient, for whilst on the right 5 U.S. Corps following up the withdrawing paratroopers, had eased the situation somewhat on that flank, the main danger came from the east. Then 15 (Scottish) Division had perforce to organise the whole of the Corps left flank as a defensive position until such time as the advance of 30 Corps caught up and rendered this unnecessary.

Turning to another aspect of the battle, it is pleasing to record that despite the already deep penetration and the numerous actions involved, the casualties so far had been comparatively light, totalling some 512 all ranks and distributed as follows:—

HQ 8 Corps and Corps troops	24
Guards Armoured Division	152
11 Armoured Division	112
15 (Scottish) Division	198
6 Guards Tank Brigade	25
8 A.G.R.A.	1

Finally, one anecdote, recorded in the history of 11 Armoured Division provides a not unfitting ending to this summary of the first two days of "Bluecoat."

General Roberts took little credit to himself for the coup of 31st July. Approaching him in the morning, one of the officers of his headquarters congratulated him on the day's performance. "Why, Sir," said this officer, sweeping his hand in the approximate direction of the Forêt l'Eveque, "two men and a boy could have held you up there." "Yes, Joe," replied the General, "but they didn't have the boy."

1st August-10th August

During the succeeding ten days occurred some of the heaviest fighting in which 8 Corps took part during the whole of the campaign, for the Germans, alarmed at the poor defence put up by Seventh Army, diverted substantial armoured reinforcements to the Corps sector, in addition to the stop-gap 21 Panzer Division. The new arrivals turned out to be old friends, 9 and 10 SS Panzer Divisions, once again cast in the familiar rôle of "fire brigade." From prisoners' statements, which were confirmed by the stubborn opposition now offered, it appeared that these divisions had received considerable increases in strength, mainly at the expense of cannibalising other enemy formations. Thus 21 Panzer Division had absorbed the remnants of 16 G.A.F. Division, largely destroyed during "Goodwood," whilst 9 and 10 SS Panzer Divisions had also been heavily reinforced. Of the new SS troops a high proportion were discovered to be "Volksdeutsche," that is, they had become Germans through the incorporation of their various homelands in the Reich proper. This development gave some trouble to the Corps interrogators, for if Poles had been comparatively common so far, now they were often confronted with Ukrainians, Latvians, Lithuanians, Czechs, Croats, Slovenes and even on one occasion by an Italian, though he, poor fellow, had found himself in the SS by accident and was in no way representative of their normal fighting spirit. Unfortunately, the mixed nationalities seemed to make little difference to the fighting ability of the SS divisions, which remained as high as ever. The turning movement and the eastwards advance had also brought the Corps against Panzer Gruppe West, now renamed Fifth Panzer Army, and commanded by General der Panzertruppen Heinrich Hans Eberbach. Unlike Seventh Army, its positions were intact, and, since it was confronting Second Army, far more strongly held. It was therefore to be expected that with the arrival of the three Panzer divisions on the Corps front, backed up by the solid ring of resistance stretching to the east around Caen, the advance would be slower. However, this suited the Commander-in-Chief, for Third U.S. Army had now begun to pass through the gap south of Avranches, and after first sending 8 U.S. Corps into Brittany was now itself swinging mobile columns eastwards towards Mortain and Domfront.

Thus, although the progress by 8 Corps in the next period was slower than hitherto, it was in reality a measured driving-back process which was to help encircle and compress almost the entire German forces in Normandy into a small area between Falaise and Argentan known forever to history as the "Falaise Pocket."

At dawn on 1st August the armour again moved forward. On the right 11 Armoured Division by 1100 hours had captured the formidable height, Point 205, overlooking Le Beny Bocage, which by evening was also in the hands of 29 Armoured Brigade. In addition a mixed force of 3 Royal Tank Regiment and 4 King's Shropshire Light Infantry was despatched to hold the bridge over the River Souleuvre east of the town, thereby cutting off any enemy attempt to retreat along this axis, and also to occupy the small village of St. Charles de Percy somewhat to the south. With its forward positions secured against surprise, the remainder of the division could then be disposed along the Le Beny Bocage feature in readiness to push on at first light on the next day. The German High Command appeared to be ignorant of the extent of British penetration to the south, for 2 Household Cavalry was able to send patrols into the ruined city of Vire, where little enemy activity was reported. However, this lay in the path of 19 U.S. Corps, now following up the withdrawing 3 Parachute Division on the right and pinching out 5 U.S. Corps in so doing. Vire was therefore not to be entered by 8 Corps. If, however, the Germans were not clear about this area, in the northern half of the Corps sector they had no such doubts, for a series of sharp counter-attacks were put in during the morning against 15 (Scottish) Division between the Bois du Homme and St. Martin des Besaces by tanks and infantry of 21 Panzer Division, reinforced by remnants of 326 Infantry Division. Unco-ordinated and lacking artillery support, these efforts were easily beaten off by the experienced Scots, who, although still aligned in a defensive position along the left bank, were able to improve their position south of Point 309 by assaulting and occupying two enemy strongpoints in La Marcellière and Galet. The main body of 21 Panzer Division, however, appeared to have formed up on the high ground between Le Tourneur and Vaumartin, where is constituted a direct block to the move-forward of Guards Armoured Division. Shortly after daybreak 5 Coldstream Guards, supported by 2 Armoured Irish Guards, launched an attack on Point 238, but heavy opposition, especially from dug-in tanks, caused fighting here to last until midday before the enemy was finally subdued.

As by this time it was evident that resistance along the divisional axis of advance was going to be strong, at 1230 hours the Corps Commander ordered 5 Guards Armoured Brigade to hold the ground so far gained, while 32 Guards Brigade cleared the country astride the centre line up to Le

Tourneur and captured the bridges to the south and east respectively. This task was completed by dusk save for a few pockets of enemy holding out around Le Tourneur, which were eliminated on the morrow. The division then pushed forward towards Vassy in two mixed columns, with a third in reserve for any further necessary mopping-up operations.

The following day, 2nd August, was to witness much harder going, since the Germans were now sited most favourably for defence and in strength along the high ridge running south-west towards Mont Pincon. As the left hand group consisting of 1 Motor Grenadier Guards and 2 Armoured Grenadier Guards advanced via Catheolles towards Montchamp, the enemy entrenched on the plateau south of Montamy and Arelais, countered with a thrust by several "Tiger" tanks, which caused a temporary withdrawal of the Guards, since tanks had not been able to support their attack up the steep heavily wooded slopes. Several more enemy sorties were made from this area during the day, and no further progress was made. The right column, too, after passing through St. Charles de Percy and cutting the main road from Vire to Villers Bocage, was heavily fired upon from the high ground on its left. At the same time, some infiltration between its units enforced a halt, for it was clear that the revived enemy strength was brought about by the newly-arrived presence of 9 SS Panzer Division. In the meantime, 2 Armoured Recce Welsh Guards, masked to some extent by the second column, had pushed ahead to within 2,000 yards of Estry, but this proved impossible to by-pass. A day of confused fighting ensued, therefore, with all three groups of Guards Armoured Division in contact with a vastly strengthened enemy.

A similar story was told by 11 Armoured Division. By the time that 2 Northamptonshire Yeomanry as right flank guard had reached Etouvy, 3 Parachute Division had begun to organise the defence of Vire, and was holding 19 U.S. Corps in desperate fighting on the western outskirts. After nightfall, German paratroopers, with considerable enterprise and daring, penetrated the positions of the Northamptonshire Yeomanry, causing a most uncomfortable night for this regiment, and, no infantry being available, a squadron of Sappers was despatched to assist it in an infantry rôle—an unusual occurrence for them. Meanwhile, 159 Infantry Brigade and 29 Armoured Brigade had set off at first light towards Tinchebray, but throughout 2nd August 11 Armoured Division, like its neighbours, encountered increasingly stiff resistance. There was a firm impression generally that the division was running into opposition moving up from the east and south-east, whilst the difficult terrain which prevented deployment, paradoxically enough caused some dispersion among its units. This in turn was aggravated by the infiltration tactics adopted by the Germans. Nevertheless, by evening, on the right 159 Infantry Brigade had reached the important lateral road about five miles east of Vire, whilst 23 Hussars accompanied by 8 Rifle Brigade, the leading units of 29 Armoured Brigade, after being halted on the outskirts of the village of Chenedolle, finally took up a position on the Perrier spur somewhat to the north.

The completely changed situation made it obvious that more infantry was needed. 30 Corps had now moved up sufficiently for 15 (Scottish) Division to be released from its flank protection duties, and General O'Connor, therefore, decided to bring the Scots forward by brigade groups in the rear of Guards Armoured Division. A newcomer to 8 Corps in the shape of 3 Infantry Division was also placed at his disposal and ordered to concentrate as soon as possible in the Caumont area, where it was joined by 4 Armoured Brigade. Corps Headquarters, too, moved during the afternoon to a new location at La Fouquerie, from whence a magnificent view extended southwards over the battlefield.

The day marked, however, the close of the period of rapid advance, for at this stage the enemy was very full of fight and lost no opportunity to counter-attack. These attacks themselves were not mounted in great strength, but were usually made by about six tanks with one or two companies of infantry, and each was preceded by heavy mortar fire. In the main they were directed against the open left flank of the Corps or the apex of the advance of 11 Armoured Division, and conducted on the basis of infiltration between the defended localities. Circumstances, moreover, favoured the enemy for the moment, for

(a) as a result of its long advance 8 Corps was not suitably disposed for defence in that it was inevitably strung out and thin along the front; and (b) the lie of the country favoured the attacker, for there were three ridges successively across the line of advance, with roads running along the valleys between them from the direction of the open flank—a notable example being the Burcy-Presles valley where 11 Armoured Division experienced so much trouble.

The next seven days were therefore difficult for the Corps and only slight progress was achieved at heavy cost. The wisdom of having organised the leading divisions into mixed infantry and armoured groups was, however, more than upheld, since had this not been done beforehand it would have been impossible to hold the positions won, once 21 Panzer Division and 9 SS Panzer Division were brought against the front. By 4th August when 10 SS Panzer Division also made its appearance, it was doubly fortunate that 3 Infantry Division and 15 (Scottish) Division were available as backing for Guards and 11 Armoured Divisions and able to place infantry brigades at their disposal.

Indeed, having collected substantial armoured forces west of the Orne, the enemy was now not content merely to halt 8 Corps, but grew ambitious and wished to re-establish a main line of resistance, based on good natural features.

The line desired ran south-west from Thury Harcourt via Mont Pincon through Estry and along the Perrier ridge to Vire. Unfortunately, in the south it had already been breached by 11 Armoured Division, but, nothing daunted, the Germans set out to recover the lost ground, first employing the infiltration tactics already described. Had the enemy been able to re-occupy the Perrier ridge, the whole area between that feature and the River Souleuvre would certainly have become untenable, resulting in both armoured divisions being forced to withdraw. However, though leading units like 23 Hussars and 2 Fife and Forfar Yeomanry were placed in a precarious and unhappy position for some days, General Roberts accepted the risk entailed in maintaining these positions. The Corps Commander, too, fully agreed with his decision, and placed 185 Infantry Brigade from 3 Infantry Division under his command as soon as possible in order to strengthen this sector, which in conjunction with that of Guards Armoured Division on the left was now organised as a firm base. In consequence many isolated pockets of enemy were mopped up, and maintenance traffic, which in some cases had been interrupted for over 48 hours, could be resumed.

General O'Connor further decided that while the armour stood fast in the centre, on the flanks 15 (Scottish Division) should begin to exploit towards Estry and Vassy and 3 Infantry Division southwards towards the hills west of Flers; furthermore, if any enemy weakness developed on the Corps front, it was to be followed up by a general advance by all four divisions.

The Germans, feeling their lack of success, changed their tactics and brought up a fresh infantry formation in the shape of 363 Infantry Division newly arrived from Denmark to take over from 10 SS Panzer Division. Two days more were spent in preparation and survey, and finally a heavy attack was launched by the latter at 1900 hours on 6th August against the apex of the Corps salient, just at the moment when 185 Infantry Brigade was relieving 159 Infantry Brigade. Much heavy fighting ensued, but despite employing more than fifty tanks in this desperate bid, only a few hundred yards were gained in the early stages, and 1 Royal Norfolk and 3 Monmouthshire Regiments subsequently held their vital positions around Sourdeval, whilst 2 Fife and Forfar Yeomanry destroyed much of the intruding armour. Further east SS Panzer Grenadiers pressed 2 Royal Warwickshire Regiment very hard indeed, but by forming a tight "leaguer" with 23 Hussars, in the gathering dusk the Germans were halted, their losses mounted, and finally the fury of the assault died down with the enemy withdrawing. The Corps and Divisional artillery during all this time was greatly in demand and concentration after concentration of fire was brought down on the SS assembly areas, where great carnage must have taken place. Once repelled, it became a question of finding out what forces the enemy had used in his venture. This proved illuminating, for while the whole attack had been led and co-ordinated by 10 SS Panzer Division, it had included a battalion of tanks from 116 Panzer Division, a battalion of engineers fighting as infantry, and a mixed force of "Tiger" tanks from 2 SS Panzer Corps Tank Battalion, strengthened with a few self-propelled guns. The divisional organisation of the enemy was beginning to break up and an orderly command becoming progressively more impossible for him.

Elsewhere Guards Armoured Division and 15 (Scottish) Division had made limited advances against fierce opposition, although Estry, which had taken a heavy toll of lives already, proved equally obstinate, and only the northern half of the village was occupied by the Scots.

6th August was, however, to be the last occasion in Normandy on which the enemy was destined to attack 8 Corps in strength, for on the following day, on the orders of Hitler, four panzer divisions, 2 and 116 Panzer and 1 SS and 2 SS Panzer Divisions, together with 84 Infantry Division, disengaged themselves from their immediate battle areas and attempted to thrust westwards to cut off the American spearheads now deep into France After some initial success in the morning against 30 U.S. Infantry Division at Mortain, two further American divisions were switched to the scene and overhead the Allied Air Forces brought their combined weight to bear against the enemy columns. Although von Kluge, who had done his best to convince his superiors of the complete impracticability of this attack, reinforced failure during the afternoon of 8th August by the addition of elements of 9 Panzer, 10 SS Panzer Division and 363 Infantry Division, through the intensity and continuity of the air attack, the issue was never in doubt. It was the gambler's final throw. On the same day the Commander-in-Chief had issued orders for a general advance to the Seine and simultaneously for Third U.S. Army to carry out a wide enveloping movement north of Paris. With the Mortain counter-stroke thrusting the Wehrmacht forces deeper into his trap, on 8th August he ordered a concurrent envelopment by American troops due north from Alencon, whilst earlier that morning a major Canadian offensive broke against Falaise. It only remained thus for 8, 12 and 30 Corps to drive eastwards against the pocket as rapidly as possible.

Awake too late to the threat to his whole force, Field Marshal von Kluge asked and received the Fuehrer's permission to retire behind the River Seine.

Hastily pulling back his armour from Mortain towards Argentan he ordered the divisions facing Second Army to hold on at all costs in order to permit an orderly general withdrawal. On the Corps front, therefore, the German soldier, obedient to the last, continued to resist staunchly. Fighting and advancing without respite under the most trying conditions for nearly a fortnight the troops of 8 Corps, as all commanders realised, were now tired. Possibly the situation was best summed up in the following message from General Roberts read to all ranks of 11 Armoured Division at this time:

" 1. I wish all ranks to know that during the present period of operations tremendous demands will be made on their powers of endurance. Although the enemy is resisting very stubbornly on our front, all our men should realise that his endurance is equally, if not more, tested than ours. The main Allied plan is developing with the greatest success, and superhuman efforts now will not only save casualties later, but have every chance of bringing the war with Germany to an early conclusion.

2. I fully realise that a stage is eventually reached when tiredness and the disorganisation caused by prolonged hard fighting results in such a loss of efficiency that operations carried out by a unit in such a condition do not pay a reasonable dividend.

I can assure you that I am watching this, and will only call upon troops to do the almost impossible and not the completely impossible.

3. This Division has already achieved so much, not only in the attack but also by stubborn defence in isolated positions that I have no doubt that I can rely on all ranks to prolong their efforts. I am only anxious that everyone should know that the stakes are high and the prize great.

It may be of interest, but perhaps not of comfort, to realise that the greatest enemy resistance at the present time is on 8 Corps front. By containing such enemy strength we are being of the utmost value to the remainder of the army."

The Commander-in-Chief, too, issued a personal message on 11th August forecasting the victory ahead and urging no relaxation of the all-out effort. This therefore continued relentlessly, for on the same day Operation "Grouse" began, with 8 Corps directed towards the high ground west of Flers, and 30 Corps making for Condé sur Noireau; though initial progress was slow and achieved at heavy cost, by 15th August it was clear that the enemy was withdrawing his armour towards the Seine. On the afternoon of that day resistance on the Corps front began to collapse, and on 16th August 3 Infantry Division entered Flers, where for the first time the thrill of liberating a town was experienced. In the words of the old song, henceforth " it was a summer of roses and wine," for the French inhabitants at last decided that their German oppressors had gone for ever, and gave the British troops everywhere a great welcome. Along the whole of this western flank, enemy soldiers now started to surrender in batches, whilst the Allied Air Forces and artillery began pounding the Germans trapped in the area enclosed by Falaise-Argentan-Trun-Chambois. The slaughter continued for the next four days, during which time the British, Canadian and American forces tightened and compressed the ring around the doomed Germans, now making repeated and desperate efforts to break out and escape. By 20th August, except for some minor mopping up operations, resistance was at an end and the battle of Normandy was over.

Not for 8 Corps, however, was the thrill of the chase and the breath-taking pursuit to the borders of Holland. The fortunes of war, the converging axes of the British and U.S. armies, together with the inadequacy of the French road system, had combined to pinch out the Corps a few miles east of Flers. 5 U.S. Corps, now once again operating on the right to the north of Argentan, and 30 Corps moving east through Falaise, did not permit of a third body of troops advancing between them, and thus from 18th August 8 Corps was out of action, save for some small clearing operations in the Bois de Messel. To say that it was a disappointment to all at Corps Headquarters, from General O'Connor downwards, is to state the obvious. It was, however, inevitable, since to collect together the Corps troops and Services strung out far to the rear, would have taken at least two days more, without any question of further preparation for a move-up of eighty miles to the River Seine. Moreover, it would have meant passing through 30 Corps on the narrow Normandy roads, considerable delay would have resulted, and, speed being vital, the Commander-in-Chief could not afford to take this risk. The shape of things to come had actually been apparent from 14th August, when 11 Armoured Division passed under command of 30 Corps, and it was some consolation that the drive eastwards was spearheaded by this magnificent formation, as also was the fact that one of the assaulting divisions over the Seine was 15 (Scottish) Division, under command of 12 Corps from the same date.

The ease with which this formidable barrier was surmounted, together with the debacle suffered on its banks by the remnants of Fifth Panzer Army and Seventh Army fleeing in disorder and second only to that of the Falaise pocket in its magnitude, were alike greater than the most optimistic predictions on the Allied side. Indeed, it had been anticipated that the British, Canadian and U.S. armies, after lining up along this water obstacle, would find it necessary to undertake an opposed crossing of the scope which was later to be carried out over the River Rhine. General O'Connor being warned of this eventuality, in fact took steps to prepare accordingly and ordered his two remaining divisions to carry out assault-crossing training at a practice bridging site on a lake west of Flers, to the vicinity of which on 21st August Corps Headquarters was also moved to supervise it. The training proceeded satisfactorily and would have been concluded by 28th August. However, on 24th August Guards Armoured Division was placed under 30 Corps and ordered to concentrate in the area of Condé sur Noireau. Three days later the Seine was crossed in force and the race by Guards and 11 Armoured Divisions to Brussels and Antwerp was on.

8 Corps back in Normandy, though now feeling a trifle lonely, was still able to assist, for the Corps R.A.S.C. transport together with many first line vehicles were called upon to help build up Second Army roadhead stocks as quickly as possible along the tremendous line of communication from the Normandy beaches to Belgium, some three hundred miles away. Certain specialised units and equipment, too, such as Air O.P. flights and high-powered wirelesses were put at the disposal of Second Army for intercommunication purposes, and a senior officer managed to get shot down, fortunately without serious damage, whilst surveying Versailles from the air! Another substantial task accruing in this period to the Corps was to organise, through intelligence channels, a check-up on the losses sustained by the German Army in the Falaise pocket—an undertaking which involved counting many thousands of vehicles and equipments.

Meanwhile the short break allowed a number of new localities to become familiar with the sign of the " White Knight "—notably Granville (wonderful bathing), Mont St. Michael (wonderful food), and the Breton capital, Rennes (wonderful shops), whilst at least one member of the Staff received permission to visit his Paris home and entered the French metropolis in triumph with the conquering 2 French Armoured Division.

For several days more the Corps was allowed to relax, enjoying the local bathing in the River Vire, exploring the countryside in a variety of luxurious cars of the Mercedes Benz and Horch variety (not for nothing was the Falaise pocket combed), and listening to George Formby and other ENSA entertainers. Finally, on the last day of the month, a warning order came for 8 Corps to establish itself, temporarily, east of the River Seine in the general area of Les Andelys-Morgny, 55 miles north-west of Paris, and on 1st September the move-up began.

The Results of Operation "Bluecoat" and a Review of the Normandy Campaign

General Dempsey at the conclusion of Operation "Bluecoat" stated that the results achieved by 8 Corps were of the highest importance to the whole Allied plan, and in particular to the break-through of the American Armies. It is also certain that the breaching of Seventh Army lines south of Caumont in the centre of the Allied front came as a complete surprise to the enemy at a moment when his attention was focused on its limits. Hence his slow reaction extending over nearly 48 hours before measures to restore the situation began to take effect. In those few precious hours took place the two outstanding features of the battle, for this golden opportunity was wholeheartedly accepted by 8 Corps. The first was the action carried out by 6 Guards Tank Brigade on the opening day of the operation, when its tanks proceeding with the utmost dash and skill across extremely difficult country to their final objective, captured the massive and dominating Point 309 far in advance of the accompanying infantry. Moreover, when it is realised that this was the occasion upon which the brigade received its baptism of fire, the greatest credit is reflected on its commander, Brigadier Verney, and all officers concerned with training it for war.

The second highlight of the battle was the manner in which 11 Armoured Division advanced through the Forêt l'Eveque and across the River Souleuvre to capture the equally dominating Beny Bocage area, a feat which was to prove decisive for closing the Falaise pocket from the west.

8 Corps can therefore be justly proud of its contribution to the overwhelming Allied victory in Normandy, the results of which are enshrined in history for ever. It is doubtful whether in so short a time as fourteen weeks an expectant, resolute and strongly entrenched enemy has ever been so crushingly defeated, least of all when the opposing side had first to launch an amphibious operation from a distant shore, endure a gruelling build-up under constant attack, and finally carry out an enveloping movement of some hundreds of miles.

Nearly 50 divisions had either been destroyed or severely mauled in the fighting at a cost to the enemy of half a million casualties, half in dead or wounded and the remainder in prisoners to 21 Army Group. A further 100,000 soldiers were locked up in the Brittany ports and the Channel Islands, and 200,000 more were to be collected during the pursuit up to the Dutch borders. Over 20 senior generals had been killed or captured whilst the enemy Supreme Commander had been twice changed, for on 17th August Field-Marshal Walter Model arrived from Russia to take over from von Kluge. So far as *materiel de guerre* is concerned, the Germans had lost 3,500 guns and 1,500 tanks, together with tens of thousands of vehicles and a vast array of equipment of all types. The losses sustained by the Allied armies, on the other hand, were a mere fraction of these staggering totals.

So far as 8 Corps was concerned, Operation "Bluecoat" and subsequently, cost in all 5,114 casualties of all types, whilst losses for the whole campaign were distributed as follows:—

	Killed		Wounded		Missing	
	Offrs	ORs	Offrs	ORs	Offrs	ORs
H.Q. 8 Corps and Corps Troops ...	4	41	10	143	6	21
Guards Armoured Division	38	317	82	1435	8	161
7 Armoured Division	7	55	28	324	—	22
11 Armoured Division	36	338	134	1708	32	394
3 British Division	5	78	61	672	4	121
15 (Scottish) Division	49	569	155	3229	20	428
43 (Wessex) Division	21	255	79	1373	18	678
53 (Welsh) Division	12	103	25	455	4	65
6 Guards Tank Brigade	10	35	16	81	2	48
8 A.G.R.A.	4	39	5	72	—	—
Miscellaneous Units	17	96	59	393	6	80
Totals ...	203	1926	654	9885	100	2018

Sad to relate, Lieutenant-Colonel Sir Walter Barttelot, who succeeded Brigadier Verney in 6 Guards Tank Brigade on the latter assuming command of 7 Armoured Division, was killed when his scout car hit a mine on the road near Estry on 16th August; whilst on 5th August Major-General MacMillan, who had done so much for 15 (Scottish) Division, was wounded, though fortunately slightly, and 8 Corps saw him no more until the winter.

Hitler, throughout his rise to power and reign, had always held a tenacious belief in the value of "will power"—*der Triumph der Wille*, indeed, was one of his favourite maxims. At last, however, he had met on the battlefield an opponent equally endowed in this sphere, for the outstanding and astonishing fact about the campaign in Normandy is that it was fought exactly as laid down beforehand by the Commander-in-Chief. The plan he had formulated had been relentlessly followed by him, despite the minor delays, criticisms and setbacks inevitable in any campaign. Had the succeeding phase of Allied operations been so planned and organised, there can be little doubt that the war would have been over long before Christmas 1944, but before passing on to the next chapter to see how operations developed during the ensuing autumn, let us glance at two final quotations which express better than anything the feelings of the opposing soldiers at this juncture.

Here is the first—a triumphant message to all Allied troops from the Commander-in-Chief, now fittingly created a Field-Marshal for his achievement:—

"1. On the 11th of August I spoke to the officers and men of the Allied Armies in N.W. France. I said we must 'write off' the powerful German force that was causing us so much trouble; we must finish it, once and for all, and so hasten the end of the war.

2. And to-day, ten days later, it has been done. The German armies in North-West France have suffered a decisive defeat; the destruction of enemy personnel and equipment in and about the so-called 'Normandy pocket' has been terrific, and it is still going on; any enemy units that manage to get away will not be in a fit condition to fight again for months; there are still many surprises in store for the fleeing remnants.

The victory has been definite, complete and decisive.

3. As soldiers, we all want to pay our tribute to the Allied Air Forces. I doubt if ever in the history of war air forces have had such opportunities, or have taken such good advantage of them. The brave and brilliant work of the pilots has aroused our greatest admiration; without their support, we soldiers could have achieved no success.

4. Where all have done so well, it is difficult to single out any for special praise.

As a British General, I can speak for all the soldiers of the Empire, and can express our high admiration for the brave fighting qualities of the American Armies in the opening stages of the 'break-in' battle on 25th July and following days; and we followed with tremendous enthusiasm their great achievements during the wheel of the right flank almost to the gates of Paris. We never want to fight alongside better soldiers.

As an Allied Commander, and the overall Commander of the land forces under General Eisenhower, I can praise the fighting qualities and tenacity in battle of the British, Canadian and Polish troops on the eastern flank; they fought the enemy relentlessly, and took heavy toll of him during the whole of this great battle.

5. But surely it matters little who did 'this' or 'that.' All that matters is that it was well and truly done by the whole Allied team.

The proper motto for Allies should be:
   'One for all, and all for one.'
And that is our motto.

I want to thank you all for the way you responded to the call.

6. The victory in N.W. France, south of the Seine, marks the beginning of the end of German military domination of France. Much still remains to be done, but it will now be done the more easily.

7. And what next?

Having brought disaster to the German forces in N.W. France, we must now complete the destruction of such of his forces as are still available to be destroyed. After knowing what has happened to their armies in N.W. France, it is unlikely that these forces will now come to us; so we will go to them.

8. 'The Lord mighty in battle' has given us the victory.

The news is very good from the war fronts all over the world.

The end of the war is in sight; let us finish off the business in record time."

The second quotation is the conclusion to a long and dignified apologia sent by Field-Marshal von Kluge to the Fuehrer on the day following his dismissal and on which he was to commit suicide:—

"My Fuehrer.—I think I may claim for myself that I did everything within my power to be equal to the situation. In my covering letter to Field-Marshal Rommel's memorandum which I sent you, I already pointed out the possible outcome of the situation. Both Rommel and I and probably all the other commanders here in the West, with experience of battle against the Anglo-Americans, with their preponderance of material, foresaw the present development. We were not listened to. Our appreciations were NOT dictated by pessimism, but from the sober knowledge of the facts. I do not know whether Field-Marshal Model, who has been proved in every sphere, will still master the situation. From my heart I hope so. Should it not be so, however, and your new, greatly desired weapons, especially of the air force, not succeed then, my Fuehrer, make up your mind to end the war. The German people have borne such untold suffering that it is time to put an end to this frightfulness.

There must be ways to attain this end and above all prevent the Reich from falling under the Bolshevist heel. The actions of some of the officers taken prisoner in the East have always been an enigma to me. My Fuehrer, I have always admired your greatness, your conduct in the gigantic struggle and your iron will to maintain yourself and National Socialism. If Fate is stronger than your will and your genius so is Providence. You have fought an honourable and great fight. History will prove that for you. Show yourself now also great enough to put an end to a hopeless struggle when necessary.

I depart from you, my Fuehrer, as one who stood nearer to you than you perhaps realized in the consciousness that I did my duty to the utmost.

Heil, my Fuehrer,
(Signed) VON KLUGE,
18th August, 1944. Field-Marshal."

CHAPTER 5

Normandy to the River Maas

The Situation in the West on 1st September 1944

THE conclusion of the supreme battle of Normandy marked also the end of the phase in which Field-Marshal Montgomery held operational command over all Allied ground forces, for General Eisenhower decided to assume direct control of the land battle from 1st September. Hitherto, as his Chief of Staff remarked at a press conference, he had not been engaged in the day-to-day operations, but in planning three months ahead. Let us therefore turn to an examination of the general situation obtaining on his assumption of command. It was a period of tense expectation, for on all sides informed opinion considered that the war with Germany was virtually over, and that in a week or two the greatly superior mobility and strength of the Allies, striking deep into Germany, would bring about the final collapse of the Hitlerite power. Supreme Headquarters until now stationed in England, was brought over to France with considerable speed and opened officially on 1st September. Meanwhile, from the middle of August onwards, an exchange of views between Field-Marshal Montgomery and General Eisenhower makes it plain that until a comparatively late date in that month the Allied plan for advancing into the Reich was not firm. Field-Marshal Montgomery favoured what he termed "one full-blooded thrust across the Rhine and into the heart of Germany backed by the whole of the resources of the Allied Armies." General Eisenhower, on the other hand, was more cautious and decided to line up the British, Canadian and U.S. armies along the River Rhine, establishing bridgeheads wherever possible, and not undertaking, for administrative reasons, operations further to the east until the port of Antwerp was captured and opened to traffic. This policy was known as the "broad front policy," and resulted in the Allies one month later manning a line four hundred miles long and extending from Switzerland westwards to the sea. A study of Allied strategy, and least of all criticism of it, has no part in this account of the operations of 8 Corps. In order, however, to understand the future development of the campaign a short explanation of affairs at the beginning of September is necessary.

For the Germans themselves it was a time of great anxiety, for the general withdrawal from France and Belgium forced upon them by the results of Operation "Overlord" could only be carried out in the greatest confusion, as the new German Supreme Commander was obliged to acknowledge in the following rallying call to his dispirited troops, issued on 3rd September:—

"*Soldiers of the Western Army:*

With the enemy advance and the withdrawal on our front, a great stream of troops has been set in motion. Several hundred thousand soldiers are moving backwards, Army, Air Force and tank units, which must re-assemble and form new strongpoints or lines according to a plan and orders they receive.

Among them there stream along, together with headquarters now superfluous, columns which have been routed, which have broken out from the front and which for the moment have no firm destination and could receive no clear orders. Town Majors' offices and headquarters of rearward towns are often taking on tasks which could not overtax a corporal and three men. So, while closely packed columns turn off the road and get themselves sorted out, the stream of the others pushes on. With their vehicles travel idle talk, rumours, haste, inconsiderateness, unnecessary disorder and short-sighted selfishness. They may bring a feeling into the rear areas and into the fully intact bodies of the fighting troops which must be prevented at this moment of extreme tension by the severest measures.

As your new Commander-in-Chief I direct this call to your honour as soldiers. We have lost a battle, but I tell you, we will still win this war ! I cannot say more now, although I know there are many questions burning on the troops' lips. Despite everything that has happened, do not allow your firm confident faith in Germany's future to be shaken one whit.

I must, however, make known to you the gravity of this day and hour. This moment will end and should separate the weaklings from the real men. Every single man carries now the same responsibility: when his commander falls out he must takes his place and carry on in his spirit.

I demand of you categorically:

1. Report without any hesitation to the nearest headquarters or collecting point. In any statements there about your withdrawal, about orders given, your destination and your tasks, stick precisely to the facts.

2. Do not expect that headquarters or collecting points can deal with you and your affairs, except quickly fix you up as suitably as is now necessary. Think over to yourself what is best and most right in the situation.

3. Don't sit back with your hands folded ! Stand up and get about actively, and don't rely on luck. Above all, don't give yourself up to the feeling that luck would never come to you. It comes to every man who has his heart in the right place. A quiet word, a sensible thought, a steady word of advice at the right moment, will give to countless others the necessary support, confidence, self-reliance, self-belief, and the right demeanour.

4. Show increasingly to the outside world a flawless discipline. I have satisfied myself that your inward spirit is flawless. Do not forget that even the slightest gesture, each word, every proof of honour, shows the population that the spirit and cohesion of the German Army are intact. So let your inward feelings be fully demonstrated outwardly ; your head high in all difficulties ; your body erect ; your salute smart and confident. By the French and Belgians too, the fighting worth of a unit and of each individual soldier will be judged by their outward behaviour. The terrorist himself, our most cowardly enemy, thinks so too ! He will sooner attack a slack unmanly soldier than one who strides along erect and confident and gives that impression by his soldierly bearing or his correct salute.

5. Let yourselves be irritated by nothing, especially not by stupid chattering, pessimistic rumours and idle talk, which the enemy seeks to bring you. Take immediate steps against all such panic mongers. The

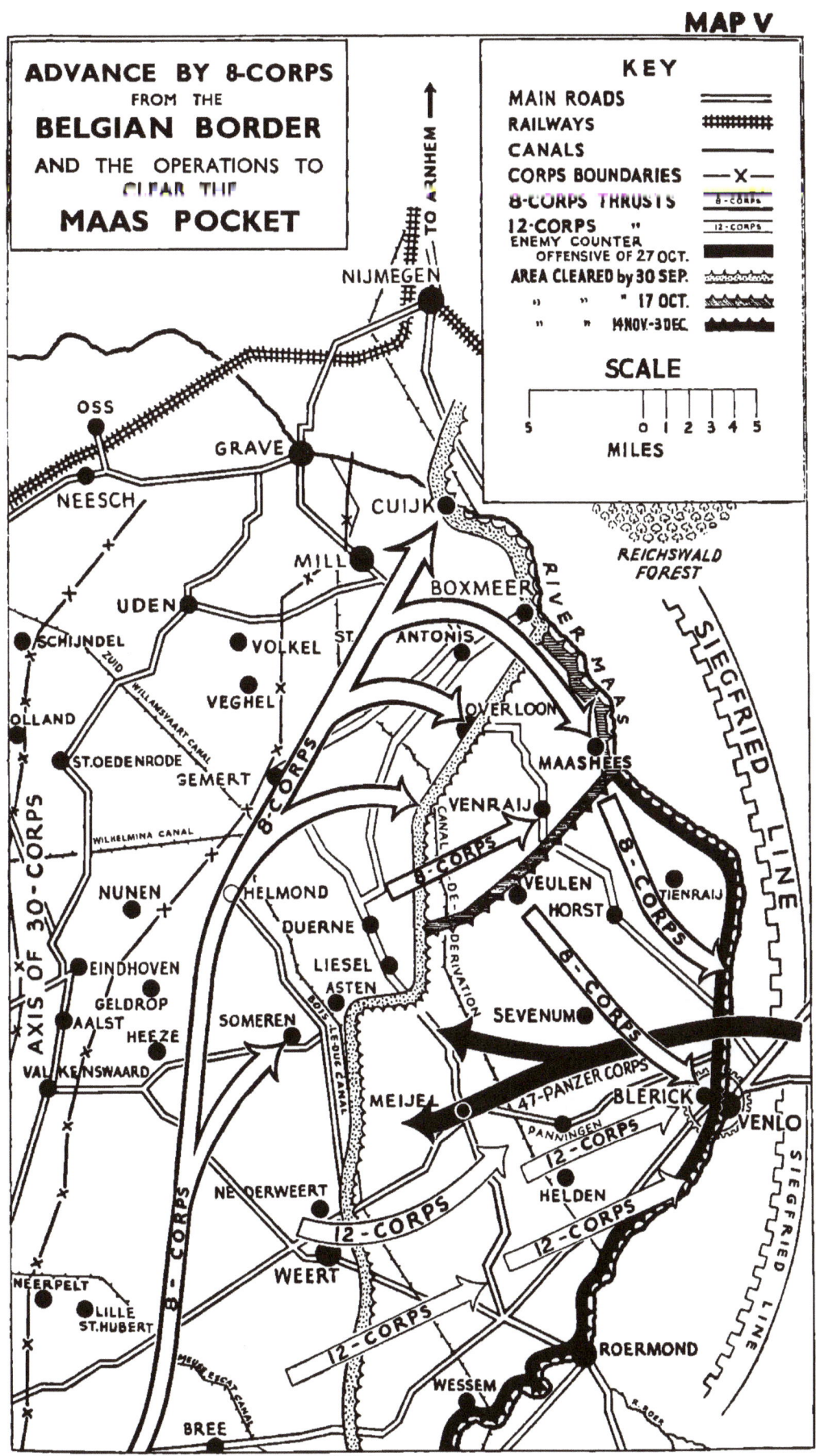

enemy has lost battles for four years. He has for the first time won a battle against us. He has not won it because he is cleverer and better and braver. He is not a magician. He is not everywhere. If one added together all the tanks which rumour mongers reported they had seen, the enemy would have a hundred thousand. In fact they were often only very small spearheads. They can be increasingly halted by defensive obstacles of all kinds. Often the rumours have done us more harm than those tanks. With courage and presence of mind make an extra effort: stop important positions being given up needlessly, necessary weapons, equipment and fortifications being over hastily blown up. For every hand grenade, every rifle, every gallon of petrol is now needed to arm the new line to receive our troops. They are more important than suit-cases or useless plunder.

6. Take thought, then, that at this moment everything adds up to the necessity to gain the time which the Fuehrer needs to bring into operation new troops and new weapons. They will come!

Soldiers, we must gain time for the Fuehrer!

(Signed) MODEL, Field-Marshal."

In the Reich itself Himmler, appointed to command the German replacement and training armies, was struggling to raise the twenty-sixth and last of the series of divisions formed during the war—the so-called "Volksgrenadier" divisions, derisively nicknamed "Götterdämmerung" by the Allies. The Volkssturm, or German equivalent of the Home Guard, was also called into existence by Goebbels, busily engaged in bolstering up the home front. In the last weeks of August these measures were in full swing, and by the end of the first two weeks of September, through remarkable improvisation, the Wehrmacht had re-established a coherent line in the West. For the Allies the rapid advance, too, brought in its train gigantic problems of administration and supply, magnified many times by the length of the front along which the British, Canadian and, especially, American armies were now extended. The principle of concentration of effort had seemingly been abandoned, with resultant benefit to the non-mobile enemy, for our weak advanced spearheads, opposed by scratch enemy battle groups armed very largely with light infantry weapons such as Panzerfausts (the equivalent of Bazookas or PIATS), suffered progressively serious checks from quite disproportionate enemy forces—e.g., General Patton's Third U.S. Army being held up for over a month before Metz, the last fort of which, defended by a German cadet school, was not in fact reduced until 13th December. The enemy was thus enabled to make a timely use of the Siegfried Line, which by virtue of being constructed in hundreds of mutually-supporting small concrete forts and emplacements and not as one continuous defence line like the Maginot Line, was ideally manned by these scattered battle groups. Nor could the overwhelming might of the R.A.F. and U.S.A.A.F. be used to advantage in close support operations like the swift concentrated blows which had paid such a handsome dividend during July and August, since the enemy forces presented no worth-while targets, and in any case the Allies were no longer strong enough to mass sufficient troops to follow any such attack without a major regrouping.

In conformity with General Eisenhower's decision, and with 21 Army Group weakened by the loss of First U.S. Army, Field-Marshal Montgomery decided to establish bridgeheads over the Rivers Maas and Rhine and to await the time when his forces would be sufficiently strong to advance eastwards and occupy the Ruhr—a task beyond the power alone of 21 Army Group, now comprising only First Canadian and Second British Armies, some fifteen divisions in all. During this period also the approaches to the great port of Antwerp were to be cleared, which would eliminate the necessity of depending on the beaches of Normandy for supplies. The latter task was to be accomplished under the direction of General Crerar, whilst General Dempsey organised the advance to the north. Although no additional American armoured or infantry divisions were available to reinforce 21 Army Group, in lieu General Eisenhower placed 1 Airborne Corps, commanded by Lieut-General F. A. M. Browning, and consisting of two U.S. and one British airborne division, at Field-Marshal Montgomery's disposal. He in turn allotted it to Second Army, where three further corps were already planning to carry out General Dempsey's plan—one to lead and two to back up. It thus became necessary for 8 Corps to be called forward with all possible speed from the Seine area to take part in the projected operations.

Headquarters 8 Corps was established on 2nd September near Morgny and adjacent to 43 (Wessex) Division, at a village called St. Germain, and for some days thereafter virtually performed the duties of a line of communication headquarters—taking charge of residues and organising their move-up into Belgium, and completing certain engineering commitments such as the construction of bridges along the axis of advance. The Corps Provost branch, too, accepted and successfully fulfilled the enormous task of signposting the main Second Army route to Brussels, while a detachment from 3 Infantry Division rounded up numbers of enemy soldiers at large in the forests south-west of Amiens. In addition, not content with having ordered 8 Corps to investigate German losses in the Falaise pocket, Second Army now asked for a further report on enemy installations between the River Seine and Arras—no mean undertaking. It was thus anything but an idle period.

Within ten days the majority of the changes had been effected, the remaining formations and units in Normandy had begun to move up and 8 Corps found itself some 60,000 strong with 3 and 43 Infantry Divisions, 6 (Guards) and 34 Tank Brigades, 3, 5, 8 and 59 A.Gs.R.A. and numerous corps troops, all under command. On 10th September orders were received for Corps Headquarters to move in stages to Nosseghem, on the outskirts of Brussels, and on the following day the advance party left for this new area, actually setting itself up in a small place with the delightful name of Erps Querps, about eight miles east of the Belgian capital.

It was hoped that the supply situation would permit the remainder of the Corps to concentrate by 15th September, but Second Army felt it necessary to call an increasing number of engineer and artillery units up into Belgium as priorities, and at length on 13th September 43 (Wessex) Division was placed under command of 30 Corps and instructed to assemble around Diest, half-way between Brussels and the Belgian-Dutch border. However, although 3 Infantry Division, 6 Guards Tank Brigade, and the three A.Gs.R.A. remained grounded and stripped of most of their transport for the benefit of those moving up, by 16th September the bulk of its troops had begun to arrive east of Brussels, and on the following day the advanced and rear headquarters of the Corps were able to join up at Coursel, a small village on the edge of the Belgian equivalent of Aldershot, and equally desolate. In passing, it must be noted that the week, during which the Staff at advanced Corps Headquarters tasted the delights of liberated Brussels, had roused no small degree of envy in the breasts of those who had perforce to stay behind on the banks of the Seine. The latter were consoled, it is true, by occasional visits to Paris, but there was no comparison between the two cities either in the warmth and friendliness of the welcome extended to the Allied forces or in the amenities provided for them. Brussels was an easy winner, and anyone who was lucky enough to enter that hospitable capital during these early days will have unforgettably happy memories for the rest of his life. However, although the utmost was made of the short period available for recreation, time was very pressing, and once the Headquarters was at Coursel, planning began immediately to put 8 Corps back into action as quickly as possible. On 16th September 3 Infantry Division started the journey northwards from the Seine, and at 1200 hours on the same day old friends in the shape of 11 Armoured Division came under command once again. This division was in contact with the enemy in the area Petit Brogel-Peer on the right of Second Army and a short distance south of the Meuse-Escaut Canal; from now on all the main barriers to movement during the autumn and winter were to be the rivers and canals in which the Low Countries abound. So far as flanks were concerned, on the left was situated 30 Corps, whilst on the right and some distance away 19 U.S. Corps of First U.S. Army was operating eastwards in the direction of Cologne. There was thus the danger of a gap arising as each formation advanced. However, for the moment a contact point was set up between the two corps at Asch, about 15 miles due east of Coursel.

On the following morning, 17th September, Corps Headquarters moved a few miles north-east to a somewhat isolated location near the village of Linde where it was well-placed to continue the advance to the north as the battle unfolded. At the same time 1 Belgian Brigade located in Bourg Leopold, joined 8 Corps and intimation was also received that 4 Armoured Brigade would move up from France with all speed to come under command. There was, in fact, extreme urgency throughout Second Army for all re-grouping to be finished as soon as practicable, since 17th September was "D" day for the new phase of 21 Army Group's activities. Having thus discussed the Allied situation on the eve of this daring and courageous enterprise officially christened Operation "Market-Garden" but known to the world, quite simply, as "Arnhem," let us cast a brief glance at how the enemy was faring by mid-September.

The Enemy Situation on 17th September

North of the Meuse-Escaut canal the German forces in Holland likely to become involved in Operation "Market-Garden" were estimated to consist of some 10,000 men, 29 field guns of various calibres, 119 anti-tank guns, together with 30 tanks and self-propelled guns. In addition, a large number of anti-aircraft (Flak) troops permanently stationed in the vicinity of the Arnhem-Nijmegen bridges were equally to be feared, for they amounted to some 30,000 men with 420 heavy and 600 medium and light guns—a formidable array, as events were to demonstrate. Reinforcements, too, were available—one division was moving down from Denmark whilst the disorganised remnants of the Fifteenth German Army, some 40,000 troops all told, were escaping from the Scheldt Islands over improvised ferries into western Holland. Most important of all, 35 miles north of Arnhem there was a large SS training centre at Deventer, which included armoured units.

There was therefore, on paper at least, an enemy force of considerable strength to be taken into account.

So far as fixed defences were concerned, neither air photographs nor agents' reports indicated any preparations other than anti-tank ditches around Nijmegen and Arnhem, together with some weapon pits in the neighbourhood of Venlo. Nevertheless, the enemy knew this country well and obviously relied upon demolitions at the major canal and river crossings, which together with the ground which was everywhere very soft and unsuited to tanks (as the armour was later to find out) would effectively restrict movement.

To sum up, the Germans had not had time to prepare a good defensive position, but against this, the natural obstacles were so placed that little work was needed to convert any canal into a good line of defence. In fact the Wehrmacht now had the advantage of defensive positions potentially stronger than at any time since "D" day, but the unorganised state of the enemy formations (for the moment in Holland there were few divisions but many miscellaneous battle groups bearing the names of their commanders, e.g., "Grasmehl," "Hardegg," "Hermann" and "Huebner," all destined to become very familiar as winter progressed) might however be expected to result in little effective control over them. If therefore surprise were achieved by means of airborne landings, General Dempsey's very dashing plan had a good chance of success in the ensuing confusion in the enemy camp.

Second Army Intention and Plan for Operation "Market-Garden"

The official intention of Operation "Market-Garden" as laid down by the Commander-in-Chief was "to place Second Army, including airborne forces, astride the Rivers Maas, Waal and Neder Rijn on the general axis Grave-Nijmegen-Arnhem, and to dominate the country between the Rhine and the Zuyder Zee, thus cutting off communication between Germany and Holland." Field-Marshal Montgomery had also given instructions that the drive northwards was to be made with the utmost rapidity and violence, and without regard to events on the flanks. Every effort was therefore made to mount the operation as quickly as possible and with all available forces.

The venture was given a double code-name—"Market-Garden"—for the first part represented operations by the ground troops and the second those of 1 Airborne Corps. The plan, briefly, was for 30 Corps to thrust northwards from the Belgian border along the single axis Eindhoven-Veghel-Grave-Nijmegen-Arnhem, an advance of over sixty miles, in the course of which paratroops would be dropped astride this route as follows:—101 U.S. Airborne Division—Son and Veghel; 82 U.S. Airborne Division—Grave and the eastern outskirts of Nijmegen and 1 British Airborne Division, most isolated of all, to the west of Arnhem. Supporting 30 Corps on the left was 12 Corps, and on the right 8 Corps, and their joint object was to broaden the base of Second Army's advance.

During the planning stage, considerable uncertainty prevailed regarding the date of the operation, for while 23rd September was originally chosen, it was later put forward no less than six days to 17th September, in order to take maximum advantage of the disorganisation of the enemy. Preparations were therefore extremely hurried, and there was little time for consultation between 8 and 30 Corps. Moreover on the day finally selected, 8 Corps, as already pointed out, was widely dispersed with one division in the line and the other in the act of moving up from the Seine area, 300 miles to the rear, whilst its two independent brigade groups were also in transit.

Thus, for the task assigned, the Corps was extremely badly situated from every point of view. In addition, although it had no responsibility whatever for protecting the main axis of advance of 30 Corps, it was clearly not in a position to start advancing until some 48 hours after the operation began. 30 Corps would therefore be on its own in a narrow corridor, together with the airborne troops. Speed however was considered, as usual, to be the overriding factor and the resultant risk was accepted by the Commander-in-Chief.

The 8 Corps plan evolved by General O'Connor, in the short time available was divided into four phases:—

Phase 1. Establishing a bridgehead north of the Escaut Canal in the vicinity of Lille St. Hubert, using 3 Infantry Division.

Phase 2. Capturing and dominating the area Leende and Weert.

Phase 3. Passing 11 Armoured Division through 3 Infantry Division to seize Helmond and over-run the surrounding country.

Phase 4. A further advance north-east in accordance with the general situation and orders from Second Army.

No air support in the form of a heavy bomber effort was available since all Allied resources were directed to the 30 Corps sector, whilst the Sappers were heavily reinforced in anticipation of the many bridging problems that would arise.

Operations 17th—30th September

On 17th September the weather was fine and generally favourable for an airborne operation. Initially, too, all went as planned—the paratroops and glider formations landed successfully in the early afternoon, whilst at 1425 hours Guards Armoured Division began to move out of its bridgehead to join up with them. Heavy fighting took place all that day and the next, but by the evening of 18th September, the Guards had relieved 101 U.S Airborne Division, captured Eindhoven and reached the Wilhelmina Canal, sixteen miles further on.

Now the moment for 8 Corps to take a share in the battle was at hand, and by 0100 hours that night in Phase 1 of the operation, 3 Infantry Division had achieved a small bridgehead over the Escaut Canal, despite determined opposition. By 0830 hours, working under continuous small arms and mortar fire, the Sappers had completed a bridge and the advance to the north began. This provoked fierce resistance and for a short while thereafter 9 Infantry Brigade was held up, but the Corps Commander ordered 11 Armoured Division to move 2 Fife and Forfar Yeomanry Group northwards over the bridge already built by Guards Armoured Division and to swing east towards Achel. However, the great mass of traffic streaming along this main axis of 30 Corps through Eindhoven and towards Nijmegen—for Guards Armoured Division had had an astonishing run in the morning of some 35 miles in five hours and was now on the banks of the River Waal—naturally hindered the passage of this regimental group and it was not clear of the bridge until 1730 hours. At about this time patrols from 50 Infantry Division (under command of 8 Corps since midday) also reported that demolitions during the afternoon over a subsidiary canal parallel to the Eindhoven road, would prevent the advance eastwards of 2 Fife and Forfar Yeomanry. In the meantime, however, 3 Infantry Division had widened the area of its bridgehead, and at the end of the day was nearly up to the Belgian-Dutch border. Fighting continued throughout the night, and by dawn on 20th September, 3 Infantry Division had joined up with 50 Infantry Division on its left, reached the general line Achel-Hamont, and built a second bridge, this time strong enough to carry tanks across the Escaut Canal. It was now possible to commit 11 Armoured Division, organised as in the battle of Caumont, in mixed groups of infantry and tanks, and at 0900 hours its leading troops, 23 Hussars and 8 Rifle Brigade crossed the canal, followed by 3 Royal Tank Regiment and 3 Monmouthshire Regiment. On the left 2 Fife and Forfar Yeomanry with 1 Herefords moved forward through Valkenswaard and Heeze to Someren encountering only sporadic resistance on the way. The advance of 11 Armoured Division was thus able to continue all that day against opposition that was often negligible though sometimes stubborn and tenacious, and by last light on the right 29 Armoured Brigade Group was disposed around Heeze and on the outskirts of the strongly defended village of Someren; on the left 159 Infantry Brigade Group was established in the area of Soerendonk and Hamont, 3 Infantry Division remained holding a firm base for the Corps and during the night frustrated several attempts by troops of the reconstituted 10 SS Panzer Division to infiltrate into its positions, whilst 4 Armoured Brigade and 1 Belgian Brigade concentrated south of the border in the general area of Caulille-Gerdingen-Asch. On 21st September, 11 Armoured Division continued its advance northwards, for General O'Connor's intention was to force the Zuid Willemsvaart Canal, seize the important town of Helmond and the enemy strong-point of Deurne to the east, as quickly as possible and thereafter to push forward armoured cars to reconnoitre north-west and north-east. The enemy had managed to accumulate some armoured forces in the neighbourhood with which to oppose 8 Corps' advance, and his main intention appeared to be to withdraw behind the Zuid Willemsvaart Canal— a barrier well sited for prolonged defence. Nevertheless 11 Armoured Division was too fast for the Germans, for by midday 159 Infantry Brigade Group was in a position to stage an assault crossing over this obstacle north of Someren, and by dusk a firm bridgehead had been established facing Asten. To the south-west the enemy had abandoned any attempt to hold his positions, for little opposition was encountered by 3 Royal Tank Regiment or 23 Hussars up to the Wilhelmina Canal (a branch of the main Zuid Willemsvaart running westwards to Tilburg) and earlier a smaller tributary was crossed beteen Eindhoven and Geldrop, but thereafter strong attacks were encountered from a new type of enemy tank unit, 107 Panzer Brigade. This unit was one of a series of "pocket" armoured divisions formed during August on Hitler's orders, and useful to the enemy in that they were not only compact but were equipped entirely with "Panther" tanks. A moderately heavy engagement was fought with this formation during the afternoon south of Nunen by 23 Hussars and 8 Rifle Brigade and eventually the enemy withdrew to the north, having lost half a dozen tanks and armoured cars. It appeared that the objective of 107 Panzer Brigade had been the important bridge at Son but that the timely arrival of 11 Armoured Division had forestalled this move. In the opinion of the Corps Commander this action saved the vital centre of Eindhoven.

It was clear that by this time the enemy had sized up the general situation and was making strenuous efforts not only to eliminate the Arnhem bridgehead, the condition of which was now causing anxiety to the British High Command, but to cut the 30 Corps corridor and thus seize the initiative. The time and place of enemy reactions to advances both by 8 and 30 Corps, began to suggest a higher degree of control and co-ordination than had been shown since the battle of France was fought and lost. Elsewhere, too, on the American and French fronts, the Allied drive had been stalled and the touch of a master hand was everywhere apparent. At this juncture it was discovered that Hitler, swallowing his pride, had felt obliged to call once again upon the services of Field-Marshal von Rundstedt, dismissed, though undefeated, in France at the beginning of July. Model despite having performed marvellous work as the "Fuehrer's Fireman" (as he liked to call himself) in rallying the beaten Army Group B, was not of much calibre as a strategist, though exceptionally good as a "fighting commander." He therefore took command of Army Group B and von Rundstedt for the second time became "Supreme Commander, West." The latter, a somewhat weary and cynical old gentleman of 70, on resuming his appointment issued the following order of the day which, concise and to the point, is a model of its kind:—

"Soldiers of the Western Front:

"On the Fuehrer's orders I have again assumed command of Supreme Command West, effective 6th September. During my absence, the Command and troops have undergone heavy fighting. I am convinced that every single officer, N.C.O. and soldier knows what we are fighting for. I trust you, as the whole country places its trust in you. Fight under me for our people, our country and our leader."

The measures which he put into force were now beginning to take effect and henceforward the remainder of the advance by 8 Corps up to the line of the River Maas was difficult and against a determined and co-ordinated defence. Moreover, from 19th September the weather, which had previously been good, turned dull and rainy, greatly hampering the reinforcement and support of 1 Airborne Division isolated west of Arnhem, and under constant attack from greatly superior enemy forces.

Early on 22nd September, 11 Armoured Division passed 2 Fife and Forfar Yeomanry and 4 King's Shropshire Light Infantry through the Someren bridgehead, where the Herefords had repulsed two heavy armoured counter-attacks in the previous twelve hours, and with a sudden thrust captured the enemy strongpoint of Asten together with over three hundred prisoners, whilst on the left 29 Armoured Brigade by midday was half a mile south of Helmond. Here the enemy put up a strenuous resistance, but notwithstanding this the town was outflanked during the afternoon and armoured cars of the Inns of Court patrolled several miles to the north. In the south of the Corps sector, 3 Infantry Division during the morning entered the important communications centre of Weert, from which the Germans had withdrawn during the night, after destroying the bridge in the town over the Voorer Canal. This, however, was repaired by midnight, so that after some further clearance operations of a minor character, both 3 Infantry Division and 1 Belgian Brigade were able to close up to the line of the Canal in the early hours of 23rd September and to enter Maeseyck during the afternoon. During this time 4 Armoured Brigade, which was holding the junction points at Asch and Lanklaer with 19 U.S. Corps, sent its first patrols into Dilsen and Opitter, likewise now clear of enemy. In order, however, to ensure against any surprise in this sector, it was found necessary, in view of the length of front which this formation was guarding, to dismount one squadron from each armoured regiment to act as infantry at strategic points along the banks of the Maastricht Canal—a somewhat unpopular proceeding with 4 Armoured Brigade.

During the morning Corps Headquarters moved to the Dutch-Belgian border north of Achel and set itself up in an old convent, the "Couvent de la Trappe," which stands in the midst of a heath as lonely and sandy as only the most enthusiastic Trappist monk could have discovered.

Whilst things were therefore going well on the right flank of Second Army, in the centre and on the left the situation was not so satisfactory. Quite apart from the desperate battle being waged around Arnhem where the marked enemy superiority had both driven the heroic remnants of 1 Airborne Division to the west of the town and prevented the relieving forces of 30 Corps from achieving their mission, the enemy to the west of the Eindhoven-Nijmegen road had grown bolder. Not only was 12 Corps being held in some fanatical fighting at a small village named Best, but to the north there had been several sporadic attacks across the axis of advance of 30 Corps, resulting in certain dangerous interruptions to its traffic. Thus at midday on 22nd September enemy infantry and tanks attacking from the north-west had straddled the main road between Veghel and Uden, and were only to be dislodged twenty-four hours later with the assistance of the infantry brigade of Guards Armoured Division despatched southwards from Nijmegen.

It was obvious that the existing method of leaving 30 Corps responsible for the protection of its own lines of communication was unsuitable in view of their extended length. The Army Commander therefore held a conference at Headquarters 101 U.S. Airborne Division in St. Oedenrode at 1215 hours on 23rd September, as a result of which this division was placed under General O'Connor from 1830 hours, becoming the first U.S. formation to enter the Corps, and 50 Infantry Division received instructions to move to the general area St. Oedenrode-Nunen-Geldrop, in order to strengthen the right flank of the Americans. In addition, the plan formulated by the Commander of 101 U.S. Airborne Division to clear the enemy from the Uden-Veghel road in conjunction with a drive from the north by Guards Armoured Division was approved and carried out later that afternoon with complete success.

During the night 22nd-23rd September in the sector of 11 Armoured Division the enemy had maintained his pressure against the Asten bridgehead, putting in two sharp counter-attacks with elements of 10 SS Panzer Division and 107 Panzer Brigade. The Germans were getting a steady flow of reinforcements from Venlo and across the Peel Marshes, though it seemed pointless to bring troops west of such a good defence line as the River Maas to an area where they might well be trapped. However, as will be apparent later, this stubborn, and seemingly inexplicable refusal of the enemy to give up any ground voluntarily, was later to pay him a handsome dividend and cause Second Army no small annoyance.

At first light on 23rd September a new advance out of the Asten bridgehead was started by 23 Hussars and 8 Rifle Brigade but met with heavy opposition, and at first progress was slow. A few hours afterwards, 3 Royal Tank Regiment with 3 Monmouthshire Regiment also crossed this bridge, directed on Liesel. This drive, too, experienced great resistance, but by dusk considerable ground had been won and 11 Armoured Division had reached the outskirts of Vlierden, knocking out four 88 mm. guns on the way, whilst Liesel was likewise occupied after a brisk and successful engagement with several more "Panther" tanks and self-propelled guns. Following up the armour as usual, 3 Infantry Division made an appreciable bound during the evening in furtherance of its role of "firm base," and Corps Headquarters, too, was thankful to exchange its bleak monastery for very comfortable surroundings in the charming little Dutch town of Geldrop, where for the first time since landing on the continent it was possible for some of the Staff to abandon their caravans and make use of buildings for their work.

On the following day events moved more swiftly on the right, for 11 Armoured Division early captured the important road centre of Deurne, as well as Bakel, somewhat further north. About 200 prisoners were taken in the process, approximately half of whom surrendered as the result of exhortations from a loudspeaker unit, marking the first occasion that any marked success had attended its efforts in 8 Corps.

On the left flank of the Corps, however, at midday on 24th September the enemy made his most determined effort to cut the 30 Corps axis once again. By 1300 hours several reports had reached Corps Headquarters that German troops, tanks and self-propelled guns had established themselves at a number of points along this route and were inflicting severe casualties on units of

101 U.S. Airborne Division. The thrust was undoubtedly carried out by 107 Panzer Brigade supported by infantry including German and Dutch SS troops, and so suddenly did it materialise that Lieut.-General Horrocks of 30 Corps on a visit to 50 Infantry Division, was cut off from his own Headquarters, whilst several senior officers of 8 Corps, notably Brigadiers Sewell and Glyn-Hughes (who gained a second bar to his D.S.O. in the course of the action) were likewise caught on the way back from Nijmegen. Next morning, 50 Infantry Division and 101 U.S. Airborne Division, aided by 131 Infantry Brigade of 7 Armoured Division attacking from the west, endeavoured to shift the enemy, though without much success, and the situation here was in fact not to be restored for another two days, during which time this sector was handed over to 12 Corps together with command of 101 U.S. Airborne Division. If, however, on 25th September this flank was unresponsive to Allied efforts, on the right 11 Armoured Division made rapid progress, advancing some ten miles through Gemert to St. Antonis and Boxmeer, whilst recce units of 50 Infantry Division passed through Mill and closed up to the River Maas east of Grave. The good news of the day was, unfortunately, marred by a disaster at St. Antonis, where four enemy "half tracks" in hiding attempted to escape and suddenly ran into an order group being held by Brigadier "Roscoe" Harvey of 29 Armoured Brigade. Two of his commanding officers, Lieut.-Colonels D. A. H. Silvertop and H. G. Orr, both survivors of the Normandy fighting, were killed, and Brigadier Harvey and his Brigade Major were wounded. It was small consolation that the enemy half tracks were destroyed.

This date, 25th September, marks the end of Operation "Market-Garden," for on this day Field Marshal Montgomery ordered the gallant remnants of 1 Airborne Division to withdraw southwards over the Neder Rijn, and with great difficulty and heroism this feat was accomplished. As a whole, the operation had been ninety per cent. successful, since crossings had been secured over four out of five major water obstacles, and the most northernly of these, the Nijmegen bridgehead across the Waal, was later to prove of decisive importance in the drive from the Rhine to the Baltic.

The role played by 8 Corps throughout Operation "Market-Garden," if subsidiary, had nevertheless been vital, and, moreover, carried out to the last letter. Of its formations, 11 Armoured Division in particular once again showed itself to be a division of the highest order, able to tackle the most diverse operations with equal skill, whilst 3 and 50 Infantry Divisions were alike excellent. The Sappers, too, did wonders in quickly bridging the countless canals and rivers lying in the path of the advance. There is, however, no doubt that the late decision to put forward the date for launching this operation by no less than six days had a considerable adverse effect on the ability of 8 Corps to initiate its own part as quickly as was desirable. Nevertheless it is amazing that not only were the bulk of its troops moved up from a concentration area over 300 miles distant, but that the Corps was able to begin broadening the base of the Second Army salient as early as 18th September. The subsequent fighting advance of nearly fifty miles in six days over the most difficult country and without the advantage of surprise or mass air support was a most creditable feat, during which the Corps sustained 663 casualties in all ranks in the heavy fighting and collected upwards of 1,100 prisoners.

The Situation on 1st October, 1944

The conclusion of the Arnhem battles, the approach of winter and the awkward salient in which Second Army found itself all combined to pose the age old question "Whither now, Master?" Before the answer to this problem had been revealed, fate dealt the Corps an unkind blow. Far away in Italy, the newly appointed commander of the famous Eighth Army, Lieutenant-General Sir Richard L. McCreery, required a Chief-of-Staff. What could be more natural than he should think of his friend and former B.G.S., Sir Harry Floyd? Unfortunately, this is exactly what happened, and to the great regret of every man in the headquarters, Sir Harry left for Italy in the first week of October. For over eighteen months he had been Chief-of-Staff, serving no less than six commanders and watching 8 Corps grow from the early days of training under General Lumsden to the smooth and efficient direction of the great battles of Normandy under General O'Connor. During this time under his guidance, 8 Corps Headquarters had not only never made a false step, but had gained a reputation throughout Second Army possessed by few, if any, of its rivals, while among the Staff, there was none who could say that he had ever seen Sir Harry either perturbed, angry, at a loss, or in fact, other than completely master of the situation. His was a term of office of which any man could indeed be proud.

Let us now glance at the overall situation in which 21 Army Group and 12 U.S. Army Group found themselves with the leaves turning brown and the first frosts of winter drawing near. By the end of September, First and Third U.S. Armies had come to a halt along the Siegfried Line around Aachen, and to the south before Metz in Alsace. The Americans were in fact becoming increasingly hampered in their operations by lack of resources, for like 21 Army Group, they still depended on the Normandy beaches for supplies.

In 21 Army Group, First Canadian Army having completed its task of reopening the Channel ports, on 17th September took over the Antwerp Sector from Second Army and was now to turn all its energies towards clearing both banks of the Scheldt estuary above Antwerp so that this great port could be opened up for use by the Allies. Second Army was, however, situated in an awkward and extended triangle, with Arnhem as the apex and the Meuse-Escaut canal as its base. On one side Herenthals in Belgium was its junction point with the Canadians, and on the other the Juliana Canal west of Maastricht formed the boundary with Ninth U.S. Army. In either case its front was nearly one hundred miles in length, and it was thus necessary before any further operations were begun, for an extensive regrouping of formations to be carried out.

So far as 8 Corps was concerned, by the end of September it was positioned on the general line Weert-Meijel-Deurne-Boxmeer and thence along the River Maas to Cuijk where it joined up with 30 Corps. There was thus a large pocket still under enemy control, west of the river in the "Peel" area, and about which a few words must be said.

The "Peel" area is a large tract of reclaimed marshland, extending along the west bank of the River Maas for about 20 miles on either side of Venlo. Every field in it is surrounded by a deep dyke which drains off the water fairly efficiently in summer, but in winter or during a rainy season, the land reverts rapidly to type and the whole becomes once again a quagmire. One metalled road of execrable quality leads across from Venlo through Meijel and Deurne to Helmond, though in addition, in dry weather there are certain tracks; these, however, disappear under water at the first shower of rain. In any event, none are capable of standing up to heavy traffic, least of all tanks and military vehicles, and later the utmost ingenuity had to be used in order to keep supplies going, even in static warfare. It is perhaps the worst country in the world for armoured fighting for no tank dare leave the track, and thus one cleverly placed minefield can disrupt a whole day's operations. The Dutch later stated that until Second Army conquered it, no invader had ever succeeded in advancing across the Peel Marsh either in summer or winter, and it is a fact that as late as 1940, they did not waste large forces in defending it, and the Germans themselves avoided invading Holland from this direction.

11 Armoured Division, towards the end of September had made several tentative thrusts from the north against this area in general, and in particular against a small town called Overloon set among the woods on the outskirts of the marshland, but the enemy proved too strong for other than a deliberate attack, and the engagements were broken off. At the beginning of October Field-Marshal Montgomery arranged for Ninth U.S. Army to extend its boundaries northwards to the general line—Weert-Deurne-Maashees, and 7 U.S. Armoured Division commanded by Major-General Lindsay Sylvester, which for some time past had been taking part in the siege of Metz, was brought north to reduce this difficult pocket quickly. 8 Corps was thus free of immediate tasks and began considering a new offensive over the Maas and into Germany. Corps Headquarters moved up from Geldrop and after a brief stay in a monastery at Gemert—Southern Holland teems with monasteries and convents—came finally to rest on 20th October in the pleasant village of Mill, three miles from the River Maas, and five miles west of the German border and the Reichswald Forest—the northern termination of the Siegfried Line. Here the Staff was centrally placed to plan Operation "Gatwick" which was to be the next move by Second Army.

Operation "Gatwick" involved an advance southwards between the two rivers, Maas and Rhine, with 8 Corps on the right and 30 Corps on the left. The latter was to move down through Cleve to Goch, whilst 8 Corps stormed the formidable Reichswald Forest by a frontal attack, and eventually joined up with 30 Corps in the vicinity of Goch. After many discussions between the Army Commander and General O'Connor, the operation was, however, deferred, for both felt that the assault on Reichswald would swallow up too many troops, and as 8 Corps consisted only of one armoured and two infantry divisions—one of which would have perforce to stay on guard west of the Maas, it was considered that the plan was too hazardous.

Meanwhile 7 U.S. Armoured Division with great gusto started operations against Overloon, but unfortunately was unable to make any progress at all. Finally, after several days of fruitless fighting in which considerable casualties were incurred, the operation was discontinued about the same time that preparations for Operation "Gatwick" also ceased. Whilst, thus, the larger plan was abandoned, it was both possible and desirable from the point of view of Second Army to clear up the Maas pocket. General Dempsey therefore gave instructions to this effect, and obtained the loan from Ninth U.S. Army of 7 U.S. Armoured Division which together with 15 (Scottish) Division was allotted to 8 Corps, so that for Operation "Constellation," as it was called, the Corps was to be a strong body of over 90,000 troops comprising the following formations:—

        7 U.S. Armoured Division.
      11 Armoured Division.
        3 Infantry Division.
      15 (Scottish) Infantry Division.
        6 Guards Tank Brigade.
        1 Belgian Brigade.

The Plan for Operation "Constellation"

By the early part of October, the enemy west of the River Maas had not only been substantially reinforced but had clearly taken heart, both from the Allied reverse at Arnhem, and his own successful defence against 7 U.S.

Armoured Division. The Maas pocket itself was completely organised with three divisions holding it made up largely of paratroopers—180 Infantry Division to the north, Division Erdmann in the centre and 183 Infantry Division to the south. 107 Panzer Brigade was also available to supply any armoured backing necessary in the event of a break through by the Allies anywhere along the front. Moreover the German High Command had not relied entirely upon the friendly offices of the terrible country over which the Allies were forced to advance, but had constructed two outer defence lines facing northwest, and a third joining up with the major fortifications already encircling the bastion of Venlo. The reduction of the area had thus every possibility of being a slow, difficult and hazardous operation, and so it proved, though none foresaw that it would not finally be eliminated until the beginning of December.

When on 9th October, he saw the enemy layout plotted according to the latest air photographs, General O'Connor determined to take advantage of the fact that the major defences faced north-west. Accordingly his plan, divided into four phases, was designed by means of an attack from Overloon towards Venraij, to draw the bulk of the enemy northwards. As soon as the Germans were fully engaged in this sector, another thrust would strike eastwards from the area Brexem-Weert towards Roermond and Venlo. During this time the bridges over the river at these two towns were to be destroyed by the R.A.F. and constant air attacks were to be maintained against the ferries and barges also in use by the enemy.

The four phases of the operation were organised as follows:—

Phase 1.

3 Infantry Division was to attack and establish itself in the area south of Venraij opening the main road forward for 11 Armoured Division. 7 U.S. Armoured Division meanwhile would operate eastwards along the roads Deurne-Venraij and Deurne-Amerika and join up with the British troops west of Venraij, thus coming in behind the first line of defence.

Phase 2.

11 Armoured Division was to pass through 3 Infantry Division and advance to the south, 7 U.S. Armoured Division continuing its task begun in Phase 1.

Phase 3.

15 (Scottish) Infantry Division was to establish itself in the general area of Horne so as to isolate Roermond, with 7 U.S. Armoured protecting its northern flank, if necessary.

Phase 4.

Finally the two armoured divisions and 15 (Scottish) Division were all to converge on Venlo. The greatest emphasis was laid throughout the preparations for "Constellation" on concealing the eventual entry of the Scots into the contest. It was, moreover, felt by everyone at Corps Headquarters, that in view of the appalling terrain, coupled with the extremely wet weather, the operation would be slow and difficult, and this certainly was the case, as a brief narrative of events will show:—

Operations 12th—17th October

The assault by 8 Infantry Brigade in the Overloon area began at midday and at first met fairly stiff opposition. It would undoubtedly have been considerably worse had not Typhoons of 83 Group R.A.F. and Marauders from 19 U.S.A.A.F. made a number of successful attacks on Venraij and the immediate battle area. Unfortunately the planes detailed to demolish the Maas bridges in Venlo and Roermond were called off to support the American attack on Aachen, with the result that these remained intact throughout the action, thereby enabling the enemy to increase his resistance. By 1530 hours, however, the leading troops of 8 Infantry Brigade were on the outskirts of Overloon itself and though 4 Tank Coldstream Guards supporting the attack was held up by an extensive minefield, the use of "flails" forced a gap and by 1900 hours the town was in British hands, with 3 Infantry Division in close contact with the enemy to the south. Over 150 prisoners had been taken, mainly from 180 Infantry Division. These Paratroopers were proving to be first class infantrymen brave and tenacious in their defence, and far superior to any troops which the Corps had fought since the days of Normandy.

Over the next two days in heavy fighting amid intense mortar concentrations and with mines scattered lavishly in its path 3 Infantry Division made steady progress, protected along its eastern flank and from the opposing bank of the river by a small force from 11 Armoured Division. By 15th October, after some excellent work by 29 Armoured Brigade, moving down on the right of 3 Infantry Division, a bridgehead had been achieved over the Canal de Derivation and early on the succeeding day 23 Hussars and 8 Rifle Brigade started to move over. Meanwhile 3 Infantry Division during the night had reached the Molenbeek, a formidable stream swollen greatly by the torrential rain, and just before dawn 1 Royal Norfolk and 2 Royal Warwickshire Regiments carried out a silent crossing—a remarkably fine achievement as the necessary Kapok equipment only reached them in the early hours of the morning and the weather conditions were so adverse.

8 Corps on the morning of 16th October was thus in a position to catch the forces of 180 Infantry Division in and around Venraij, in a pincer movement carried out by 29 Armoured Brigade from the west and 3 Infantry Division from the north. In addition, 7 U.S. Armoured Division, which up till now had been "demonstrating" only as part of the deception plan, was ordered to bridge the Canal de Derivation on its front so that 159 Infantry Brigade could be brought in behind the main German positions. In every way it was a most successful day, for by early evening the whole enemy defence system was crumbling, he had begun to fall back to his second withdrawal line, and large numbers of Germans had been killed or captured, the total for the operation so far being over 2,000. Most important of all, reinforcements from the southern sector around Maeseyck were identified west of Venraij. The enemy was thus reacting as the Corps Commander had hoped, and now was the opportunity to launch the Scots in the south. Alas, at the very moment when directions were being given to put this intention into effect, a telephone call from Second Army ordered the immediate withdrawal of 15 (Scottish) Division to a concentration area around Helmond, as a matter of extreme urgency, for employment as soon as possible in the final operations to clear the Scheldt estuary. Against these instructions no appeal was possible, for obviously with winter setting in, at all costs Antwerp must be put into working order as quickly as possible. It was, however, disappointing both for the Corps Commander and the divisions which had fought so doggedly to wear the enemy down and had been so clearly within sight of complete and final success in the Maas pocket. As it was, with the enemy reinforcing the northern sector, at the expense of his forces in the south, now to escape attack, there was no hope of driving the Germans back as far as Venlo. Limited advances were undertaken over the next day or two, during which Venraij was captured, as well as a further

500 prisoners, but thereafter a defensive position was adopted (for 8 Corps was still extended along a 69-mile front) and the operation was at an end.

Results of Operation " Constellation "

Reviewing Operation " Constellation," one cannot help feeling that here was a flawless plan spoiled in the very moment of its triumph, for the successive stages of introduction of the three divisions had had the effect desired and it is fair to suppose that if 15 (Scottish) Division had been allowed to carry out the tasks allotted, the whole Maas pocket would have folded up. However, the reason for the withdrawal of this division from 8 Corps was of the greatest importance and it is at least consoling to know that shortly afterwards the approaches to Antwerp were finally freed. As a remark at the time put it: " It is unfortunate that it was not possible to foresee these operations earlier, but it is easy to be wise after the event."

The first day of the operation was marked by a notable event, for Corps Headquarters had been honoured by a visit from His Majesty the King, then touring 21 Army Group. Senior officers of the Headquarters, as well as Major-Generals Roberts, Barber and Sylvester, were presented during the afternoon, and the King later inspected the Command Post discussing the situation at length with General O'Connor. It was considerably heartening to see His Majesty, wearing battle dress, among his troops again and so far forward, for one of the roads used by the Royal convoy was shortly afterwards endangered by the enemy counter-offensive. The visit also created a deep impression on the Dutch population.

From 18th October onwards, a period of uneasy calm set in, since the future was uncertain, although it had now become apparent that the Allies would, without doubt, have to wage a winter campaign. Moreover, it seemed unlikely that 8 Corps could experience any great changes until the general offensive was resumed. The weather, in addition to being extremely wet, was beginning to turn very cold, and no more cheerless prospect for troops than a winter amid the Peel marshes can be imagined. Nevertheless a close watch was kept on the enemy, busily engaged in thickening up his defences running through Horst and Sevenum as well as digging extensive trenches and anti-tank ditches on the far bank of the River Maas. The Dutch Resistance Movement about this time became more and more useful, for Holland abounds in private telephone systems, and it was possible from Eindhoven, to ring up almost any part of the Kingdom, including the area still under German occupation, with due discretion, of course. Much valuable information obtained in this manner was passed on to the Artillery and the R.A.F., and resulted in many satisfactory attacks on enemy headquarters and dumps. However, the Reich still had its sympathisers in the territory controlled by the Allies and it is more than probable that they were able to make equal use of the many unofficial telephone lines, for about 25th October a map was captured by First French Army, far distant in the Vorges area of France, which showed, with a very fair degree of accuracy, the entire layout of the three Allied Army Groups, even down to locating Headquarters 8 Corps at Mill ! The German High Command was thus aware, so far as 21 Army Group was concerned, that all energies were being directed towards clearing the Scheldt estuary and southwest Holland, and that Second Army was otherwise entirely on the defensive. Moreover, it had not escaped its attention that General Dempsey having taken a calculated risk in concentrating every available man against Antwerp, the British eastern flank, mainly guarded by 8 Corps, was extremely lightly held, especially in the sector of 7 U.S.

Armoured Division. Field Marshal von Runstedt therefore determined to see the effect of a limited offensive.

Operations 27th October—4th November

Between 0700 and 0730 hours, following an artillery bombardment lasting one hour, three attacks were launched by 9 Panzer Division, two westwards across the Canal de Derivation from Helenaveen, whilst the main thrust came against the village of Meijel. Initially, amid the early morning mist, all went well for the Germans, for the American garrison at Meijel was surprised and the greater part overrun, together with much equipment and transport. Later in the morning, tanks crossed the canal and turned left down the Deurne-Meijel road. In the afternoon Germans were observed moving further south at a place named Stokers Horst, whilst the remnants of the Meijel garrison, fighting hard, had withdrawn to the west of the village. It was clear that the Germans, attempting something more ambitious than for some time past, had launched a spoiling attack by 47 Panzer Corps, a newcomer in the area, with the object of drawing off British troops from the Scheldt operations. The German drive had come as a complete surprise after a week of fog and almost zero visibility, whereby little evidence of the build-up of 9 Panzer and 15 Panzer Grenadier Divisions had come to light. In fact the only signs of life latterly on this front had been enemy infantrymen in Panningan, the noise of a number of trains arriving in the Venlo area on 24th October, and finally the sound of tanks and vehicles moving behind the canal during the evening of 26th October. Although a clever move on the part of the enemy, it was, however, made under the most adverse circumstances, for there was but one road across the marshes to serve his attacking formations. Moreover, the heavy "Tiger" tanks were as helpless as those of British formations when they attempted deployment in this treacherous country. The only two factors which favoured the enemy were, first, the achievement of surprise, and, secondly, the bad weather which prevented air operations in the early stages. The Corps Commander fortunately quickly realised the importance of the move, and as a first reinforcement, since 7 U.S. Armoured Division was weak in artillery, sent 25 Field Regiment R.A. to support its defence. The story of this unit is an epic in itself. Arriving in position south-east of Asten early on the morning of 28th September, it found the enemy resuming the attack westward from Meijel. By its concentrated fire this thrust was brought to a halt, whereupon the Germans attempted an outflanking move to the north through Neerkant with two battalions of infantry and approximately 30 "Tiger" tanks from 15 Panzer Grenadier Division—a substantial force. However, in conjunction with the American infantry, now very reduced in numbers, by dusk this attack, too, had been held. The night, except for some extensive patrolling on both sides, was quiet, but at 0730 hours on 29th October, 9 Panzer Division made its greatest effort and was supported on the right by a simultaneous drive up the main road towards Liesel by 15 Panzer Grenadier Division. This latter village fell during the morning, and "Tiger" tanks and Panzer Grenadiers advanced some distance along the road towards Asten and Deurne.

On the previous afternoon, however, the Corps Commander had requested additional forces for this flank from Second Army, which readily ordered 15 (Scottish) Division, immediately fresh from its victorious capture of Tilburg that same day, to return to the spot it had vacated only ten days earlier. Somewhat unwillingly the Scots forsook the delights of the liberated city and began to concentrate east of Helmond, which experienced a fairly heavy raid from the Luftwaffe during the night as a consequence. As it had recently become the location of the main headquarters of Second Army, this raid and the dangerous proximity of the German advance, less than five miles distant, caused great excitement there. Distinctly hurried efforts were made to safeguard secret documents, while for the first time its Headquarters Defence Company, strengthened by personnel from the Second Army staff, felt conscious of an ultimate purpose in life; all of which, of course, caused much sardonic amusement to subordinate formations.

Before the arrival of the Scottish infantry and by the afternoon of 29th October the enemy attack had exhausted itself against the gallant stand of the Americans and, especially, of 25 Field Regiment, which, firing concentration after concentration, over 600 rounds per gun or some 10,000 rounds in all, decimated the attacking Germans. 131 Field Regiment of 15 (Scottish) Division sent on ahead in the early hours of the morning, had also been able to take part and used nearly 6,000 rounds. By dusk 227 (Highland) Infantry Brigade was in position east of Asten, and the danger period was over. 53 (Welsh) Division, which had also been pinched out in the Tilburg operations, followed 15 (Scottish) Division, coming under command of 8 Corps on 1st November and assembling west of Maeseyck in order to relieve 7 U.S. Armoured Division at the earliest opportunity. Thereafter it was merely a question of pushing back the battered Panzer Divisions behind Meijel, a not particularly difficult task, for between them they had suffered heavy casualties, losing upwards of 50 tanks and nearly 600 prisoners apart from many dead and wounded. Moreover, the diversion had now served its purpose and gradually therefore 47 Panzer Corps withdrew over the river Maas to prepare further exploits, the next of which in fact was to be the Ardennes offensive. By 6th November all the lost territory had been regained, with the exception of Meijel itself which the Corps Commander decided to leave in enemy hands until the whole operation of clearing the Maas pocket was once again resumed, thereby avoiding unnecessary casualties. Indeed, repelling the offensive had been expensive enough, for including 7 U.S. Armoured Division which suffered most, the losses in killed and wounded up to 6th November totalled 1,265 all ranks. At the height of the battle it is of interest to note that 8 Corps contained no less than five divisions, three armoured brigades, three armoured car regiments, one A.G.R.A. and one Canadian A.G.R.E., or more than 110,000 officers and men, the greatest number which it ever reached. It was certainly more than 47 Panzer Corps had bargained for, or could confront for long.

During the offensive it was found that Mill was an extremely awkward centre from which to control operations, and on 2nd November after a preliminary reconnaissance, Corps Headquarters moved to the small village of Mierloo, three miles west of Helmond where it settled down very comfortably among the hospitable though hungry Dutch inhabitants for a sojourn that was to last throughout the bitter winter of 1944-45 and until the following spring. For 21 Army Group too, the campaigning for the moment had everywhere ceased, and it was now a question of building up for the next major offensive agreed upon by Field Marshal Montgomery and General Eisenhower. This was planned to be an envelopment of the Ruhr from the north around Nijmegen, whilst 12 U.S. Army Group thrust up from the south. Before, however, this project could begin, and since against overwhelming forces the Germans would be unable to offer any successful resistance, it was firmly decided to eliminate the Maas pocket. This time no unforeseen circumstances should interfere with this thorn in the flesh of Second Army. An extensive regrouping of formations was thereupon put in hand, and 12 Corps took over command of the sector south of the Noorer Canal on 9th November, when

7 U.S. Armoured Division returned to Ninth U.S. Army. Though inexperienced at first, this division rapidly gained knowledge and fought valiantly though heavily outnumbered around Meijel. The congratulations which General O'Connor was able to bestow on all ranks on their departure, were echoed throughout the Corps.

Operations 14th November—3rd December

The final operation of the year was appropriately entitled "Nutcracker," for it was planned as a joint effort in conjunction with 12 Corps. The latter was to lead off on 14th November against the southern sector of the pocket with 51 (Highland) and 53 (Welsh) Divisions, whilst 8 Corps later began by forcing crossings over the Deurne Canal, using 15 (Scottish) Division. Subsequently 11 Armoured Division was to advance eastwards towards the quaintly named "Amerika" settlement in the very middle of the marshland, and 3 Infantry Division southwards on Horst and Tienraij. The plan was thus a series of inter-related operations, beginning with 12 Corps on the right and followed in succession by 15 (Scottish) Division, 11 Armoured Division and finally 3 Infantry Division. By this means the enemy would be dislodged from his powerful position without either corps sustaining heavy casualties. Time, for once, was not an important governing factor.

This plan worked very successfully though, as might be expected, slowly, for in front of 12 Corps the Germans withdrew, laying mines and booby traps, and blowing every possible bridge, no matter how small. On 19th November, 15 (Scottish) Division started to advance, followed on 22nd November by 11 Armoured Division. Little active opposition was offered by the Germans, but there were plenty of minefields and demolitions. The greatest hindrance of all, naturally, was the bad weather combined with the frightful country. Never before perhaps have troops successfully coped with such discomfort or so many difficulties, and that fighting was possible at all, was very largely due to the patience and perseverance of the Royal Engineers, whose problems were enormous. Special roads and tracks laid down, soon sank beneath the rising tide of mud and waters; tanks and transport became bogged and stranded; supply was maintained by carrying parties on foot, and even vehicles built specially to work in these conditions such as the "Weasel," were defeated by the Peel marshes. Nevertheless gradually and irresistibly the two corps surged forward. On 22nd November, Horst and Sevenum were occupied and the second German defence line protecting Venlo thus breached. Before November was out, junction had been made with 12 Corps, and save for two or three stoutly defended "Kasteels" along the banks of the Maas manned by the enemy as outposts together with the massive perimeter defences of Venlo, along the western bank of the river no territory remained in German hands. By 3rd December only the latter held out and on that day they were taken by storm together with their whole garrison.

Thus ends this account of the operations of 8 Corps and just as it marked the close of a phase in the Allied campaign in North Western Europe, so too it was the curtain to a happy era in the life of the Corps, for General O'Connor said goodbye at the beginning of December. On more than one occasion India had asked for his services, but until now he could not be spared. With, however, the prospect of a four months' stalemate ahead, permission was finally given for his appointment to command the Eastern Army in India, which had become the main base for the victorious advance in Burma. Nor was the farewell a happy occasion for either the Corps Commander or his Staff assembled in the tiny school at Mierloo, since both felt the parting keenly.

Under his command 8 Corps had performed great deeds, advanced over 500 miles and everywhere defeated the finest troops the enemy had hurled against it. The issue of the war against Hitler, too, was no longer in doubt, for the death-throes of the Nazi Reich were to produce only that forlorn hope, the Ardennes counter-offensive. This venture, Hitler's last supreme gamble, had Brussels and Antwerp as its objectives and its aim was to split the Allied forces in order to defeat them in detail—glittering prizes indeed. Its decisive and costly defeat produced, however, fatal consequences for Germany, for the destruction of the armies employed in the undertaking eliminated the main German reserve in the West. With the disappearance of this, across the River Rhine the way into the plains of Northern Germany lay open and unbarred.

Thus the stage was now set for the assault over the Rhine during the month following, after which were possible the victorious operations under General O'Connor's successor, Lieutenant-General Sir Evelyn Barker, which carried 8 Corps in a magnificent sweep to the shores of the Baltic and provide so fitting an epilogue to Normandy. The story of these later exploits has, however, already been told by Lieutenant-Colonel J. G. Hooper in his book "The River Rhine to the Baltic Sea," and thus, with this account, the life story of the Corps is now complete. The deeds of 8 Corps are recorded in the annals of the war against Germany and Hitlerism, yet their renown rests more surely in the hearts of those who served it, whilst its spirit lives on in the traditions of the British Army. The call of duty will sound again—who shall doubt that the " White Knight " will be there ?

HEADQUARTERS EIGHTH CORPS

A list of Officers who held appointments during the campaign in Normandy and the Low Countries up to 1st December, 1944

COMMANDER

Lieutenant-General Sir Richard N. O'Connor, K.C.B., D.S.O., M.C.

Aide de Camp
1. Captain H. Garnet
2. Captain S. G. Gill, M.C.

Military Secretary
Major R. B. Freeman-Thomas

CHIEF OF STAFF

1. Brigadier Sir Henry R. K. Floyd, BART., C.B.E.
2. Brigadier R. G. V. Fitzgeorge-Balfour, M.B.E., M.C.

THE GENERAL STAFF

Operations Branch

G.S.O. 1 (O)	Lieutenant-Colonel J. G. Hooper
G.S.O. 2 (O)	1. Major J. A. R. Freeland
,,	2. Major W. H. C. Luddington, M.C.
,,	Major M. A. L. F. Pitt-Rivers
G.S.O. 3 (O)	Captain R. M. Farmer
,,	Captain T. Russell-Cobb

Intelligence Branch

G.S.O. 2 (I)	Major G. S. Jackson
G.S.O. 3 (Ia)	1. Captain B. I. Hunt
,,	2. Captain P. Cherrington
G.S.O. 3 (Ib)	Captain H. Russell Ross
I.O. (Ia)	Captain T. Peters
,,	1. Captain P. Low
,,	2. Captain H. A. Hetherington
I.O. (Ib)	1. Captain P. H. Kelly
,,	2. Captain I. R. Bell
A.P.I.S.	Captain W. S. Butler
INTERROGATOR	Captain T. B. Higgins
,,	Captain W. Dewhurst

Staff Duties Branch

G.S.O. 2 (S.D.)	Major J. D. Paybody
G.S.O. 3 (S.D.)	Captain G. G. Rogers

Liaison Branch

G.S.O. 2 (L)	Major L. R. N. Clifford-Smith
G.S.O. 3 (L)	Captain W. M. Duane
„	Captain I. M. Hulburd
L.O. ATTACHED	Captain G. Strakosch
„	Lieutenant E. B. Scott
L.O. ATTACHED (2 HOUSEHOLD CAVALRY)	Captain N. Ford

Air Branch

G.S.O. 2 (AIR)	Major F. E. Beer
STAFF LIEUT. (AIR)	Lieutenant N. Lermon

Miscellaneous Appointments

G.S.O. 3 (CAMOUFLAGE)	Captain G. F. Willmot
STAFF LIEUT. (CAMOUFLAGE)	Lieutenant A. D. Wimbush
TECHNICAL OFFICER (C.W.)	Captain J. C. Simmons
STAFF CAPTAIN (P.A.D.)	Captain F. M. Roe
OFFICIAL OBSERVER	Colonel A. J. Clifton, O.B.E.

THE ADMINISTRATIVE STAFF

Brigadier i/c Administration

Brigadier E. P. Sewell, C.B.E.

Adjutant General's Branch

D.A.A.G.	Major H. R. Leslie
STAFF CAPTAIN (A.) 1.	Captain R. J. A. Watt
„ 2.	Captain C. M. Rose
J.A.G.	Major G. F. Leslie

Quartermaster-General's Branch

A.Q.M.G.	Lieutenant-Colonel A. B. Coote, O.B.E.
D.A.Q.M.G.	Major C. T. Fellowes
D.A.Q.M.G. (MOVEMENTS)	Major J. Mitchell, M.B.E.
STAFF CAPTAIN (Q)	Captain G. H. Simpson
STAFF LIEUT. Q. (ATTACHED)	Lieutenant H. C. Williams

THE SUPPORTING ARMS

Royal Artillery

C.C.R.A.	Brigadier A. G. Matthew, D.S.O.
G.S.O. 2 (R.A.)	Major H. F. W. Fox
G.S.O. 2 (A.A.)	Major E. F. Pinkney, M.C.
STAFF CAPTAIN (R.A.)	Captain J. A. Whitcombe
I.O. (R.A.)	Captain L. Fraser
I.G.	Major J. S. Cobley
E.M.E.	Captain G. Kerensky

Royal Engineers

CHIEF ENGINEER	Brigadier H. H. C. Sugden, D.S.O., O.B.E.
S.O. 2 (R.E.)	1. Major C. R. Nicholls
,,	2. Major R. O. K. T. Moodie
S.O. 3 (R.E.)	1. Captain W. F. G. Crozier
,,	2. Captain F. W. Goddard
,,	Captain J. B. Kelsall
A.P.I.S.	Lieutenant R. Stewart
E.M.E.	Captain K. Whitfield

Royal Signals

CHIEF SIGNAL OFFICER	Brigadier C. Knowles, O.B.E.
S.O. 2 (R. SIGNALS)	Major H. S. Thompson
S.O. 3 (R. SIGNALS)	Captain L. J. Brunner
,,	Captain D. R. Thompson
CHIEF CIPHER OFFICER	1. Captain M. F. K. Fraser, M.C.
,,	2. Captain D. V. Wellings

Civil Affairs

S.C.A.O.	Colonel G. H. Phipps Hornby
S.O. 1 (ADM.)	Lieutenant-Colonel A. W. E. Crawford
,, (EXEC.)	Lieutenant-Colonel R. S. Manley
S.O. 2 (ADM.)	Major A. G. Puttock
,, (EXEC.)	Major R. C. Peltzer

THE SERVICES

Supply and Transport

D.D.S.T.	Colonel W. H. Blackie, M.C.
D.A.D.S.T. (S.)	Major K. B. Taylor
,, (T.)	Major W. H. Dixon
STAFF CAPTAIN (S.T.)	Captain J. P. G. Lowe
,,	Captain N. W. A. Penn
,,	Captain W. R. Williams

Medical

D.D.M.S.	Brigadier H. L. Glyn Hughes, D.S.O., M.C.
D.A.D.M.S.	1. Major R. Gwyn Evans
,,	2. Major R. G. Ormerod
A.D.H.	Lieutenant-Colonel A. M. Michie
CORPS PSYCHIATRIST	1. Major R. J. Phillips
,,	2. Major G. P. Spillane

Ordnance

D.D.O.S.	Colonel W. T. Grimsdale, O.B.E.
D.A.D.O.S.	Major C. D. Key
STAFF CAPTAIN	Captain R. N. Mellor
I.O.O.	Captain J. N. Jones

R.E.M.E.

D.D.M.E.	Colonel M. A. W. McEvoy
D.A.D.M.E.	Major J. R. Matthews
STAFF CAPTAIN	Captain L.M.H. Elias
A.I.A.	Lieutenant R. A. J. Newman

Chaplains

D.A.C.G.	Reverend O. D. Wiles, D.S.O., M.C.
S.C.F. (R.C.)	Reverend W. W. Welchman
S.C.F. (J.)	Reverend L. Hardman
S.C.F. (CORPS TROOPS)	Reverend G. C. Potts

Provost

A.P.M.	Lieutenant-Colonel G. P. H. Fitzgerald, O.B.E.
D.A.P.M.	Captain A. G. Churchward

Postal

D.A.D.A.P.S.	1. Major J. C. Cashin
,,	2. Major W. F. Barnes

Welfare

D.A.D.A.W.S.	Major A. L. Verriour
LIEUT. (WELFARE)	Lieutenant W. Willis

Education

S.O. 2 (EDUCATION)	Major R. H. Tibbits
LIEUT. (EDUCATION)	Lieutenant N. Lee

Miscellaneous

D.A.D. (SALVAGE)	Major G. A. Palmer
STAFF CAPTAIN (CLAIMS)	Captain J. F. Robertson
CATERING ADVISER	Major B. W. Franks
CATERING ADVISER (CORPS TROOPS)	Captain A. Connorton-Shaw
FIELD CASHIER	Captain D. Jackson
METEOROLOGICAL OFFICER	1. Flight-Lieutenant L. S. Bill
,,	2. Flight-Lieutenant B. C. Lack

Headquarters Squadron Staff

O.C. HEADQUARTERS SQUADRON	Major M. G. H. Brown
O.C. DEFENCE COMPANY	Captain G. Newton
PLATOON COMMANDER	1. Lieutenant M. Sawyer
,,	2. Lieutenant E. A. C. Lascelles
CAMP COMMANDANT	Major G. H. J. Fleming
QUARTERMASTER	1. Captain (Q.M.) W. W. Eggison
,,	2. Captain J. W. Waters
O.C. 778 CAR COMPANY	Captain G. Jackson

ORDER OF BATTLE

EIGHTH CORPS TROOPS

Royal Artillery

O.C. 91 (A. & S.H.) ANTI-TANK REGT., R.A. Lieut.-Colonel J. W. Tweedie, D.S.O.
O.C. 121 L.A.A. REGIMENT, R.A. Lieut.-Colonel R. H. L. Brackenbury
O.C. 10 SURVEY REGIMENT, R.A. Lieut.-Colonel E. A. Spencer
C.B.O. 8 CORPS Major A. L. Temple
ASSISTANT C.B.O. 1. Captain A. N. Anderson
„ 2. Captain E. R. Footring
O.C. 659 AIR OP. SQN Major E. D. V. Prendergast, D.F.C.

Royal Engineers

C.R.E. 8 CORPS TROOPS Lieut.-Colonel J. E. Marsh
O.C. 100 FD. COMPANY Major T. Burrowes
O.C. 101 FD. COMPANY Major I. W. Taylor
O.C. 224 FD. COMPANY Major H. E. A. Donnelly
O.C. 508 FD. PARK COMPANY Major R. G. D. Vernon

Royal Signals

O.C. 8 CORPS SIGNALS Lieut.-Colonel J. M. S. Tulloch

Royal Army Service Corps

C.R.A.S.C. 8 CORPS TROOPS Lieut.-Colonel G. C. W. Neve
2 IC. R.A.S.C. Major H. D. Gravelle
22 COY. R.A.S.C. Major R. L. Leathwaite
35 COY. R.A.S.C. Major C. G. M. Marsh
703 COY. R.A.S.C. Major J. R. Hickman
227 M.A.C. Major D. H. Middleminn
122 D.I.D. Captain S. J. T. Durrell
137 D.I.D. Captain D. Sayer
230 PET. DEPOT Captain H. Stokes
118 FD. BAKERY Captain H. Kell
46 FD. BAKERY Captain W. K. Drow
132 D.I.D. Captain A. L. Jackson

Royal Army Medical Corps

O.C. 33 C.C.S. Lieut.-Colonel F. Heywood-Jones, T.D.
O.C. 34 C.C.S. Lieut.-Colonel R. Gwyn Evans
O.C. 1 F.D.S. Major H. L. Wolfe
O.C. 24 F.D.S. Major N. R. Butcher
O.C. 17 m. Ivn. one. Major R. M. Gordon

Royal Army Ordnance Corps

O.C. 8 CORPS ORD. FD. PK. Lieut.-Colonel W. Elliott
A.D.O.S. 8 CORPS TROOPS 1. Lieut.-Colonel J. Hall
                ,,   2. Lieut.-Colonel N. E. R. Carroll
I.O.O Captain R. T. P. Fletcher
O.C. 106 M.L. & B.U. Captain J. McK. Ferrier
O.C. 51 F.M.A.S. Captain J. R. Muller
O.C. 52 F.M.A.S. Captain G. Olding
O.C. 53 F.M.A.S. Captain W. I. McIntyre
O.C. 63 F.M.A.S. Captain K. Thacker
O.C. 46 ARMY KINEMA SEC. Captain J. Turser

Royal Electrical and Mechanical Engineers

C.R.E.M.E. 8 CORPS TROOPS Lieut.-Colonel F. A. Goodman, M.C.
2 IC. R.E.M.E. Major J. R. Edgar
O.C. 8 CORPS TPS. WKSPS. R.E.M.E. Major F. Hill
O.C. 813 (11) ARMD. TPS. WKSPS. Lieut.-Colonel C. B. Grandfield
O.C. 801 (15) INF. TPS. WKSPS. Major G. S. Couper
O.C. 822 (6 GDS. TK.) TPS. WKSPS. Major R. Arbuthnot
O.C. 3 REC. COY. Major T. C. Payne

Miscellaneous

O.C. 60 PIONEER GROUP Lieut.-Colonel L. W. Giles, M.C.
O.C. 105 CORPS RECEPTION CAMP Lieut.-Colonel P. W. Hargreaves, M.C.
O.C. 257 CORPS DELIVERY SQUADRON Major R. T. G. Lyons
O.C. 53 FIELD SECURITY SECTION Captain K. M. Stephens
O.C. 109 SPECIAL WIRELESS SECTION Captain J. Fletcher
O.C. 110 PROVOST COMPANY Captain J. D. Brown
O.C. 413 SPECIAL MAILS SECTION Captain J. Knock
O.C. 34 GRAVES REGISTRATION UNIT Captain W. G. Ratcliffe
O.C. 2 C.C. F.M.C. Major G. A. B. Jenkins
O.C. 6 C.C. F.M.C. Major J. F. Nevin

FORMATIONS UNDER COMMAND OF EIGHTH CORPS

FOR OPERATIONS DURING THE PERIOD JUNE—DECEMBER, 1944

Armour

Guards Armoured Division
7 Armoured Division
11 Armoured Division
4 Armoured Brigade
6 Guards Tank Brigade
31 Tank Brigade

Infantry

3 (British) Infantry Division
3 (Canadian) Infantry Division
15 (Scottish) Infantry Division
43 (Wessex) Infantry Division
50 (Northumbrian) Infantry Division
53 (Welsh) Infantry Division

Artillery

4 A.G.R.A.
8 A.G.R.A.
100 A.A. Brigade
106 A.A. Brigade

Allied Formations

7 U.S. Armoured Division
101 U.S. Airborne Division
1 Belgian Infantry Brigade

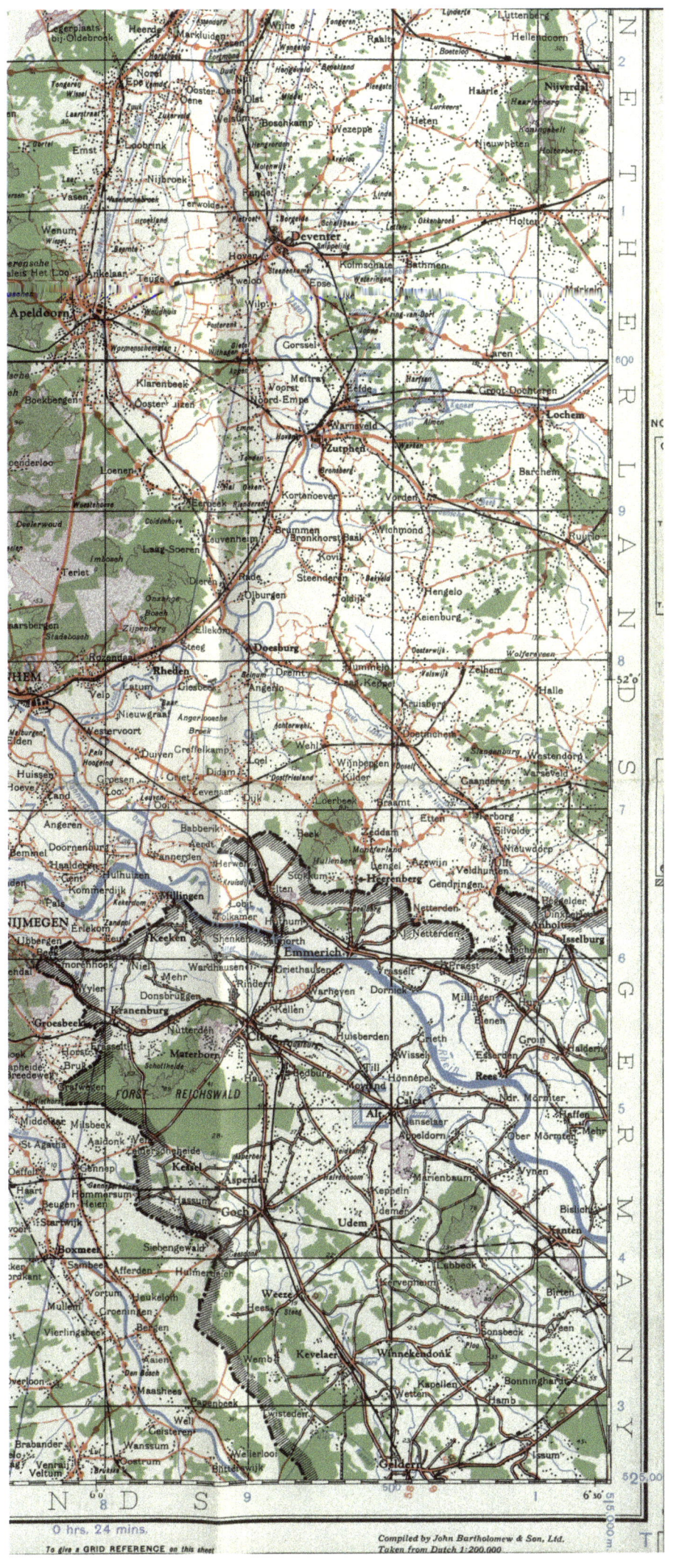

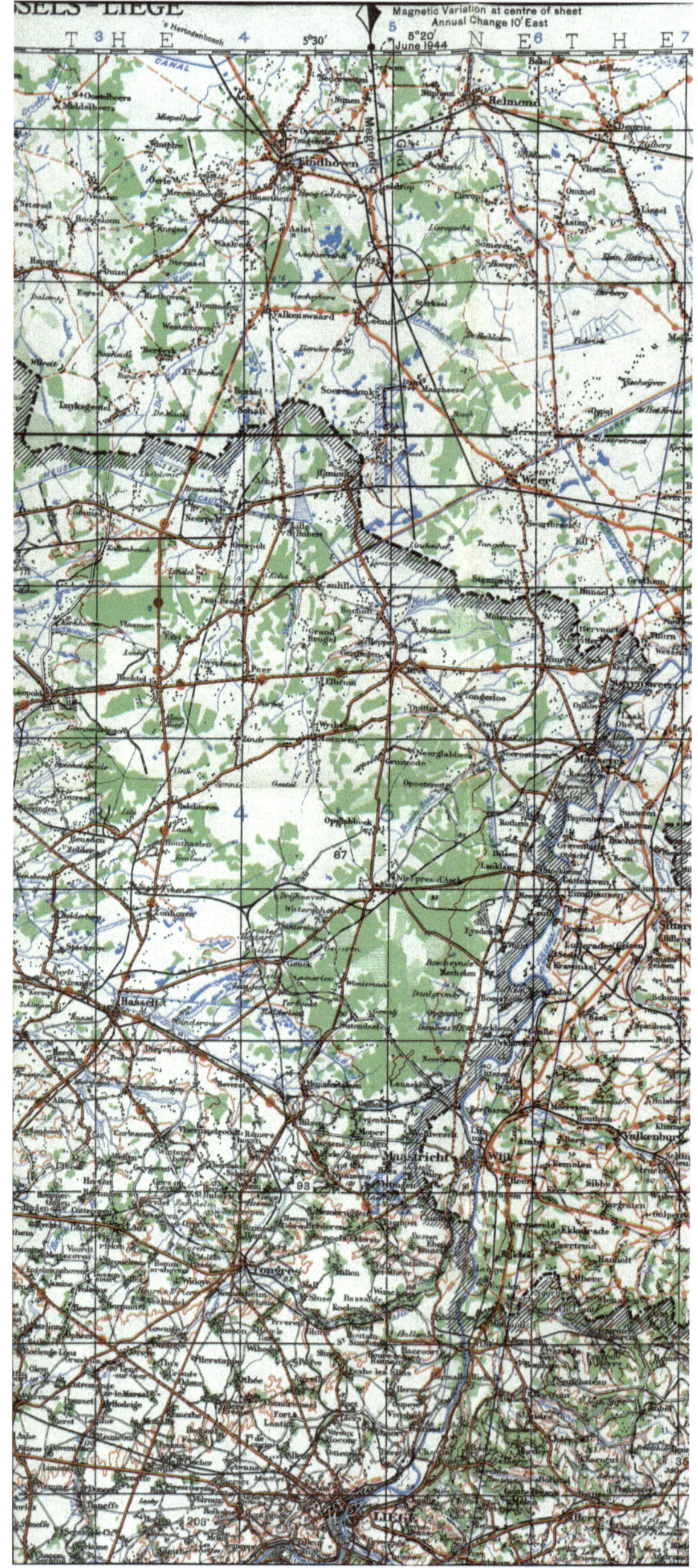

SECOND EDITION ARMY/AIR SHEET N° 3.

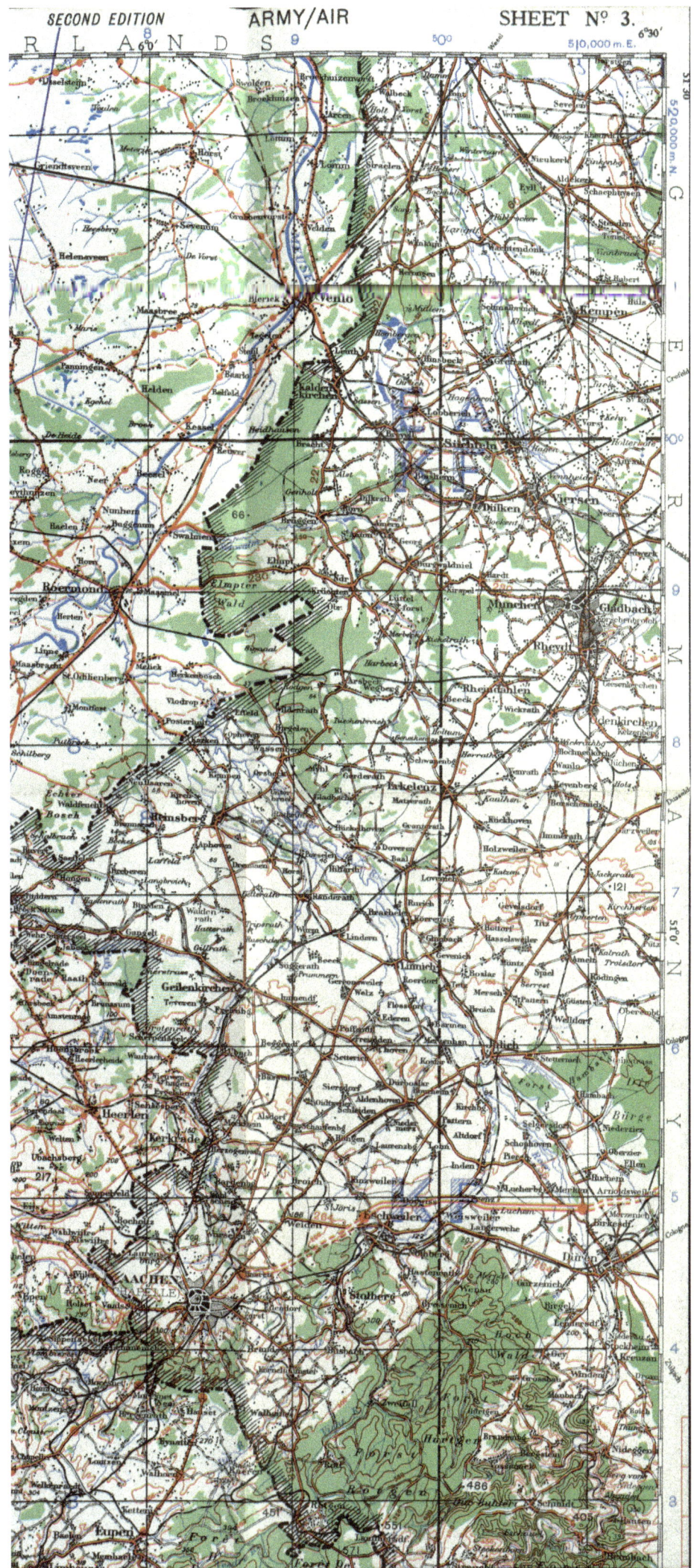

www.ingramcontent.com/pod-product-compliance
Lightning Source LLC
Chambersburg PA
CBHW061546010526
44114CB00027B/2948